THE
NEW ENGLAND
Herb Gardener

THE
NEW ENGLAND
Herb Gardener

YANKEE WISDOM FOR
NORTH AMERICAN HERB GROWERS

by Patricia Turcotte

Photographs by Ronald W. Turcotte

The Countryman Press, Inc.
Woodstock, Vermont

Library of Congress Cataloging-in-Publication Data

Turcotte, Patricia
    New England herb gardener: Yankee wisdom for growers and users/
by Patricia Turcotte; photos by Ronald W. Turcotte
          p. cm.
    Includes index.
    ISBN 0-88150-188-3
    1. Herb gardening. 2. Herbs 3. Herbs—Utilization. I. Title.
SB351.H5t78 1991
635'.7—dc20   91-2132
                                          CIP

Cover and text design by Ann Aspell
Photographs by Ronald W. Turcotte

10 9 8 7 6 5 4

Contents

Notice to the Reader

This is not a medical book, but rather a sharing of one person's experience in cultivating and using herbs.

The simple herbal medicines discussed in this book are only one aspect of a medical care program. Any serious illness or warning symptom calls for diagnosis and treatment by a qualified physician.

Remember, each individual will respond differently to herbal treatments. Not all applications are effective in every case for every person. Therefore, it is necessary to use herbs with care and moderation, keeping track of individual responses to carefully limited applications.

Some herbs may cause slightly undesirable side effects. Therefore, be sure to try only one herb at a time in small dosages and then record any such side effect. If none is present, increase the dosage or frequency *cautiously* and on a limited basis and continue to monitor for any adverse reaction. Take the same precautions with herbal medicines that you would with other medicines in your home. Label all containers.

Preface

Wormwood Farm is the realization of a dream, a dream to live in the country, to have a place to garden.

Mother Nature gives everything a purpose. Without bugs there would be no birds, without caterpillars there would be no butterflies, and without bees no pollination of vegetables, flowers, and herbs. One of my purposes, I discovered, is to grow herbs and teach others about them.

My husband, Ron, came in for lunch; I was making grilled cheese sandwiches. "That old Foran farm up on Route 9 has a FOR SALE sign on it. Pretty bad shape, barn's falling down, house needs tons of work, if it can even be saved. Probably priced too high anyway, probably not even worth looking at. Hey, don't burn those sandwiches."

"Oh, please, please, let's just look at it," I pleaded.

We had been looking for an old farmstead in the area for over a year, one that was in our price range. Real estate was rapidly rising in price. Ron laughed as he told me that we had an appointment just as soon as I served those sandwiches.

It was a cold February day; the sun was shining on four inches of crusty snow. Years of neglect had taken their toll on the 200-year-old, ex-dairy farm. Many seasons had passed since cows filled the barns and chickens roosted in the hen houses. The farm had been vacant for over a year.

We looked past the present condition and into the future possibilities of the place. Other than the rotted sills on the north side, caused by years of banking up hay against them, the house was basically sound. However, it did need tons of work. The dirt and stone cellar was full of water; Ron jumped back just in time as a cellar step broke under his weight. Ceilings and walls were blackened from years of wood stove heat. Mice holes lined old plastered walls, with tin can covers nailed onto them. In the tiny bathroom, a hole in the ceiling was the only entrance to the upstairs, where old blue wallpaper clung to the walls.

I sat in an old rocking chair on the glassed-in porch, heated by the sun. I knew, I just knew this farm was to be my destiny. This is where I wanted to be. The price was right and, three months later, the final papers were signed. It was ours! We cleaned and cleaned, trying to make it livable so we could stay here until we decided exactly what we wanted to do with it. It didn't take long before we felt we had been here forever. There are special spirits and characteristic qualities about an old house. The huge, hand hewn, pegged beams were impressive; such good workmanship of so long ago. It didn't take long for us to fall completely in love with the old farm, even when friends and family were using the word *bulldozer* in every conversation. Some were sure we had lost our minds.

Our first priority was not to replace the rotted sills or the rattling glass in the windows: it was to hire someone to rototill garden space for use. "Isn't fifty by seventy-five feet a little large?" Ron asked. But the garden was quickly filled with many vegetables and colorful flowers. For the previous eight years my gardening had consisted of flowers on a postage-stamp-size lot, with a small vegetable garden three miles away at Dad's. Now, finally, I could devote my time to what I wanted out of life: to garden and to do some serious studying of plants. An herb garden, however, was not in my plans at that time. Other than the basic eight herbs I used for cooking purposes and a fragrant lavender, herbs were a complete mystery to me.

Burdock, clover, and alfalfa were abundant throughout the fields, a good sign of fertility of the soil. The small front yard area was the only place the previous homemaker had had for her flowers; the rest of the land was utilized for dairy farming. I was delighted to be poking around in the weeds, discovering a treasure of flowers, fragrant old roses, lemon-scented day lilies, mature peonies and the nice surprise of a small bed of asparagus, just enough for supper.

Poppies and lily of the valley were trying to overtake the other plants. The old herb, cranesbill geranium, was a special find. In back of the barn stood a pile of "black gold," a well-aged manure pile. It took me five years to deplete that pile.

The first year at the farm was spent in backbreaking cleaning up of the fields and tearing down unusable outbuildings.

One afternoon, while weeding the lavender, Ron asked, "Why don't you grow more of the fragrant plants like lavender?" I made up my mind to learn everything there was to learn about herbs and plant them for their fragrance. Nine years later, I am smart enough to know that no one can ever learn all there is to know about herbs. The subject seems to be endless, always just one more plant to identify or new uses to discover.

Spring and summer are spent with hands-on growing and observing; fall and winter in deep study; cold wintry days curled up in front of the wood stove, with a cup of herbal tea (made with herbs from my own garden), and my reference books.

As the garden increased, I found myself with more herb plants than I needed. Notes from my diaries read "southernwood—from one plant last year I now have four." Soon friends were shaking their heads to signal *no* when they saw me coming with plant in hand.

One weekend I had about three dozen tomato, cabbage, basil, and parsley plants I didn't know what to do with. I set them beside the road with a "free" sign on them. They were gone by that evening. I thought about trying to sell a few plants. My gardening hobby was growing (no pun intended) and I could use some money to buy more new plants and gardening books. And I did not want to work outside the home again. That first year, I sold all the extra plants I had. The next year, when I put out my little sign, the State Agriculture Inspector stopped by and asked if I was going to be selling the following year, because if I was I would need to get a license. He was very nice and informative and, after talking with him for awhile, I decided to try it. This ended my hobby status and was the beginning of a business. Ron would start me off with a thousand dollars, my "seed" money. Being a do-it-yourself family, we erected a 14 by 14 foot plastic addition onto the old milkroom for a greenhouse. We didn't advertise in those early days. People would stop by when they saw the sign and the business grew from word of mouth. Now since we were to become a business it would need a name. I had decided to specialize in herbs and wanted to keep the old farm look, so we needed an herb name for the farm. I picked out three herb names I liked and let Ron choose the final one. He chose "WORMWOOD," not so much for the herb name but because of all the wormy wood around the farm. Here was a name with a double meaning for us.

Friends and customers began asking me to give workshops so they could learn about herbs too. That led to lectures at garden clubs and other organizations. People who stopped at the farm asked if they could look at the garden too. We now had over one hundred herbs in various garden areas.

All the money I made went back into my expanding business and the researching of herbs. I had become addicted to herbalism, a common malady among those who catch the herb bug. By 1988, Wormwood Farm was boasting of growing two hundred fifty herbs in its gardens, along with a few backaches and dirty fingernails for the owners.

For several seasons my customers have asked, "Why don't you write a book?" So here it is! My hope for *The New England Herb Gardener* is to provide basic, practical, growing information and to answer, in writing, some of the varied questions on herbs we receive at workshops, lectures, and garden tours. I want this book to be fun, yet well used, not just another garden book to sit on a shelf gathering dust.

This book will take you through all stages of herbalism, from studying the soil and starting seeds to the many uses of herbs. Seventy-five herbs will be profiled in the thirteen chapters. So turn to Chapter 1 and plan to get your hands dirty in the soil.

Herbally yours,
Patricia Turcotte

Introduction:
Welcome to the World of Herbs

Herbs are for everyone! Our two-year-old granddaughter gently caresses the soft, maple-shaped leaf of the peppermint-scented geranium, capturing its pungent aroma in her tiny hands and breathing "ah" as she inhales the fragrance. The older boys enjoy our zoo garden, a theme garden with each plant having the common or botanical name of an animal, insect, or bird. The lamb's ear is a touchable plant for adults and children alike. The boys are often seen with the velvet, gray-green leaves sticking out of their small human ears, as they *baa* at the smaller children. Besides being a fun plant, applying the leaf of lamb's ear to cuts and bee stings will feel good, along with a *boo-boo* kiss from grandmother, of course. Lamb's ear, like many herbs, has antiseptic properties.

New England has a long history of herbs, dating from the early days of the settlers who brought herbs with them to the New World. Our climate is ideal for those herbs that need a cold dormancy time, such as chives and horehound. There are many uses for herbs other than just looking pretty. We use thyme to season fish chowder, globe thistle for drying to make wreaths, sage tea for pleasure and for medicine. Tansy in the cellar repels ants, and the scent of homemade potpourri fills the home with a longer-lasting fragrance than the commercially made kind. Relax in a hot tub after a long day working in the garden, with the scents of mugwort and agrimony to surround you.

Herbs are easy to grow. You can have five acres, 25 acres, or a windowsill; sun, shade, wet or dry soil. Mother Nature has generously provided a plant for every situation.

Tiny, one-inch rupturewort grows out of a crack in the cement; the six-foot, fragrant valerian provides a background in the border garden. In the windowbox of an apartment, the culinary herbs chives, sage, and parsley are grown for use in a gourmet dinner.

I have tried to write this book for the average gardener, using common names as we know them in New England. However, I highly recommend that you learn the botanical names. Knowing these names makes learning easier and makes it easier to look up herbs in reference books. One way I learned them was to put a label on each plant in the garden. Then, as I weeded, I memorized them. My second recommendation is to buy a magnifying glass. Look closely at the leaf and flower to see interesting patterns and textures. St. Johnswort has tiny pores on the leaf, which gave early herbalists reason to think it was good for the skin. This practice of associating herbs with how they look is called the Doctrine of Signatures.

Lungwort leaf was thought to look like diseased lungs, so was used in the treatment of lung diseases. Today, lungwort is sold as a perennial landscape flower under its botanical name Pulmonaria. The flowers come in pink and then turn blue, giving them an interesting characteristic.

Cultivating your own herbs not only provides you with a ready supply but may also help to save some of the wild native herbs. As land is being bulldozed and buildings put up, many of the wild herbs are disappearing. You don't always know if chemical sprays have been used in a harvesting area, so growing your own herbs will prove to be the safest method. Most wild herbs can be started with seeds or plants purchased from reliable herb growers. Cultivating your own will provide you with a pure unadulterated product, fresh air, exercise, and a relaxing hobby. Not everyone can attend my workshops so I hope this book will provide you with the answers to some of your herbal questions. As you read this, don't just read words, but think of us as talking about herbs, gardener to gardener.

Note: For all recipes included in this book using *Parts:* Parts can signify various units, such as quarts, cups, etc., depending on their context in each recipe. Example: 1 part can equal 1 quart or 1 cup, 2 parts can equal 2 quarts or two cups, etc.

ONE

Potato Peelings, Grass Clippings, and Egg Shells

(Preparing the Soil)

HERBS HAVE BEEN tolerant of man and his ways for many centuries. They have survived wars, climactic disasters, bulldozers, chainsaws, and poor placement. The early American settlers brought herbs with them. These herbs were very important for cooking and medicine. As living conditions improved and science and technology became dominant factors, many herbs were discarded, left to flourish for themselves in the wild. Examples of this are motherwort, mugwort, and shepherd's purse. Today's herb gardeners are now returning these and other herbs to the cultivated garden. An interest in gourmet and ethnic cooking has brought about the introduction of herbs from other countries, now added to our New England herb gardens. Among these are shisho perilla, mitsuba, and epazote.

Anyone who is willing to learn the basic information about individual herbs and the proper conditions for cultivating them can be a successful herb gardener. It is important to cultivate each herb under the proper conditions for best results. Each chapter in this book features "Plant Profiles," which contain this information for selected herbs. In addition, Chapters 3 and 4 cover this in more detail and there are other reference sources listed which cover the ideal cultivation conditions for every herb.

Soil Preparation

Basic Soil Types

There are three basic types of soil found in New England:

Sandy Soil: This type of soil provides the excellent drainage most herbs need, but it is so porous it can drain away some important nutrients. It does warm up quickly in the spring for earlier planting and it's easier to pull weeds out of a sandy soil.

Clay Soil: We have a lot of this type of soil at Wormwood Farm. It is heavy, with small, fine particles that compact together. This makes the soil hard as a rock when insufficient water is supplied. It is slow to warm up in the spring and often has standing water after a heavy rain.

Loam Soil: This type of soil provides the happy medium we all strive for in our gardens. It is light with a medium texture. It drains well and yet has good moisture-holding capabilities that also retain nutrients well.

Improving The Soil

Both sandy and clay soil will benefit from the addition of organic matter. Sandy soil will develop the necessary moisture-holding capabilities and clay soil will loosen up for better drainage. Two ways to deal with heavy clay soil are to make raised beds or plant moisture-loving herbs. See the plant profiles at the end of this chapter.

The late Jim Crockett of "Victory Garden" fame said on his show, "You should add as much peat moss as your pocketbook can stand." This is also true of compost and manures. You cannot overdose your soil with too much organic matter. Since peat moss is slightly on the *acid* side, which herbs do not like, it would be necessary to add a substance to raise the pH-level to *alkaline*, which they do prefer. Those substances include lime, bonemeal, and wood ashes. In applying lime, clay soils will need a larger amount than sandy soils and it will aid in loosening the clay soil. It is a good idea to have your soil tested for its pH-level. This test will tell you how acid or alkaline the soil is. If you have pine, spruce, and fir trees growing on your land, the soil is probably on the acid side (as much New England soil is). Your county agricultural extension agent (listed in your phone book) will furnish you with a container and testing information. Test kits are also available at farm supply stores. The test results will tell you how much lime, if any, to add to your soil type.

Composting

Compost is a mixture of organic materials that will decay into *humus*. Added to the soil, compost produces a better quality soil for growing plants. Mother Nature composts naturally in woodlands with decaying leaves, dead insects, spent mushrooms, and wilted flowers. A good supply of compost in your garden will produce strong, healthy plants. My compost pile is layered on the ground next to the garden. It is made in large quantities and it can be turned over with the tractor. Smaller piles can, of course, be turned over by hand, using a shovel or fork. Turning helps to speed up the decomposition of the materials in the pile. My family members are sport fishermen, so they often can be seen turning the compost by hand to find the abundant number of earthworms that appear in good compost. In town, you want to enclose your compost in a bin for a more attractive look. My son has a compost bin made with wood slats on three sides. The rhubarb growing behind the compost bin benefits from the nutrients leaching from the compost. Commercially-made compost bins are available, but homemade bins are easily made by the do-it-yourselfer. A 5 by 6 foot size is easy to turn. It should be at least five feet high for the best composting condition. The length will depend on what you have room for and what material you fill it with. Remember this: A five-foot-tall pile will shrink to half its original size as it decays. Your compost bin can be made from wood, bricks, or cement blocks. Leave a space between blocks or wood pieces for air circulation. Screens fastened together in a square with hinges on one side can be used to get at the compost.

The secret of making good compost is to use *a variety of materials*. Use what is normally available in your area.

Recommended Materials	Materials to Avoid
animal manures	cat or dog manure
leaves (best if shredded)	plant material that is tainted by
seaweed and shells	herbicides, pesticides, insects,
garden vegetation	or disease
hair (high in protein)	greasy, oily foods
grass clippings	meat scraps or bones
sawdust	
straw and hay	
wood ashes (cold)	
weeds (dry out roots first)	
kitchen wastes (tea, coffee grounds, etc.)	
fish by-products.	

Ingredients Needed for Compost Making—There are three major ingredients needed for making compost:

Nitrogen: This is found in manures, egg shells, dried blood, and cottonseed meal. Without enough nitrogen-producing materials, the compost will not decay effectively. With too much nitrogen and not enough carbon materials, a rotten aroma will occur.

Carbon: This will come from straw, hay, weeds, leaves, and grass clippings. Since grass clippings tend to mat down, they should be mixed lightly with other material. Also, soil added to the compost will help it decay faster.

Water: The compost pile should be moist, but not soggy. Too much water will wash away nutrients and cause an odor. Make an indentation on top of the pile so water will penetrate and not just run off the pile.

Shredding all material that goes into the compost pile will help speed the process. There are shredders available to buy or rent. A shredder is a good investment if you're doing extensive gardening, but it is too expensive to buy for a small home garden.

Manures are extremely important ingredients. Therefore, try to make contact with a farmer or commercial vendor who can supply you at a reasonable price. Dried manures can be purchased at garden centers.

It is nice to have three compost piles: one that is completed and ready to use in the garden, one that is in the composting stage, and a third that is in the making.

Finally, use *caution* when putting wood ashes in the compost pile because ashes can remain hot for a long time. One winter, I set the compost pile ablaze with a bucketful of ashes that had a hidden glowing ember inside. Wood ashes can also be spread right on the garden itself. Lavender and roses are especially grateful for a yearly application of wood ashes.

Black Plastic Composting—In recent years, black plastic has been an aid in decomposition of the compost pile. When the pile is five feet tall, water well, then cover with a sheet of black plastic. Weigh it down with rocks or posts so wind does not blow it away. The plastic holds moisture in and warms up the material quickly. Compost is then more quickly made.

Compost can be added to the garden any time of the year, with spring being the preferred time. Turn compost into the top four inches of soil with a tiller or by hand. Compost can be used to mulch new seedlings when they are planted in hot weather or to help established plants anytime.

Preparing the Soil

In a large garden or one accessible for a rototiller, mechanical rototilling is the easiest way to turn the soil. Rototillers can be purchased (expensive), rented, borrowed from a friend, or you can hire someone who does that kind of work. Tillers come in all sizes, from small and easy to handle to large tilling attachments for a tractor. Many herb gardens, however, will be too small for a tiller or otherwise inaccessible, such as next to a foundation. These gardens must be turned by hand. I prefer to prepare the garden plot in the fall, but it seems most people wait until spring when the warm sun provides the inspiration and energy that beckons us to the garden. *Beware of trying to work the soil when it is too wet.* It will only be clumpy and hard to work with.

Fall Preparation

- Cover area with compost and manure (fresh manure is fine).
- Sprinkle with lime, bone meal, or wood ash.
- Water well.
- Cover with black plastic and weigh down ends.

By spring, the area will be composted and the weeds killed. At that time, digging in the soil will be easy. Turn the soil over with a garden fork and then rake out rocks and roots.

Spring Preparation

- Dig or till soil, remove all sod, grass, and weeds, shaking off soil from sod if hand digging. Put sod and weeds in your starter compost pile.
- Add well-aged compost or dried manure.
- Mix any additives well into the soil.
- Rake out any roots or rocks for a smooth surface.

Raised Garden Beds

Raised beds are ideal because you can control the type of soil used in them. They make it possible to have a garden in areas with very poor or wet soil. They warm up quickly in the spring. Also, you can sit on the edge of these beds for easier weeding. Raised beds make gardening available to those in wheelchairs or with bad backs. They should not be wider than six feet across; this will give you an arm's length from both sides for weeding. Any wider and paths will be needed to weed in the center.

Filling a raised bed; notice the double tiers to provide proper height.

Making the Raised Bed

1. Rototill or turn soil by hand in a measured area.
2. Frame out area with wood, brick, cement blocks, or rocks.
3. Fill with soil. There are no set rules for what you fill the bed with. It should be light in texture for easy working. A mix I often use is:

> 3 parts garden soil
> 3 parts gravel
> 3 parts peat moss
> 2 parts compost
> 1 part vermiculite
> $^1/_{16}$ part bone meal or lime

4. Water bed well.
5. Let set two or three days to settle. Do not firm down.
6. Plant.

Raised beds have good drainage which most herbs prefer. However, note that moisture-loving herbs will *not* do well in raised beds. These herbs will thrive in soil with a very high moisture content, some even in wet soil. At Wormwood Farm, we have an area that is clay-type soil with large amounts of standing water in the spring and after a rain storm. Here we are able to grow the native joe-pye weed, normally found in boggy areas. Comfrey and mints tolerate this area along with purple loosestrife, red cardinal flower, marsh marigold, and yellow and blue flag iris. These herbs will brighten up that damp area.

To plant these herbs in a drier area, mulch heavily and water if rain is not sufficient.

Hay and grass clippings are mulched between the rows of an annual herb garden.

Mulch

Mulch is a material that is put on the ground to keep moisture in and to keep weeds down. When organic material is used, it will break down the soil adding humus and nutrients. Among organic materials to use are wood chips, bark, grass clippings, straw, pine needles, sawdust, and cocoa hulls. Non-organic materials include plastic, aluminum foil (expensive and blows around if not weighted down), stones, and weed screen, a new plastic weave fabric that lets water and air through, but keeps weeds at a minimum.

Black plastic added in early spring will aid in warming up the soil. However, this will not work well when it is very hot as it keeps the soil too warm.

Summer Mulching—Mulch for summer plants should not be applied until the soil has warmed up. Most herbs are sun lovers and mulching too early will keep the soil too cool. Many herbs are from the Mediterranean area, and these I prefer not to mulch at all. Included are lavender, savories, and thymes. Do not apply mulch too closely to stems or it will rot the stem. Silver and gray herbs are not partial to very much mulching.

Winter Mulching—We do very little winter mulching at Wormwood Farm simply because we have clay to loam soil and mulching would keep our soil too moist and cool. If I had a good sandy soil, I would mulch for winter. In winter, use straw and evergreen boughs, which will not mat down on the herbs and cause them to rot under the snow. The reason for a winter mulch is to protect the herbs from constant thawing and freezing. In high wind areas, winter mulch will help protect the herbs. Lavender in particular dislikes a windy area. A winter with no snow cover will do more damage to herbs and to other plants than a good snow cover. In some instances, hay mulch will encourage slug, mole, or mouse activities.

Plant Profiles

American Ginger (*Asarum canadense*)

Family—Aristolochiaceae (birthwort)

Synonyms—Canada snakeroot, wild ginger, colic root.

Description—12-inch tall ground cover, the herbaceous perennial has kidney-shaped, medium green leaves; the brownish-purple flowers are quite shy, hiding beneath the leaves; look for them in early spring; native to Canada and New England areas.

Cultivation—Likes partial or filtered shade, slightly acid soil; mulch lightly and keep weeded and its creeping rhizomes will spread over area.

Propagation—Rhizomes are fleshy horizontal stems that grow underground, spreading yearly; these are taken in the spring and cut into

Comfrey can be cut several times a year to add nutrients to compost piles.

sections; each must have an eye, which is the green part growing out of the rhizome. (See Chapter 2 for propagation of rhizomes.)

Part Used—Rhizome

Harvest—Rhizome is harvested in midsummer, when still full of food; rhizomes shrink in fall for lack of food; to dry rhizome, clean well with water, slice and dry in lowest oven temperature possible, with door open.

Uses—Culinary: The American Indians used candied ginger as a sweet and they seasoned their foods with it in the same way we use the tropical ginger in seasoning foods today.

Medicinal: Most native herbs were utilized by the Indians and the American ginger is no exception. It was valuable for indigestion, either chewed or in the form of a tea; women took it for pains at childbirth; an important "belly ache" herb; the name colic root comes from the fact that it was used in a tea for children with colic. It is also used to help treat fever, convulsions, and nausea.

Comfrey *(Symphytum officinalis)*

Family—Boraginaceae (borage)

Synonyms—Knitbone, knitback, ass ears, bruisewort.

Description—Large herb to 3½ feet; invasive, herbaceous, perennial; the name ass ears comes from the shape of the leaf (straplike) and the slightly hairy leaf and stems. Like all members of the borage family it has blue flowers, often coming out pink and later turning blue; flowers all season. Comfrey is not always welcomed in the small garden because of its invasive habit. But its sister, the Russian blue comfrey *(Symphytum uplandicum)*, has smaller leaves with light blue flowers and is not invasive. Both are used in the same way with the same culture and propagation methods.

Cultivation—Comfrey prefers a rich soil but will grow anywhere. It is a heavy feeder and one of the few plants that will accept fresh manure as a fertilizer. It will grow in sandy soil but won't realize its full potential unless it receives a substantial amount of water. Grows in full sun to partial shade; plant in an area where it will stay, because once planted it is hard to eradicate. Cut down to within 3 inches of root several times a year to keep it from becoming too large and weedy looking; it regrows quickly.

Propagation—It can be started by seed but is slow to mature; spring root cuttings are preferred.

Part Used—Leaf and root.

Harvest—Use young leaves and growing tips since the larger, older leaves are hairy. Dry leaves on screens and don't let them touch each other or the parts touching will turn black. Dry root in fall (see Chapter 8 for drying roots).

Uses—Use in tea *with caution*. There is controversy on just how safe comfrey is for internal use.

Medicinal: Comfrey contains mucilage, allatoin, and tannic acid. It is one of the few plants that takes vitamin B from the soil. It is reputed to help in intestinal problems, diarrhea, whooping cough, bleeding piles, and as a blood purifier. Its external use gave it the common name of knitback, knitbone, and bruisewort because it was thought to mend broken bones and fractures; what it does do is to aid in taking the swelling down. Often used as a poultice on wounds, bruises, ulcers, and fractures.

Miscellaneous: Good herb for beekeepers; bees love the flowers all season.

Elderberry *(Sambucus canadensis)*

Family—Caprifoliaceae (honeysuckle)

Synonyms—Mother elder, pipe tree.

Description—Actually a small tree to 15 feet; medium sized, oval leaves are poisonous, creamy white flowers and blue berries are not; an attractive tree for an herb garden. Folklore tells us that it is the protector of the herbs and herbalist. The tree is always presented in the female gender, and permission must be asked before harvesting any of her products or before it can be cut. This perhaps could be true: one day while gathering flowers from the tree, I looked up only to have mother elder poke me in my eye. I had not asked permission first. Then there is the English doctor who always tipped his hat in respect to mother elder as he passed an elderberry tree. In Denmark, it is thought that Hylder (mother elder) lives in the tree and will haunt anyone who cuts her down without permission. If a cradle is made from her wood, she will pull the leg of the child put in it in order to make it cry. Gypsies would never use elder wood in their fires at their camp for fear of evil happenings. Elderwood branches hung over doorways offer protection from witches. Branches were once laid on grave sites to protect loved ones from evil spirits in the afterworld.

Cultivation—Sandy to clay soil with good drainage. Full sun to partial shade; often found wild on banks by streams and old roadways. Easy to care for; trim dead branches in spring (of course, ask permission first).

Elderberry Sauce

Stew your berries in water, just enough to barely cover them, for 20 minutes. Remove from stove and strain through cheesecloth. To each gallon of juice add

½ ounce whole ginger
¼ cup whole cloves

Boil for one-half hour. Then stir in *2 cups of sugar* to each gallon of juice. Boil for 10 minutes. Strain and bottle. Keep in refrigerator. Can be used on vanilla ice cream, pancakes, waffles, french toast.

Propagation—Usually from suckers off the mother plant. Seeds are slow to become a mature plant. From eating the berries, birds often plant seedlings in their droppings.

Part Used—Leaves (poisonous); flowers and berries more often used.

Harvest—Leaf all season; flowers as they come into full bloom; dry on paper towels on screens since they are tiny; berries, when blue-black in color. Flowers can be microwaved. If flowers are not dried quickly, they will turn brown. I watch the birds; they will not eat the berries until they are fully ripened but they can also strip a tree in a day. Dry leaves on screen and *be sure to label the poisonous leaves* and do not dry them near other herbs you use in food or medicines.

Uses—Culinary: Flowers can be dipped in batter and fried, or used in tea blends (they are too bland when used alone). Fresh berries should not be eaten in large quantities—they may make you sick. They are perfectly safe when cooked. We use the berries in pies, jellies, wines, and sauces.

Medicinal: Elderflowers are slightly astringent and soothing. They are used in the form of a salve to treat hemorrhoids, burns, and wounds. Internally, they are used in a tea taken for colds, headaches and flu; especially effective taken with hyssop and peppermint. The berries were often taken in the form of wine mixed half and half with water for rheumatism, colic, as a laxative, or for diarrhea.

Cosmetic: Because of its soothing qualities, elderflower makes an excellent lotion for skin care; it is used as an herbal water or diluted elderflower vinegar. Useful on sunburns, in facials, or for helping to keep the skin free of blemishes. It was a favorite of Victorian ladies, along with other floral waters.

Miscellaneous: Leaves can be rubbed on the skin to deter mosquitos and black flies. Use as a landscape specimen on its own or to provide shade for those herbs that like shade.

Elderberry Wine

I serve elderberry wine at some of my workshops and even those who don't normally drink wine find its taste smooth and sweet.

Pick *3 gallons of elderberries,* put in crock. Pour 2 gallons of boiling water over berries, cover and let stand for 24 hours. Strain through cheesecloth. Squeeze cloth to remove all the juice from the berries. Measure amount of juice. Put in large stainless steel kettle. To each gallon of juice add the following:

3 pounds of sugar
½ ounce sliced ginger root
¼ ounce whole cloves
¼ ounce whole allspice
1 pound raisins

Bring this mixture to a boil, then simmer for 1 hour. Skim froth off the top frequently. Pour mixture back into clean crock. Cool slightly and add *1 cake yeast* and *1 piece of hard toast* (make toast two days ahead of time). Cover with cheesecloth and set to ferment for two weeks. Then bottle and cap and store in cool area. Let age for two months before serving; the longer it ages the better it tastes. It can be diluted with ginger ale for a weaker drink and for medicinal purposes.

Elderberry Fried Flowers

Mix batter of:

2 cups flour
4 tsps baking powder
½ tsp salt (optional)
½ tsp paprika
¼ tsp black pepper
2 well-beaten eggs
1 cup milk (or beer)
½ cup water

Dip flower heads in batter and deep fry in *shortening* until crisp. Serve immediately.

Joe-Pye Weed *(Eupatorium purpureum)*

Family—Compositae (daisy)

Synonyms—Gravelroot, purple boneset, marsh milkweed.

Description—Joe-pye stands over 6 feet tall; even so, this hardy, herbaceous perennial does not need staking. The thick, round stems are very strong. Leaves are lance-shaped, slightly rough, and pointed; dark green on top of leaf, slightly downy on the underside. Terminal mauve-colored flowers in mid summer. Native to the New England landscape; its name came from an Indian named Joe Pye, who was an herbal medicine man. He reputedly cured the typhus fever with a decoction from the plant's root and the plant was then named in his honor.

Cultivation—Even though it grows in boggy areas in the wild, joe-pye adapts very well to the cultivated garden. Use a good mulch and supply water during dry spells. Plant in full sun to partial shade.

Propagation—Can be grown from seed but germination is poor. It will take two years for a mature plant to grow from seed. Root division in spring, use sharp shovel as roots are strong and intertwine in a heavy mass. Do not dig from the wild. Trying to transplant large plants almost always ends in their dying.

Part Used—Flowers and roots.

Harvest—Harvest root in fall. Flowers are harvested only in budded stage of growth. Once flower opens it will "fluff out" while drying. (Fluff out is when a plant is picked too late in its growth stage. It continues to open while drying, scattering its pollen everywhere.) Most flowers stop growing once picked; joe-pye is one of those that does not. Timing is very important when picking these kinds of flowers.

Uses—Decorative: Flowers used in floral arrangements and wreaths.

   Medicinal: The main use of joe-pye is in medicine. In a tea or tincture, the roots are used for fevers and as a gentle laxative; also helps treat gout, rheumatism, and kidney stones.

Marshmallow *(Althaea officinalis)*

Family—Malvaceae (mallow)

Synonyms—Hockherb, mortification root, cheeses.

Description—A moisture-loving herbaceous perennial growing to 5 feet tall with velvety grey-green leaves; small pink and white flowers in summer followed by little round seed pods (called cheeses). It was once

Sauteed Marshmallow Roots

Rinse roots well, boil until tender. Slice and sauté in *vegetable oil* with *sliced onions* and *sliced green peppers*. Nice served over a steak.

Marshmallow Cough Medicine

Steep leaf or root in boiling water for 2 hours. Bring to a boil and let set overnight. Strain. Use alone as a gargle or mix with *orange juice* and drink as a cough medicine.

Marshmallow Cough Syrup

Mix *½ cup marshmallow water* (see above recipe) with *1 cup brown sugar* in saucepan. Bring to a boil. Boil for 1 minute. Use by the teaspoonful for coughs.

a very important part of the herb garden because of its many uses; can be found near brackish waters in the wild.

Cultivation—Plant in full sun to partial shade; likes an alkaline soil and lots of water, but adapts to the cultivated garden very nicely. For a summer hedge, plant three feet apart. A mulch will help keep it moist; during drought periods supply it with water.

Propagation—Easy from seed, which is abundant from the cheeses; takes two years to mature. Division of roots is easy in spring.

Part Used—All parts, making this a worthwhile plant. This is one of my favorite herbs; I always delight in giving high praise to it during my garden tours. Since every part is usable and safe, it is a most practical herb.

Harvest—Leaf has most essential oil just before it comes into flower. Flowers collected in full flower are best used fresh. Second-year roots are gathered in the fall. Dry leaves on screens; (see Chapter 8 on drying roots). Seed pods are gathered in the green stage and eaten fresh like nuts. When seed pods are brown they can be collected for the seeds to start new plants.

Uses—Culinary: When young shoots are only 3 inches high they can be harvested and cooked like a vegetable, tasting like spring peas. The edible flowers can be used in tea or salad. Bland as a tea alone, it is nice combined with rosemary and/or mints.

Medicinal: Both leaf and root contain a mucilaginous substance, making this herb valuable in medicine and cosmetics. Especially useful in cough medicine and for sore throats.

Cosmetic: Marshmallow water is one of the best herbal lotions for hands; very good for softening the dry, chapped hands of the gardener. Make herbal water in the same way as in the cough medicine recipe. Rub into skin; it will feel sticky at first but smooths into the skin quickly, making it soft. This herbal water needs to be kept in the refrigerator. Remember, this is a pure natural product with no chemical preservatives added to give it a long shelf life.

Sweet Cicely *(Myrrhis odorata)*

Family—Umbelliferae (carrot)

Synonyms—Shepherds needle, cow chervil, myrrh.

Description—Herbaceous perennial to 2½ feet tall. Sweet cicely has delicate, fern-like foliage with terminal white, dill-like flowers. These are followed by bright green seeds that stand upright on the flower stems; as the seeds mature they turn a shiny black. The whole plant has an anise taste and aroma. Flower heads can be kept cut off for more leaf production.

Cultivation—Partial shade for sweet cicely, a nice herb to plant in a lightly wooded area that receives some filtered shade or a few hours of direct sun. Needs good drainage and prefers a slightly alkaline soil.

Propagation—The viability of the seed is short lived. Gather and plant seeds in the fall. If seeds are left on the herb, it will self-seed around its base; you can then gather seedlings in spring to put in other locations.

Sweet Cicely Cough Syrup

Mix together:

> 2 tbsps honey
> 1½ tbsps lemon juice
> 1 tbsp strong sweet cicely tea

To make a strong tea, pour boiling water over the herb and let steep for 30 minutes. Strain and use. Take as often as needed for coughs or sore throat. Other herbs that can be used instead of sweet cicely are marshmallow, sage, fennel, anise seed, and elecampane.

Part Used—Leaf and seeds.

Harvest—Leaf is harvested all season; does not dry well but can be frozen for winter use or put in a sugar pack; layering sugar and leaf in an airtight container will give the sugar an anise taste and aroma. Harvest seeds while they are green.

Uses—Culinary: Seeds can be eaten in the green stage but never when they turn black. Leaves are used in desserts with fruit (especially tart fruit such as rhubarb), and in teas. This is a sweet herb, making it useful to diabetics and dieters. When used in cooking, less sugar is needed in the recipe.

Medicinal: Valued as a diuretic and as a cough syrup ingredient.

Watercress *(Nasturtium officinale)*

Family—Cruciferae (mustard)

Synonyms—None.

Description—Herbaceous perennial growing in wet areas; needs cold moving water with high lime content. Oblong-toothed small leaves are high in vitamins C and E; small yellow flowers.

Cultivation—To grow in cultivated garden, follow these special steps:

Dig a hole and sink a large plastic container into the ground with the rim at ground level, in an area that gets at least four or five hours of morning sun and afternoon shade. Fill the container one-quarter full of good soil mixed with bone meal or lime; cover with inch of heavy gravel to prevent washout. Plant seedlings, adding just enough water to cover the watercress stems half way.

The secret to growing watercress is not to let the water become stagnant. Let the hose run several times a week on low volume into the container, creating a stream effect. Be careful not to wash away the seedling roots with a strong force of water.

Propagation—Seeds are easy but must be kept moist at all times; division of plant in early spring.

Part Used—Leaves.

Harvest—All growing season; use fresh.

Uses—Culinary: popular in a cream cheese sandwich. Because of its peppery taste, it can be used as a substitute for black pepper. Try adding some watercress to your spaghetti sauce and salads.

Medicinal: Used in tea to help pass kidney stones.

Cosmetic: Eating high-vitamin watercress will help keep the skin clear.

TWO

From Seed to Ground

(How to Start and Care for Your Seedlings)

He who sees things grow from the beginning will have the best view of them.
—Aristotle

Getting Started

Starting Seeds Inside

Starting seeds inside gives the New England herb gardener, who is faced with a relatively short growing season, a good head start. It produces an earlier harvest of annual herbs like fennel, which needs extra growing time to produce mature seeds.

In addition, starting seeds inside allows you to save money, especially if you need a large quantity of one kind of herb. One plant of dill, basil, or chervil never seems to be enough. Also, you can grow rare and unusual herbs not always available from local nurseries. Finally, there is a great deal of personal satisfaction in seeing those tiny seeds emerge from the soil and become full-fledged plants because of your own work.

To become totally acquainted with the growth process of each herb, start it from seed and observe its growth pattern right through to the *seed pod* stage. A seed pod is nature's seed holder, a seed-filled vessel which forms after the flower dies.

Packaged Seed

If you purchase packaged seed, following the correct procedure will enhance your chances for success. Most seed companies are reliable. They have a lot invested in their operation and they depend on a good reputation to remain in business.

Some herbs require fresh seed for successful germination, while others will do well with older seed from previously opened packages. I have used basil seed from the same package for the last three years with good results. However, herbs such as angelica, lovage, and sweet cicely will need fresh seed to germinate. They are best planted in the fall or within three months of harvesting the seed.

If you use only a portion of the seed in the package, seal the remainder in an airtight container. Plastic bags that self lock are good. Store them in a cool area away from direct sun or heat. Beginners are advised to try annual herb seeds first for good results.

Gathering Your Own Seed

Since most herbs have not been hybridized, gardeners can gather their own seeds in the fall. This is a good way to save money, develop a hardy strain of herbs, and increase your own plant supply considerably.

Starting Your Seeds the Wormwood Farm Way

Depending on the variety of herb, start your seeds six to eight weeks before the normal last frost date in your area. Check package directions.

Tips from Wormwood Farm

Here is a proven procedure for gathering your own seeds:

- Mark early in the season, with a colored tape or cloth, the herb from which you want to gather seeds.
- Harvest only from healthy, strong herbs.
- Select those with best color, size, or earliest flowers.
- Harvest only when seeds are fully mature.
- Clean away all debris, pods, leaves, and dirt.
- Label seeds.
- Dry in an open but not windy area, or dry in a warm room.
- When fully dried, store in envelopes or jars and label. Any seeds not completely dry will mildew and be useless.

If you start your seeds too early, you will end up with tall, "leggy" plants. I recommend starting half your seeds eight weeks before the planting date and the other half six weeks before the planting date.

After nine years of experimenting, trial and error, success and failure, we have developed a method for starting seeds that produces excellent germination for us. According to folklore, parsley seed "must go to the devil and back seven times before it germinates." With our method, it germinates in one half the normal time.

Step 1 (The Containers)—Any container with a depth of three inches and drainage holes on the bottom is suitable. Peat fiber flats, plastic flats, even cottage cheese and milk cartons will make suitable containers. It is important that the container be *sterile* and have *drainage holes* in the bottom. These drainage holes prevent the soil from becoming soggy and rotting the seed. Sterile containers will help prevent dampening-off disease, a disease caused by a fungus, which can make the seedlings rot off at the base of the plant and topple over. This disease occurs in unsterile or soggy soil, or in high humidity and high temperatures.

Step 2 (The Starting Medium)—You want to fill your container three-quarters full with a sterile medium. There are several good soilless preparations on the market. These may contain peat moss, perelite, vermiculite, a starter fertilizer, and often a *wetting agent*. The wetting agent is an element which helps hold moisture in the soilless medium. Perelite, used alone, is too cold and produces poor germination, while vermiculite *can* be used alone with very good results.

If you use your own soil, it should be sterilized. This can be done in the oven, but I must warn you, it is a very messy, smelly job. If you prefer to make your own soil mixture, here is a recipe that has worked well at Wormwood Farm:

Homemade Starter Medium

Mix together:

> 3 *parts sterile soil* (you can also buy soil)
> 2 *parts perelite*
> 2 *parts vermiculite*
> 2 *parts peat moss*
> ¼ *cup bonemeal to 9 quarts mix*
> *Wetting agent (optional)*

Follow manufacturer's directions.

Step 3 (Water)—Whenever possible, it is best to water by *capillary action*. This is a process by which the water is absorbed into the container from the bottom to the top. This is accomplished by filling a tray or sink with warm water and setting the soil-filled container in the water. The water will soak up through the container to the top. When the top of the soil is moist, you know the container is well saturated. Set on a drainer for one-half hour, then plant your seeds.

Step 4 (The Seeds)—Some seeds will need special treatment to ensure their success. Two such treatments are mentioned below. In addition, the Plant Profiles at the end of each chapter may mention any special treatments needed for particular herbs.

Stratification is a cold treatment sometimes needed by seeds for good germination. The seeds are planted in flats, enclosed in a plastic bag, and put in the refrigerator for the number of days or weeks suggested on the seed package. Many seed companies will have completed this dormancy period for you, so read the directions on the package carefully to determine if this step is needed. Some of the herbs which need stratification are aconite, sweet cicely, and the wild rose.

Soaking is another special treatment which is sometimes required. I can remember my grandfather always soaking his vegetable seeds before planting. I didn't know exactly why he did this other than it seemed to help. Indeed, soaking some seeds in water *will* shorten the germination time. This is especially useful for hard seeds as it makes their outer coat soften. Also, some seeds contain a built-in, natural chemical inhibitor which prevents germination until all of the proper conditions exist. Soaking helps to leach out these unwanted chemicals. Two hours are usually sufficient. Herbs that will benefit from soaking include scotch broom, parsley, and castor bean. Keep in mind that this treatment is *not* necessary for germination.

Step 5 (Sowing the Seeds)—Reap what you sow! Scatter your seeds *lightly* over the top of the soil. Even experienced gardeners sometimes overseed a flat, but remember that seeds planted too thickly will have to be thinned out later. Overcrowded seedlings will be starved for air and food and be subject to dampening-off disease, resulting in leggy, weak stems. Our goal is stocky, strong seedlings. If you do overseed, simply pluck out the excess seedlings as they grow, taking care not to disturb the remaining plants. If a plant is getting too big too rapidly, lowering the temperature will slow down its growth. Correct temperature is discussed later in this chapter.

I do not cover very tiny seeds at all but simply firm them into the soil with my hand. Larger seeds the size of basil should be lightly covered. One of the major problems in seeding is burying the seed too deeply.

Sowing coriander seed into the flat; this larger-sized seed should be slightly covered with soil.

Step 6 (Label - Label - Label!)—Unless you are planting only one kind of seed, you will need to label each variety carefully. Containers of tiny seedlings look very much alike at the early stage of growth. Some young plants will not look at all like the mature version. Be sure to use a waterproof pen, as water and rain will quickly erase common pen marks. There are many labeling devices you can use, from cut-up bleach bottles or milk containers to commercially made labels. I use popsicle sticks from the craft store.

If you are going to be starting seeds every year, I recommend using a notebook to keep track of important records. Here are a few things to list:

- name of seeds
- seed company (or home harvested)
- date planted
- date germinated
- any special treatment given

This information will be invaluable in future years. Note also any recommended changes in procedure, for example an earlier or later planting date. Notes are much more reliable than memory from year to year.

Step 7 (Using Plastic Bags)—When the previous steps have been followed, put your container into a clear plastic bag, making sure the plastic *does not touch* the soil. Any type of plastic bag will do, even bread bags.

Prop up the bag with popsicle sticks (or something similar) to keep it above the soil. You could also cover the container with a piece of glass or clear plastic wrap, which will serve the same purpose of keeping in the moisture. Check daily. If you find a little fungus growing, the container is too wet and you should remove the plastic. Be careful the soil does not dry out too much or the seeds will not germinate.

Step 8 (Heat and Light)—Using *bottom heat* will help seeds to germinate in one-half the normal time. My first set-up each year is using the bottom of the fish tank with a heating pad below and a fluorescent light above. This starts off some of the earlier herbs before I open the greenhouse. In the greenhouse (or in a cold frame), I lay heating cables on the floor under an inch of gravel. Commercial heat propagation mats are also available in all sizes and prices.

For correct air temperature, check the recommendation on the seed package. In the house, I usually keep the air temperature at 70°F during the day and 65°F at night. In the greenhouse, the night temperature is lowered to 60°F. If your seed needs a higher temperature, put your containers in the warmest place available. By using fluorescent lights, you can make a seed starting set-up in any room.

In the past, I went to the trouble of putting herb seeds which were supposed to require darkness to germinate in a dark place. These herbs did well. However, as I observed a lot of herbs over time, I noticed that the borage herb, one supposedly needing darkness, would self-germinate in the sunlight, even if not covered by soil. Soon I experimented with starting more of these "darkness-loving" herbs under the lights. Germination was good to excellent so I have not bothered to separate these plants anymore. Try this and other experiments for yourself. It's fun!

Step 9 (Plants Up)—As soon as the tiny leaves emerge, remove the plastic wrapping and the container from the heat source. Seedlings can be grown under fluorescent light or in a sunny window. If grown under lights, make sure the tops of the seedlings are always kept 2 to 6 inches from the bulb. If the plants are on a windowsill, beware of the sun's drying rays. Dried-out soil can kill the seedlings or seriously stunt their growth, so be sure to check the soil conditions regularly. You must also remove the containers from the windowsill at night because of the danger of chill to the seedlings. Or, you can place a piece of cardboard between the window pane and the plant. If the seedlings are leaning toward a light source, it means they are not getting enough light.

Step 10 (Caring for the Seedlings)—With a shelf full of seedlings, this is no time to take a vacation! These seedlings will need daily care. With just a few flats, it will take only minutes a day. Watering with the correct frequency and amount is the most important job in gardening. Too much water and the seedlings will rot; too little and the roots will dry out, killing the seedling. To much force of water can wash the seedlings right out of the flat.

Most of us do not enjoy a splash of cold water thrown on us as we bask in the sun. Neither do these little seedlings. Always use room temperature water for all watering before the hardening-off period. Rather than watering "on schedule," water when the seedlings need it. You can determine this by checking the soil with your fingers to see how dry the middle of the soil is. If it feels nice and moist, water later. If not, water now, preferably by capillary action (discussed earlier).

A few other hints:

- Check for insect problems regularly.
- If the seedlings topple over, they probably have dampening-off disease. If you catch it early enough, just scoop out the diseased part and separate the flat from other flats. Watch the remaining seedlings carefully.
- Give the plants a drink of chamomile tea on occasion. It is one of the healing herbs for fellow plants.

First Transplants

The first leaves that appear on the herb plant are called *seedling leaves*. Next comes a pair of leaves that are the *true leaves*. When this occurs, it is time for the first transplant. Some people leave the seedling in the original container, but I disagree with that method. Those seedlings tend to become leggy and weak stemmed. Those seedlings that are transplanted (into individual containers or six-packs) will develop strong, stocky stems. Water your seedlings about two hours before any transplanting; this fills the stems and leaves with water. Keep in mind that whenever a plant is transplanted, it loses a lot of moisture through its leaves.

For this first transplant, you can use good garden soil or the soilless mix you used previously. Do not fertilize for about a week after transplanting. Then start a fertilizing program using any good commercial fertilizer or a home mix such as manure tea (a cup of manure steeped in a gallon of water for several days). In commercial fertilizers, I like a 5-10-5 or 5-10-10 mixture and then I use it at only half the recommended strength. *Brand names are not important, only the number sequence.* The numbers represent, in order, nitrogen, phosphorus, and potassium. The numbers tell the percentage of each in the mix. For growing, we want a mix with a higher *phosphorus* content.

Nitrogen is found in the natural state in manures, dried blood, and fish emulsion. A lack of nitrogen causes slow, stunted growth and pale leaves. Excess nitrogen will produce too many leaves, not enough of the essential oils, and fewer flowers. Soils that receive sufficient compost will naturally have enough nitrogen for herb plants.

Phosphorus (the middle number) is found in bonemeal or phosphates. A lack of phosphorus will result in a purplish-colored leaf, and less flowers. Organic matters mixed with the soil will help "unlock" the phosphorus contained in the soil.

Potassium, or potash (the third number), is found in wood ash, green-sand, and Muriate of potash. Scientists are not exactly sure why potash is so important to plant growth. However, we do know that a lack of it will result in smaller herb plants with slightly brownish, dry leaves.

Hint: I am a fond believer in misting all plants to keep them clean and to provide extra moisture on the leaves. Also, using a bit of chamomile, yarrow, or garlic in the mister will promote plant health.

If newly transplanted herbs go limp, they are:

- Not getting enough water.
- Getting too much sun.
- Stored at too high a temperature (usually a greenhouse problem).

Hardening off

Hardening off is the process of introducing your safe, secure little seedlings to the harsh realities of the outdoors. They must face the perils of fluctuating weather, pouring rains, insects, soil-borne virus, fungus, and small animals. A cold frame is the ideal home for a small number of herbs. Cold frames are discussed in depth later in this chapter.

An alternative is to take your plants out in the morning and in at night, eventually leaving them out all the time. Be prepared to cover them if cold weather is predicted. Since New England is famous for its unpredictable weather, be ready "just in case".

At this time, you can start giving the plants colder water. In fact, I often start giving colder water just *before* the hardening off period. Remember that just because these plants have become hardened off does not mean they are hardy enough to withstand a frost. If you do get caught with a light frost, get up before the sun does and hose your plants *gently* with water. This gives them moisture and prevents the sun from breaking down the plant fibers; I have saved a few plants this way on unexpectedly frosty mornings.

In the Ground

In New England, there is a real risk of planting too early. A warm spell in the early spring can be very tempting. Year after year, people come to Wormwood Farm to buy replacement plants after they have gone to all the trouble of starting their own seeds, only to plant too early and lose them. Before planting, I like my soil temperature at a *minimum* of 45°F. An inexpensive soil thermometer will be very helpful. As a general rule, when the soil is dry enough to "work" and the general temperature is satisfactory, the seedlings can be planted. It is very difficult to give specific dates because of the great variations from region to region. If you do plant too early, be prepared to cover your plants in the event of cold weather.

The garden plot is well prepared. The seedlings were watered two hours ago. Hand tools are ready. It is evening or a cloudy day. *Now is the time.* If I plant on a sunny day, I cover the plant with a pot or basket to protect it from the hot sun, which can quickly dry out leaves and stems. The plants need some time to adjust to their new surroundings and they are quite vulnerable when first planted.

Hold the seedlings by the leaves or the root ball, not the stems. Gently tuck them into well-prepared soil. Firm in *gently*. Spacing will depend on the ultimate size of the herb plant. Very large plants such as borage or comfrey will need 2 to 3 feet while smaller herbs, such as sweet marjoram, can be placed 8 inches apart. The average is about 1 foot apart. Water the area well once the seedlings are snugly planted in the ground.

Many people think spring is the only time to plant. However, the fact is that you can put in herb plants any time during the growing season. Remember that during the hot months of July and August, the plants need to be protected from the broiling sun for several days. I do not recommend planting after late August in very cold areas (zones 3 and 4). An early frost will heave the plants right out of the soil before they have a chance to root.

The Cold Frame

The cold frame mentioned earlier is an enclosed box frame with the back higher than the front. This design provides light reflection and warmth for your plants. The cold frame can have a bottom or be bottomless, just setting on the ground. It needs a cover that lifts up for ventilation or complete removal. It is useful for starting seeds early, hardening off, all-season growing, and extension of the fall season. You can make your own or purchase a ready-made one.

The cold frame should be set up with a southern exposure. It can be made against a cellar window, allowing the warmth to flow into it from the house and the sun. A glass cover is recommended, as plastic only lasts a year or so. Old windows can be purchased at secondhand stores. Build the frame around the dimensions of the window that you are able to get.

Propagation

There are other ways to increase your supply of herbs other than by the seeding process. Some herbs, like French tarragon, produce sterile seeds and therefore must be propagated by asexual means. Note that while seeded plants will sometimes produce offspring different from the parent, asexually produced plants will all be identical clones. For the home gardener, these asexual methods are easier and quicker, especially when working with perennials. Check the plant profiles at the end of each chapter for the best method of propagation.

There are three basic propagation methods:

Division of Plants—This method involves separating the plant by its roots. I usually use this method in the spring before the plant becomes too large. I then have the entire growing season for it to become established. To divide the herb, push into the root system with a garden fork and pull the roots apart. You can use a spade on herbs with a tighter root system (such as lady's mantle).

For smaller clumps of tightly woven plant roots, cut into the clump with a knife and pull it apart with your hands. If you can pull it apart without using a knife, even better.

Often a plant produces little offspring next to the mother plant's root system. These are called *offsets* and can be removed simply by cutting the umbilical cord between the plants. Roman chamomile and allheal (prunella) produce offsets.

Another kind of plant division is from *bulbs*. These can be separated by hand, hand tools, or garden fork. Most of the alliums (onions) are separated by bulbs. The dwarf curly onion will form a rosette and each bulb can be separated. The Egyptian onion can be propagated by the bulbs that grow on top of the stalk or by the bottom bulb. Each can be planted in the ground or, if left alone, will replant itself.

Some herbs, iris florentine for example, are divided by the rhizome. Simply separate it with a hand tool as it grows very close to the top of the soil. Wash and check it for soft spots and worms. If a soft spot is found, take a spoon and scoop away the mushy part until you feel hard root. Then sterilize the rhizome with a solution of one part household bleach to one part water, mixed thoroughly. The plant can then be divided into pieces;

A knife is often used to cut through the tightly woven roots of some herb plants. Each clump will be a new plant.

each must have roots and eyes (the top green part) on it. Let a callous form on the cut parts before replanting.

Stem Cuttings—This is another asexual method of propagation. I have found that the best time to take stem cuttings is during the noon hours, when the herb is full of food. *Remember*, if possible, to water the plant two hours before taking the cuttings. Do not take cuttings from flowering stems. The following procedure is recommended:

1. Remove stem cuttings with a knife or scissors.
2. Remove the lower leaves so none will touch the soil medium or water.
3. Dip in a rooting mixture (This is optional; I do not use it).
4. Place cuttings in a soilless medium, water, vermiculite, or perelite. Pack the cuttings in thickly so they will root better.
5. Wrap in a plastic bag to maintain high humidity.

Watch the cuttings. If leaves start to brown, you have too much humidity and not enough air. Both are necessary in the right amounts. Remove the bag. Rosemary, pineapple sage, oreganos, and scented geraniums are

A flat of sage cuttings; notice how the lower leaves are removed to prevent rotting.

good species for stem cuttings. In August, take the garden cuttings of basil, thyme, and sage to place on the windowsill for your winter herbs.

When taking cuttings from scented geraniums, follow the basic instructions with one exception. After you remove the lower leaves, let the cuttings sit on the shelf for two hours. This will form a callous on the cut end and prevent it from rotting in the medium.

If you are away from home and someone gives you a cutting, place it in a container of water until you can plant it at home. Many people start their cuttings in water alone; this sometimes produces soft roots but this will vary with individual herbs. Dittany of Crete, for example, does best started in water alone.

Layering—This propagation process involves starting a new plant from the mother plant without cutting it off from the mother plant. Woody herbs in particular take well to layering. Here is the procedure:

1. Bend the woody stem to the ground.
2. Wound the area that will touch the soil. This is done by scraping off a little wood or slightly (but not completely) breaking the stem.
3. Push the wounded stem into the ground.
4. Cover with soil.
5. Secure it. This can be done with a heavy rock, brick, or wire.

Examples of woody herbs include lavender, rosemary, southernwood, hyssop, and wormwood. Some herbs (such as thyme) will root themselves wherever the stem lays. They can then be cut out just like offsets.

Plant Profiles

Borage *(Borago officinalis)*

Family—Boraginaceae (borage)

Synonyms—Bee bread, burrage.

Description—Annual, height to 2½ feet, width to 3 feet; the hollow, hairy stems have dark green, oval-shaped leaves that are also slightly hairy. Flowers are blue (sometimes they bud out pink and then turn blue), five pointed, star shaped, flowering all season. Borage is the symbol of courage. It is said that those who eat of the borage herb will be given strength of heart and joyfulness along with courage.

Cultivation—Borage will grow in just about any soil, as long as it has good drainage available; plant in full sun or partial shade. A good 3 by 3 foot area is needed for this herb; because of weak stems it tends to sprawl down instead of standing upright. Borage is loved by bees and therefore is a good pollinating herb; plant with tomatoes and strawberries for this reason. Beekeepers will want this honey-making herb near the beehives.

Propagation—Borage is generally started outside by seed; however, small seedlings to 3 inches high can be transplanted. Give a lot of water and put a pot over the herb for two or three days; it will wilt, but take root in a few days. Large plants almost always die when transplanted because of their long tap root.

Part Used—Flowers and leaves

Harvest—Flowers are harvested all season for fresh use; they do not dry well. Leaves should be harvested when young, or just take the growing tips since the older leaves are just too hairy. Dry on screens.

Uses—Culinary: The blue flowers can be used in salads, cakes, decorations, and for floating in drinks. The slight taste of cucumber from the leaves makes them good in tossed salads, or on cream cheese sandwiches. Young leaves can be cooked with peas, or served like spinach. Borage is one of the ingredients in our popular Wormwood Farm Punch.

Medicinal: Borage tea is used internally to reduce fevers and act as a calmative. Externally, the herb can be used as a poultice for abcesses.

Herbal Punch

Take *one handful of borage leaves and flowers, one handful of lemon balm leaves,* and *one handful of Lebanese mint and curly spearmint* (or any two mints mixed). Steep for two hours in 1½ quarts of boiling water. Strain and add the following:

¾ cup of sugar
1 quart of black tea (using 4 tea bags)
½ cup lemon juice
1 large (46 oz) can pineapple juice
1 large (46 oz) can orange juice

When ready to serve, add *three 2-liter bottles of ginger ale or Sprite.* Mix can be frozen in portions if all is not needed at one time.

I serve this punch in a large bowl at all our herbal functions. The punch is decorated with orange slices, lemon slices, and a pretty herbal wreath. During the Christmas holidays, green and red cherries are placed on the lemon slices and cinnamon sticks are added. During the summer, you can freeze edible flowers in ice cubes. Dried herbs can be substituted for the fresh herbs, using ¼ cup dried to equal one handful of fresh.

The herbalist Gerard says, "A sirup concocted of the flowers quietith the lunatick person."

Coriander *(Coriandrum sativus)*

Family—Umbelliferae (carrot)

Synonyms—Cilantro, dizzycorn, Chinese parsley

Description—This 24-inch annual has bright green leaves divided into segments. The white terminal flowers sometimes have tinges of pink in them. The seeds are little round balls that turn brown when ready for harvest. This herb is often confusing for the beginner, as it is sold under two names, coriander and cilantro, but it is all one and the same plant: it is called *coriander* when the seed part is used and *cilantro* when the leaf part is used. The fresh plant emits an unpleasant aroma, but the seeds develop a pleasant aroma as they age. This herb can be kept a long time before using the seeds since it gains in aroma as it ages. One of the oldest herbs known to mankind, it was found in ancient tombs, where it was used to preserve bodies. The Chinese thought it would bestow immortality on the dead. It is mentioned several times in the Bible; from Exodus, "And it was like wafers made from honey." In the Arabian *Thousand and One Nights*, coriander was mentioned as an aphrodisiac. A popular herb in witchcraft, it was thought to have the power of love when used in sachets and charms. Also, witches said that when combined with fennel, it could conjure up the devil himself.

Cultivation—Plant in full sun and good soil; does not like to compete with weeds. Apply a good mulch in hot, dry weather to keep the roots cool.

Propagation—Seeds germinate easily; they can be started inside or seeded directly outside. For a continuous supply of leaf (cilantro), plant weekly for three weeks. The herb goes by quickly, especially in hot dry weather. Coriander will self-seed the following year.

Part Used—Leaf and seed

Harvest—Leaf is best used fresh; does not dry well; can be frozen in ice cubes for winter use. Harvest seeds when the leaves begin to turn brown by putting seeds in a paper bag with air holes and hanging in a warm place; seeds will fall to the bottom.

Uses—Culinary: Cilantro has become popular in the past few years because of an interest in ethnic cooking. Mexican, Indian, and Oriental recipes often call for it. Leaves are good in salads and soups. The seeds (coriander) are tasty when ground into apple sauce, puddings, Danish pastry, curries, beets, and soups. I use a pepper mill just for coriander,

Spicy Bread Pudding

Butter a one-quart casserole dish. Fill three-quarters full with bread pieces (I like to combine white and brown breads). In a small mixing bowl combine:

4 cups milk
2 medium eggs beaten
1½ cups brown sugar
2 cups raisins
½ tsp vanilla
½ tsp ground nutmeg
½ tsp ground coriander

Pour over bread in casserole dish. Bake in 350° oven for about 40 minutes or until firm in the middle. Serve with vanilla ice cream and a little grated coriander on top if desired.

keeping the seeds as whole as possible for a fresher taste, grinding as needed. My favorite recipe for bread pudding includes coriander.

Medicinal: An herb as old as coriander would naturally have found its way into the world of medicine. Internally, it is used to relieve cramps, expel gas, and strengthen the stomach. Externally, it is used as a massage oil to rub on painful joints and to ease rheumatism.

Cosmetic: Use as an ingredient in cheesecloth bath sachets for aroma.

Crafting: A good textured seed for potpourri that adds a spicy aroma.

Caution: The name dizzycorn comes from the fact that eating the seeds in very large quantities has a narcotic effect and will make you dizzy.

Calendula *(Calendula officinalis)*

Family—Compositae (daisy)

Synonyms—Pot marigold, Mary's gold

Description—Hardy annual to 15 inches tall. Leaves are pale green and oblong, with rounded points and a slightly sticky feel. Flowers are orange or yellow, flowering all season. This herb also became hybridized. In older herb books, calendula is often referred to as marigold.

Cultivation—Calendula enjoys full sun with good drainage and alkaline soil. A soil that is too rich will produce more leaves and less flowers. Calendula can be potted to add patio color or to grow on your windowsill.

Propagation—Easy by seed; start inside four weeks before last frost date; will self-sow the following year.

Part Used—Flowers

Harvest—All season; dry only the colored petals on paper towels or screens; can be microwaved.

Uses—Culinary: Leaves were sometimes used in the past in salads but are too bitter for modern-day taste buds. Use flower petals in rice, cheese dishes, egg dishes, soups, salads, and desserts. Calendula is often used as a substitute for the very expensive saffron. Calendula tea can be made alone or mixed with equal parts of thyme and elderflower for pleasure.

Medicinal: Used as a wash for sore eyes or in a tea to bring out measles and treat colds, fevers, and cramps.

Cosmetic: This slightly mucilagenous herb makes a good lotion for softening the skin. Also, use in bath water and as a hair rinse for light-colored hair.

Dye Herb: Petals produce a creamy yellow dye.

Crafting: Orange and yellow petals are a colorful addition to potpourri mixes. See Chapter Eleven for potpourri recipes.

Marigold Flower Cake

Cream ½ *cup butter* with ½ *cup sugar* until soft and fluffy. Add *6 egg yolks* that have been well beaten; add to the mixture below, alternating with *1 cup milk*.
  Mixture:

  3 cups flour
  4½ tsp baking powder
  ½ *tsp cinnamon*
  2 tbsp finely cut calendula flowers

Stir in *1 tsp vanilla* and *1 tsp lemon juice*. Bake in greased 9 x 13 cake pan in 375° oven for 25 to 30 minutes. To serve, sprinkle on a little confectionary sugar and decorate with calendula flowers.

Chamomile, German *(Matricaria chamomilla)*

Family—Compositae (daisy)

Synonyms—Wild chamomile

Description—Hardy annual to 15 inches. The differences between the German and Roman Chamomile are:

German	Roman
appears early in spring	appears late in spring
hollow yellow disk	solid yellow disk
erect growth	prostrate growth
annual	perennial

Cultivation—Full sun, alkaline soil, and good drainage; keep weed-free.

Propagation—By seeds; start inside six weeks before last frost date in your area.

Part Used—Flowers

Harvest—Flowers as white petals start to turn backwards. Dry in microwave or on paper towels on screen. A lot are needed as the flowers are very small. Foliage can be dried for use in potpourri.

Uses—Medicinal: As a tea for pleasure and medicine. *Caution:* May have an adverse affect on persons with hay fever and may increase the appetite. Use the tea for a cold and as a gargle for a sore throat. Make an antiseptic for a douche, hemorrhoids, and external wounds. Large doses are emetic (induce vomiting).

Cosmetic: As a skin and bath herb; use in hair rinse for light-colored hair.

Chamomile, Roman *(Anthemis nobilis)*

Family—Compositae (daisy)

Synonyms—None

Description—Perennial to 6 inches high, with small daisy-like flowers. A good herb for growing between rocks or bricks in walkways. Can easily be mowed to keep it low and prevent flowering. It is said the more it is walked on, the more it grows. Has an apple-like scent when touched. Has a green, ferny leaf.

Cultivation—Full sun or partial shade; good drainage; alkaline soil. Keep weeded; it will choke out weeds as it grows.

Propagation—By seeds, six weeks before last frost; root division any time.

Part Used—Flowers

Harvest—Flowers as their yellow rays start to turn backwards. Dry in microwave or on paper towels on screens.

Uses—Medicinal: *See German chamomile* for use as a medicinal tea. Excessive use can cause vertigo and vomiting (excessive use consists of several cups a day over a prolonged period of time).
    Cosmetic: Same as for German chamomile.
    Miscellaneous: It is said that if you rub this herb on your skin before entering the woods, you will be protected from mosquitos. A healing herb for other plants; use in a mister or in a watering can to prevent dampening-off disease.

Epazote *(Chenopodium ambrosiodes)*

Family—Chenopodiaceae (goosefoot)

Synonyms—American wormseed, Mexican tea

Description—Annual herb growing to 3 feet tall; lance-shaped leaves; flowers are greenish.

Cultivation—Likes full sun to partial shade, good drainage; will grow in sandy soil.

Propagation—By seed; will self-seed abundantly.

Part Used—Leaves only. *Caution:* Flowering tips may be poisonous. Do *not* use these tips internally.

Harvest—Lower leaves all season; best when fresh; hang-dry the entire herb for making wreaths.

Uses—Culinary: Use with baked beans, corn, and fish dishes.

Medicinal: An herb used to expel intestinal worms. The Mexican people use it as a spring tonic. The American Indians also used it as a medicine for intestinal problems. *Caution: Do not use epazote medicinally unless under medical supervision.*

Crafting: The entire plant can be dried and used in wreath making.

THREE

Cracks and Crevices

(Garden Design and Plant Placement)

"To prescribe one form (of garden) for every man to follow were too great a presumption and folly, for every man will please his own fancie."
—John Parkinson (1629)

KNOWING THE characteristics of the herbs you are working with and having a plan in mind will help you achieve a successful garden.

Garden Size and Placement

Gardening should be fun, a pleasure not a chore. Matching the size of your garden to the level of commitment you can make to it will help to ensure that it remains fun. Start with a small garden if you are a beginner or if you cannot devote much time to it. Increase the size of your garden as your interest and commitment increase. Ask yourself these questions as you are planning:

- How much time can I devote?
- Will I have help? From whom?
- How much money do I want to budget?
- How much space do I want to commit to an herb garden?

If you do wish to plan for a large garden, you may want to develop it over a period of several years. Finally, remember that a large variety of herbs can go into a fairly small space. You can also plan for container gardening.

Placement of the Garden

As you plan the placement of your herb garden, consider the following:

- Do I want to be able to see the garden from a certain window?
- Will I have foundation plantings?
- Do I have a choice of front, back, or side yard? Which offers the best conditions for the herbs I want to grow?
- What type of soil will I be working with?
- Will the garden interfere with the space requirements of other family members or pets?
- What are the sun/shade conditions in various areas?

When you have answered all of these questions, you should be ready to select your garden area.

Herb Garden Style

Here we will describe some ideas and choices which have worked for us here at the farm. There are many other options, so do not be afraid to try out your own ideas.

There are basically two general styles of garden, *formal* and *informal*. The formal garden is characterized by:

- geometric shapes
- a balance among plants and statues
- planting in evenly numbered rows
- less variety but more of one herb
- neatly trimmed edgings
- a focal point
- a requirement for perfect maintenance
- paths of brick, stone, cement, etc.

Formal gardens can be as simple or as elaborate as you choose. Quilt patterns provide good ideas for shapes and layout of the formal garden.

Informal gardens are characterized by:

- a wider variety of herbs placed in more random settings, well planned but less structured
- planting in unevenly numbered rows
- placement in herbaceous borders, foundation planting, islands, or other natural settings

Tips from Wormwood Farm

- Plan your garden on paper first: Here you can make changes before too much time and energy are involved.
- Herbs can be in a separate garden but they are also right at home intermingled with flowers and vegetables.
- Keep in mind that you are working with living things and changing weather. Plants will change from week to week; keep an eye on them throughout the growing season to learn more about their individual needs and how they develop into mature plants.

Early informal colonial gardens were normally for practical use, not decoration. They were placed as near the house as possible with no special design. These gardens were called "yarb patches."

Your garden can be determined by the style of your house, the layout of your land, or the time and energy you want to put into planning and maintenance. A slope is a good place for a rock garden or a terraced garden. A flat area can be made into an attractive formal or island bed. Wooded areas lend themselves to naturalist gardening.

Exposure to the Elements

The amount of light a plant receives will determine the amount of chlorophyll it manufactures. You must know in advance how much light an individual herb requires.

Check your garden area to see how the sun plays out its drama during the day. If you are planning during the winter or early spring, remember that the sun is lower in the sky at that time of the year and adjust accordingly.

There are several light conditions we work with. Keep these in mind as you read the plant profiles:

Full Sun: provides at least seven hours of sunlight.

Partial Shade: minimum of five hours of full sun.

Filtered Sun: bright light with partial shade provided by the leaves of deciduous trees; may include several hours of full sunlight.

Full Shade: this does not mean *no sun* (only moss, ferns, and lichen grow without sunlight). It is a condition of diffused light wihout direct sunlight.

High winds in exposed areas can sometimes do more damage to plants than extreme cold. Certain plants, lavender, for example, and other Mediterranean-type herbs, do not like the wind. They must be planted in a protected area behind fences, walls, or buildings.

New England normally receives ample rain for most herbs. However, if you plant under trees the amount of rain getting through the leaves may be insufficient for the herbs. Keep your herb plants away from the wash-off from roofs. Note areas where water puddles after a rainstorm as that area may have poor drainage for your herbs. Finally, in your planning be sure to figure a way to water those plants that may need it.

Design Considerations

Pathways

In gardens wider than three feet (or however far your arm can reach), the need to weed requires that you create pathways. Plan for these early. Paths can be made out of any accessible material, for example brick, flagstone, crushed stone, wood chips, gravel.

Give some thought to the purpose of your path before you construct it. If you do have a large garden, you will want to make the pathways wide enough for your garden cart or wheelbarrow, as well as for evening strolls.

Brick pathways in Wormwood Farm's Chimes of Thyme *garden.*

If you just want access for weeding, a smaller path will do. In a garden full of fragrant herbs and flowers, you may want the path close to the plants so you can brush against them as you walk by.

To decorate brick and stone paths, try planting herbs which can be walked upon. These include creeping thymes, rupturewort, and Roman chamomile. The flowers of these herbs should be cut off because they attract bees and you do not want to step on bees.

Walls and Fences

Walls and fences are a welcome addition to your garden, whether you build them or use those already in place. They provide privacy, good background for taller plants, wind protection, and warmth. Because of this protection, they can help your plants mature faster, providing an earlier harvest. Plan your herb colors for the type of wall or fence you have. Gray plants look washed-out against cement but contrast nicely with red brick. Use bright colors against a cement background.

Focal Points

A focal point is a special interesting item added to your garden to provide your own personal touch of beauty and to make a statement. It is a very popular addition to many theme gardens. It can be a:

- specimen plant (such as a large rosemary in an urn or raised planter)
- sundial
- bee skep
- statue
- bird bath
- specially handcrafted art work

You can use your focal point as the centerpiece of the garden or you can add it as a complementary item.

Garden Shape

During planning, give some thought to what shape you would like your garden to be. Plan for a circle, square, rectangle, triangle, or a combination of shapes. The layout of your land may dictate what pattern you will be able to use.

A couple of simple designs for *beginners* or those with a *small area* are:

- an old wooden wheel set on bricks off the ground with herbs growing inside the spokes. The center hub can have a focal point of your choice.

An old bicycle wheel is used as a focal point
in a raised bed of annual herbs.

- an old wooden ladder set on bricks with plants between the rungs. This is a good layout for those who want only a few herbs.

Theme Gardens

Developing a theme garden is creative and a lot of fun. It is an art form of gardening. Our gardens include a culinary herb garden, a saint's garden, and a zoo garden.

Here are some ideas you can try or think about. This list may give you some ideas of your own for creating an herb garden to go with your own hobbies and interests.

Culinary herb garden—This can be a collection of your favorite culinary herbs or it can be a specialized garden with just salad herbs, soup herbs, or culinary flowers. Some culinary herb garden tips:

- Place the garden as near the kitchen as possible. Gathering herbs for that last-minute dish will be faster.
- A path made of clean, solid material will be less muddy in the rain. You can even walk on it with slippers on wet mornings.
- Locate your garden away from roads. They produce lead, salt, and dirt you do not need.
- Do not use chemical sprays on culinary herbs. See Chapter 9 for a list of culinary herbs to use.

Fragrant herb garden—Who doesn't enjoy the wonderful aroma of herbs? The ancient Greeks planted their fragrant plants near doors and windows so the fragrance would float into the room on a gentle breeze. You can have fresh arrangements on the coffee table and you can dry fragrant herbs for use in winter, when everyone will really appreciate them.

Some fragrant herbs will give generously of their aroma For example, valerian can be enjoyed from twenty feet away. Others, like lemon balm and southernwood, wait until they are caressed to release their scent. A sampling of fragrant herbs to use:

Annuals	Tender perennials	Biennials
ambrosia	lemon grass	clary sage
basil	lemon verbena	wallflower
marjoram	rosemary	
mignonette	pineapple sage	
sweet annie	scented geraniums	

Hardy perennials		
anise-hyssop	lemon balm	thymes
bee balm	lemon catnip	southernwood
clove pinks	meadowsweet	Russian sage
costmary	mints	tansy
gnaphalium	old roses	valerian
hyssop	pennyroyal	violets
lavender	santolinas	winter savory

Cosmetic herb garden—Herbs have been used for centuries to enhance beauty. Place these herbs away from roads and do not use chemical sprays. A focal point might be a Greek or Roman statue. The following is a list of herbs appropriate for your cosmetic herb garden:

Herb	Part Used	Purpose
agrimony	leaves, flowers	healing and soothing aching muscles
borage	leaves, flowers	heals dry skin

Continued on next page

calendula	petals	nourishes and softens skin; shampoo and hair rinse
chamomile	flowers	moisturizes; shampoo, dandruff control
coltsfoot	leaves	helps prevent red thread veins
comfrey	leaves	healing
elderflower	flowers	softens dry or aging skin
fennel	leaves	healing; wrinkle removal
lady's mantle	leaves	healing; for sensitive skin
lavender	flowers	fragrance; astringent
lemon balm	leaves	soothing; wrinkle removal
lovage	leaves	natural deodorizer
marshmallow	leaves, root	emollient; healing
mints	leaves	astringent; healing
mugwort	leaves	relaxes muscles
parsley	leaves	prevents dandruff
rosemary	leaves, flowers	rejuvenating; shampoo and hair rinse (will darken hair)
roses	petals	fragrance; moisturizer
sage	leaves	astringent; for oily and itchy skin
salad burnet	leaves	softens dry skin
soapwort	leaves	shampoo
southernwood	leaves	prevents dandruff and strengthens hair
thyme	leaves	stimulating; acne control
valerian	leaves	calming
vervain	leaves	relaxing in bath
yarrow	leaves	astringent for oily skin; shampoo and hair rinse

Biblical garden—There has been a close relationship between herbs and religious ceremonies since the early pagan era. Scented herbs and flowers were even used to cover up the putrid smell of burning flesh when sacrifices were made to the sun gods. Christian religions changed the role of plants to a more positive one of decoration for rites and ceremonies. Certain herbs were rededicated to Christian beliefs.

During the Dark Ages, the monasteries preserved this herbal tradition and history for mankind. Monks grew medicinal herbs near the infirmary, culinary herbs near the kitchen, and a paradise garden of fragrant herbs and colorful flowers for decorating the church.

Biblical gardens can be developed around several sub-themes:

Our Lady's Garden: herbs dedicated to the Virgin Mary; includes lady's mantle, lady's bedstraw, and teasel (called Our Lady's Basin).

Herbs from the Bible: includes herbs or flowers actually mentioned in the Bible, such as wormwood, dill, coriander, leeks, garlic, and thyme.

Saint's garden: includes those herbs that have special correlation to a saint. These would include basil for St. Basil, St. Johnswort for St. John, and herb Robert for St. Robert. An appropriate focal point would be a statue of a saint. At Wormwood Farm we have a special garden which is a combination Saint's and Biblical gardens. St. Francis stands at the head of the raised bed with a background of red roses for love and purity. At his feet grows thyme, signifying courage and its use in the manger. In front of the saint statue is a cross of bricks filled with thyme. Other herbs include: lady's mantle, the herb dedicated by the Virgin Mary to women's medical problems; calendula signifying the sun against the darkness of sin; costmary, also called Bible leaf, was used in Bibles as a book mark and also chewed during long sermons; St. Johnswort, the herb Robert, wormwood, and blue flax fill the center. Rue, the herb of grace, Johnny-jump-up, or viola tri-color, to signify the Holy Trinity, are also included in our Saint's garden.

Medicinal herb garden—Some of the earliest uses of herbs were medicinal. Hippocrates listed over 300 medicinal herbs in his works. See Chapter 13 for more details on medicinal herbs. As with a culinary garden, keep a medicinal herb garden away from roads and use no chemicals. Several of the medicinal herbs are invasive so you may want to isolate them. Some wild medicinal herbs can be grown in lovely natural settings.

Dye herb garden—This could be called the garden of tinctoria, the botanical name for dye herbs. Our ancestors raised sheep to produce wool and flax to produce linen. Dye plants were used to add color to these materials. They were also used to give color to food and cosmetics. When aniline, a synthetic chemical dye, was discovered (about 1850) herbs were replaced by the more efficient chemicals.

A fixative substance (called a mordant) is used to make the material receptive to the natural herb dye and to make the color longer lasting. Mordants are alum, iron, chrome, cream of tartar, tin and copper sulfate. Herbs used for dye include:

Herb	Color	Mordant
agrimony	yellow from leaves	alum
bloodroot	red and orange from root	none
comfrey	brown from leaf	iron oxide
dyer's broom	yellow from flowers	alum
elderberry	violet from berry	alum
gipsywort	black from leaf	none
lady's bedstraw	red from root	alum
madder	red from root	alum
madder	orange from root	tin
St. Johnswort	yellow from flowering top	chrome

Monochromatic gardens—This is a garden of herbs and flowers of one color. These can be combined for a dramatic effect. Use your favorite color with a small number of plants of a contrasting color to add interest. All one color can become boring, especially without a suitable background or focal point. Here is an idea for a *gray and silver garden* with red brick pathways for contrast. Or, you can use burgandy foliage plants for good contrast.

Example of a Monochromatic Garden

edelweiss	8-inch perennial from the Swiss Alps; gray flowers and foliage
gnaphalium	10-inch curry-scented perennial, gray leaves with bright, woolly, yellow flowers
lamb's ear	12-inch perennial with velvet leaves and soft, pink, woolly flowers
mullein	6-foot wild biennial for a background, self-seeds, spike yellow flowers
Roman wormwood	15-inch perennial, spreads quickly, silver-gray, fragrant
rose campion	3-foot biennial, soft gray foliage with crimson red flowers, second season
santolina	(lavender cotton) 15-inch silver-gray tender perennial for zone 4, yellow flowers
silver king	3-foot invasive perennnial, silver-gray leaf, white-gray flowers
silver mound	12-inch mound of ferny leaf, silver-gray foliage, white-gray flowers
white peppermint	3-foot perennial, non-invasive mint, gray-green foliage with white flowers
wormwood	3-foot gray-green leaves, insignificant yellow flowers

Shakespeare garden—Shakespeare's plays and poems are full of references to herbs and flowers. The Elizabethan gardens were located close to the house, often enclosed with fences and hedges. They varied from simple front yard cottage gardens to elaborate estate gardens with gates, intricate hedges, urns, statues, and fountains.

The women of the time were well-schooled in the use of herbs. The "still room" was a special part of the house where all the work with herbs was done. People of wealth often employed several herb ladies to prepare special recipes, which were passed down from mother to daughter. See Chapter 10 for our Shakespeare tea recipe.

The following herbs, mentioned in Shakespeare's plays and poems, can all be easily grown in the Northeast:

aconite	heartsease	salad burnet
bay leaf	hyssop	sampire
broom	lavender	savories
calendula	lemon balm	southernwood
chamomile	mints	sweet marjoram
clove-pink	parsley	thyme
dill	rosemary	violets
fennel	roses	wormwood
flax	rue	

Colonial garden—This type of garden is a favorite of people with colonial homes. It includes herbs commonly used by the early American settlers for cooking, medicine, and cosmetics.

Gardens were enclosed by wattle fences (fences made with young saplings woven together). Later, split rail, picket, and other types of fences came into use. Fences were used to keep animals out. Today we fence the animals *in* and leave the gardens *open*. Paths of brick and gravel were commonly used. Sundials were a favorite focal point. Herbs, flowers, and vegetables were often grown together. Logs were used to make raised beds.

Flowers were dried for winter use and herbs were hung in bunches near doorways to ward off evil spirits.

Here is a partial list of herbs favored by colonial people:

agrimony	dill	lungwort
angelica	elecampane	mallows
basil	fennel	marigold
betony	feverfew	marjoram
borage	figwort	mints
bouncing bet (soapwort)	flax	mugwort
chamomile	gipsywort	parsley
caraway	herb Robert	pennyroyal

Continued on next page

catmint (catnip)	hollyhocks	salad burnet
celandine (swallowort)	horehound	southernwood
chervil	hyssop	strawberries
chives	lady's bedstraw	sweet cicely
clary sage	lavender	thyme
comfrey	leeks	valerian
coriander	lemon balm (melissa)	violets
costmary	lovage	wormwood

Bee and butterfly garden—See Chapter 6 for details on this garden.

Old English wort garden—Wort is an old Anglo-Saxon word meaning root; it was once used for all plants. Eventually, it came to mean specifically herbs. Although the word is no longer in popular use, some herbs still retain the wort, for example mugwort, soapwort, motherwort, and lungwort. Wort names are often seen in folklore and old herbals.

Wort gardens are characterized by stone seats in a private enclosed area, with fountains or ponds or some sort of water supply. Stone paths and statues are used to create a medieval garden effect. We can't put a moat around a castle and garden, but wouldn't it be fun? Perhaps you could create something like this in miniature. Here is a list of herbs which have retained the word wort in their names:

figwort	motherwort	soapwort
gipsywort	mugwort	spiderwort
lungwort	rupturewort	St. Johnswort

This list of wort herbs includes the old name (no longer used) and the modern name:

Old Name	**Modern Name**
banwort	sweet violets
blackwort	comfrey
bloodwort	yarrow
churchwort	pennyroyal
elfwort	elecampane
fingerwort	foxglove
flirtwort	feverfew
foalswort	coltsfoot
hillwort	pennyroyal or wild thyme
maderwort	wormwood
sealwort	Solomon's seal
smerewort	Good King Henry
sneezewort	yarrow
sticklewort	agrimony
wolfswort	aconite (now called wolfsbane)

Wormwood Farm's fun zoo garden attracts children; it's a good way for them to learn the herb names.

Zoo garden—My zoo garden is a delight to children and adults alike. It is a combination of herbs and flowers with names of animals, birds, insects, and fish. This garden teaches children about herbs in an interesting way. Focal points can be statues of animals. My unicorn plant (martynia) grows beside a ceramic skunk holding its own nose to show the terrible smell of the plant's beautiful flowers.

Here is a list of herbs appropriate for a zoo garden:

bee balm	hens and chickens
catnip	horehound
dandelion	lamb's ear
fat hen (Good King Henry)	red chickweed (scarlet pimpernel)
fleabane (erigeron)	snakeroot (black cohosh or cimicfuga)
foxglove	Solomon's seal
goat's rue	turtlehead (chelone)
gooseberry-scented geranium	wolfsbane (aconite)

Children's garden—It is very important to start children early in gardening. When they are young they get a feeling for the joy and satisfaction of working with plants. You can let them help you with your garden or have one of their own. A children's garden should include a variety of herbs, flowers, and vegetables which they help choose. You can provide guidance based on your experience. A 6 by 8 ft. raised bed will be large enough to grow a good variety of plants, yet small enough for a child to keep up. Some hints for a children's garden:

• A trellis at one end will support beans or gourds.

- Use a plastic animal as a focal point.
- Teach the child which plants are poisonous.
- Include a root vegetable (carrots, beets, or potatoes).
- Tiny Tim tomatoes and bush cucumbers take up very little room.
- Include fragrant flowers.

Here are some herbs I know children enjoy:

- alpine strawberries—for that weeding snack
- bee balm—to attract hummingbirds
- catnip—if they have a cat so they can make their own catnip toys
- Egyptian onion—it grows its onion bulbs on top of the stem, an edible novelty
- hens and chickens—easy to grow and multiplies quickly
- Johnny-jump-ups—grows all season and is self-seeding
- lovage—a tall herb for the background; the hollow stems are cut and used as straws (and pea shooters).

One species garden—If you have a favorite family of herbs, make a garden of all the members of that family which will grow in your area.
Some of the large families of herbs are:

achillea (yarrow)	salvias (sage)
alliums (onion)	scented geranium
artemisias	thyme
basil	wormwood
lemon-scented herbs	

Indian herb garden—Our Indian tribes have a long history of using natural herbs for cooking and medicine. Many of these are wild native American herbs; some can be harvested from the wild, others cultivated in our gardens. Here are some to consider.

1. Herbs found near pond edges and bogs:

blue flag iris	purple loosestrife
goat's rue	turtlehead
joe-pye weed	yellow flag iris
marshmallow	

2. Herbs found near wooded areas in partial shade:

agrimony	mountain mint
American ginger	snakeroot
black cohosh	tansy
bloodroot	white yarrow
May apple	

3. Herbs found in full sun areas such as fields:

alfalfa
allheal (prunella)
American elder
American mountain ash
bergamot (bee balm)
betony
blackberry
celandine
coltsfoot
great blue lobelia
Indian tobacco

mullein
New Jersey tea
pearly everlasting
red clover
scullcap
soapwort
stinging nettle
tansy
valerian
yarrow

Drying garden—Some plants lend themselves especially well to drying and later use as crafting material. The following list includes only those that are considered members of the herb families. See Chapter 11 for using dried material.

Herb	Part Dried
ambrosia	fragrant green foliage
anise-hyssop	purple flowers
bee balm	mixed flowers
Chinese lantern	orange pods
chives (most alliums)	mixed flowers
cinnamon basil	pink flowers
epazote	green foliage
feverfew	white or yellow flowers
gnaphalium	yellow flowers
hollyhock	mixed colors
hop vine	green strobile
joe-pye weed	mauve flowers
lady's mantle	green-yellow flowers
larkspur	mixed colors
lavender	lavender flowers
mugwort	flowering green tops
pearly everlasting	white flowers
showy marjoram	purple rose flowers
silver king	silver foliage
silver mound	silver foliage
tansy	yellow flowers
teasel	pod
tri-color sage	purple and pink leaf bacts
wormwood	flowering yellow tops
yarrow	assorted colored flowers

Witches brew garden—There has been a fascination with witches since ancient times. Stories and legends about witches and their use of herbs have been passed down through the years. Herbs were used by witches to work charms and cast spells. They were also used by common folk to drive away witches and other evil spirits. Sometimes, women who were interested in herbal medicine became known as witches and were executed for their practices.

The characteristics of a witches garden are:

- round shape
- focal point such as a black cauldron, black cat, rooster statue, etc.
- poisonous plants in a black witches garden
- healing plants in a white witches garden

The white witch used herbs only for good purposes like love and healing; the herbs can be used for love charms and "protection" amulets. Herbs to include in your witches garden are:

Herb	Purpose
angelica	protection, exorcism
basil	purification, protection, carried in your pocket to attract money
bay leaf	neither witch nor devil will harm those that grow bay leaf
betony	protection, used in pillows to prevent nightmares
caraway	kept near valuables to prevent stealing; keep straying husbands home
chamomile	charm to bring money
coriander	used in love charms
dill	protector of children
elecampane	love charm, used with vervain
flax	protector of small children
hop vine	put in pillow for good dreams
juniper	planted near doorways; no witch could enter a house without counting all the needles on the juniper bush; she would soon tire and leave
lovage	use in bath water to attract the opposite sex
mugwort	brings good luck and money; hung over doorways to keep the devil out
mullein	carried when walking in the forest to protect you from wild animals

Continued on next page

rosemary	hung over babies' cradles for protection
roses	love charms
rowan tree	berries were strung as necklaces and hung around the necks of pigs and cows to protect them
rue	protection and exorcism
sage	exorcism; planted on graves to give immortality
scarlet pimpernel	a charm to keep witch craft from being used on you
St. Johnswort	used at summer solstice rituals to keep evil spirits away
valerian	aphrodisiac; love sachets for squabbling couples
vervain	love charms; to repel witches
wormwood	protection; used in clairvoyance with incense
yarrow	hung by doorways on summer solstice to keep evil spirits away for the following year

Tea garden—If you enjoy herbal teas, you may want your own tea garden. Or, you may want your tea garden to be a place where you can enjoy that cup of tea. Plant near a patio or gazebo so you can snip a sprig of herb for that herbal tea. Dry your herbs for winter time teas. See Chapter 10 for tea recipes. Here are some tea herbs which can be grown in New England gardens.

agrimony
alfalfa
anise-hyssop
basil
bee balm
caraway
catnip
chamomiles
clover-red
dill
fennel

hyssop
lavender
lemon balm
marjoram
mints
mugwort
parsley
pineapple sage
rosemary
scullcap
thyme

Plant Profiles

Sweet Woodruff (*Galium odorata or Asperula odorata*)
The accepted botanical name today is usually Asperula, but its old name Galium is still used in many herbals. I am presenting both names to avoid confusion when you see it listed differently in various books.

Family—Rubiaceae (madder)

Synonyms—Master of the wood, wood rove

Description—Herbaceous perennial is only 8 inches tall, making it a good ground cover for shady areas. Shiny, bright-green leaves are palm shaped, growing in succession up the stem. Rough, textured leaves with white, star-shaped, tiny flowers in early spring. Its creeping root habit gives it its German name, master of the wood. Sweet woodruff has no aroma when fresh; however it has a hay-vanilla smell when dry.

Cultivation—Sweet woodruff seems to be the exception to the rule in herbs as it prefers shade and an acidic, rich, moist soil. Good ground cover for use under acidic plants such as rhododendrons, azaleas, or pine and fir trees.

Propagation—By root division any time. It does produce a small amount of seed but is difficult to gather. The ants often eat the seed before it is gathered.

Part Used—Leaf and flower

Harvest—Harvest in full flower or leaf all season.

Uses—Culinary: Most popular use is in making the May wine bowl, a popular drink in Germany to celebrate May Day.

Medicinal: During the Middle Ages, sweet woodruff was used to treat jaundice, liver complaints, and external wounds. Today it helps migraine headaches, depression, and fevers. *Caution:* Overuse of sweet woodruff may cause symptoms of poisoning and dizziness.

Miscellaneous: Useful in potpourri and for moth bags. This herb will repel insects around books and help prevent that musty smell from developing in packed-away items.

Restharrow *(Ononis spinosa)*

Family—Leguminosae (pea)

Synonyms—Thorny ononis

May Bowl

Fill container with sweet woodruff. Pour in a bottle of Rhine wine (any good white wine will do). Let steep for two weeks. Strain herb out. Serve with strawberries floating in a glass. Some people like to use half champagne; I prefer to cut mine with ginger ale for a weaker drink.

Description—Herbaceous perennial to 3 feet tall; root is long and hard to eradicate once established. Its name is from the root, which would become entangled in plows and harrows. One of the few thorny herbs; they appear during the second year. Pink, pea-like flowers in July are long lasting.

Cultivation—Full sun, good drainage; may need staking in windy areas. In Western states, it is considered an obnoxious weed, but in New England it does not spread as quickly and is therefore better tolerated.

Propagation—By seeds eight weeks before last frost; also, you can divide the roots in early spring; often self-seeds.

Part Used—Roots

Harvest—Roots in the fall

Uses—Medicinal: The roots are diuretic; when used in a tea, they will help pass bladder stones. Parkinson says that restharrow, sliced and steeped in wine for 24 hours, is good for tender stomachs. The root can also be dried and powdered and taken in fruit juices.

Lovage *(Levisticum officinalis)*

Family—Umbelliferae (carrot)

Synonyms—Love parsley

Description—Herbaceous perennial to 5 feet tall. Looks like a giant celery plant and has a celery taste and aroma. The name love parsley comes from the fact that it was once used in love charms and as an aphrodisiac. Umbel flowers are yellow.

Cultivation—Likes to have its roots covered with other vegetation or to be well mulched. Sun to partial shade with a rich soil; leaves will be darker if plant is in the shade. Supply water when needed in dry season.

Part Used—Leaves, stems, and roots

Harvest—Leaves all season, stems when needed, and roots in the fall; screen dry.

Uses—Culinary: Use the leaves in any dish in which you would normally use celery, such as soups, salads, rice, vegetable dishes, and casseroles. This is one of the herbs that will survive long simmering without losing its flavor. Hollow stems can be cut and used as straws in tomato juice or bloody marys. Roots can be boiled for a vegetable but are probably too bitter for most modern taste buds.

Medicinal: Tea is diuretic; also used for flatulence and fevers. Gargle a tea for a sore throat.

Cosmetic: A natual deodorizer; leaves or roots are cleansing in a bath.

FOUR

Getting Intimate with Your Herbs

(The Characteristics of Herb Plants)

"Why should a man die while sage grows in his garden."
—from an ancient herbalist

THE MORE YOU KNOW about your plants, the more successful your garden will be. Creating the right environmental conditions for each plant is an important part of your planning. Casual planting may produce unsatisfactory results. Consider the following characteristics of your plants *before actually planting*.

Growth Patterns

A key to proper choice of herbs and placement in the garden is the life cycle of the plant. There are four types of cycles. (We are using members of the salvia [sage] family for examples of each cycle).

1. *Annual*—these plants complete their life cycle in one growing season. An example is tri-colored sage (also called painted sage).
2. *Biennial*—growth cycle takes two years, the first year produces leaves and the second produces flowers and seeds. An example is clary sage.
3. *Tender perennials*—these are long-lived plants which are sensitive to frost and thus must be taken in each fall. If the plant has grown too large outside, cuttings can be taken in August and new plants started for winter growing. An example is pineapple sage.

4. *Hardy perennials*—these are long-lasting plants which survive cold weather and may even require it. Some varieties live only three or four years, others as long as fifty years. An example is garden sage.

Zone Hardiness

Zone hardiness is a function of a plant's natural resistance to cold weather. New England has four zone areas, 6 through 3, each with its own topographical climate. Your State Agricultural Department can supply you with a zone map. Wormwood Farm is in zone 4, with a tolerance of –30°F. However, many plants recommended for zone 5 will do well here. With special protection and care, even some zone 6 plants will survive a normal winter in zone 4.

Height

It is important to know the final height of mature plants so you can allow them enough room in your garden. It is easy to underestimate the ultimate height of a tiny seedling. Besides the natural height of the plant, soil conditions and the weather will play a role in final plant height. Height charts can show you averages for your plants, but poor soil will produce shorter plants and rich soil overly tall plants. Arrange your herbs so that none are hidden by others and each one shows off at its best. In a

Castor bean offers a tropical texture to the annual garden; the seeds are poisonous.

Tips From Wormwood Farm

- Medium-sized herbs (12 inches to 3 feet) should be used in the middle of the border or for hedging material (try santolina, lemon balm, hyssop, lavender, rue, or chives.)
- Small herbs that make great-looking edges include alpine strawberry, dwarf curly onion, spicy globe basil (annual), catnip mussinii, parsley, winter savory, and silver mound.
- In the cracks and crevices of rock walls, plant herbs that will tolerate heat and lack of sufficient water. These include hens and chickens, rupturewort, allheal, thymes, Roman chamomile, alpine lady's mantle, hardy oregano, woolly yarrow, gnaphalium, deadnettles, and lady's bedstraw.
- For the tops of stone walls, try herbs which will tolerate dryness and cascade over the walls.

border or foundation arrangement, place the tall herbs at the back with others planted according to descending height down to the lowest border. In an island bed (one which you can completely walk around), place the tall herbs in the center with others graduating to the outer edges.

Textures and Shape

There is a wide variety of textures and shapes in the foliage of herb plants. If possible, study a mature plant or a picture of a plant and try to select what you like best. Visiting professional gardens will give you a lot of ideas. A combination of several different textures and shapes will give you an interesting garden.

Create a soft look with the gray foliage of lamb's ear, woolly thyme, and gnaphalium. For a tropical look, use castor bean along with comfrey, elecampane, angelica, lovage, and coltsfoot. For an airy, ferny look, use herbs such as ambrosia, sweet annie, lady's bedstraw, yarrow, and fennel.

Finally, remember that flowers on perennials will last only for a short time, so consider the look of the foliage, which will last all season.

Shade and Trees

In Chapter 3, we discussed shade conditions. Now we will consider which herbs like what degree of shade. Generally, *most herbs do well with full sun or partial shade.* Those requiring *filtered or full shade* are:

aconite	May apple
ajuga	snakeroot
American ginger	Solomon's seal
bloodroot	sweet cicely
foxglove	sweet woodruff

Planting under certain types of trees can be a problem. The shallow roots of maple, horse chestnut, or beech trees, for example, will absorb all the nearby water and nutrients. Some herbs, however, can tolerate these conditions. A creeping thyme does well under our big maple tree. Be sure not to plant any closer than six feet from the trunk.

Evergreen trees prefer a slightly acid soil. Herbs that will grow well with these trees are sweet woodruff, bloodroot, and snakeroot.

Color

The mix of colors will be your personal choice—and what a beautiful mix to choose from! Those who think herbs are just a bunch of green plants have not yet met the bright red bee balm, the sunshine yellow dyer's chamomile, the airy blue of blue flax, or the brilliant orange of the Siberian wallflower.

Experienced gardeners know that the perfect color scheme is never achieved because of the constant change taking place. Flowers fade and wither; light changes, enhancing some colors while diminishing others. Whites and pastels look brighter at dusk or under artificial lighting.

Variegated herbs have a more prominent coloring when planted in the shade; when planted in full sun, they produce too much chlorophyll, which makes them lose their variegation. Feeding variegated herbs will also produce too much green coloring.

Look to nature for the variety of greens in a forest area. Mother Nature plants in harmonious colors, but man plants in contrasting colors. A harmonious green oasis can be designed with various shades and tints of green foliage. The bright light green of lemon balm, the deep, dark green of Good King Henry, the blue-green of rue, and the gray-green of horehound can, when combined with a variety of different textures, be a very attractive garden.

Refer to the following chart for information about growth pattern, color, size, and bloom time:

Annuals	Height	Color	Bloom Time
ambrosia	18"	green	summer
basil	12"-14"	pinks	summer
borage	3'	blue	all season

Continued on next page

calendula	12"	orange, yellow	all season
castor bean	6'-8'	red	late summer
chervil	18"	white	spring
coriander	20"	white	summer
dill	3'	yellow	summer
epazote	24"	green	summer
fennel	5'	white	late summer
German chamomile	8"	white	summer
mignonette	8"	green	summer
parsley	12"	white	2nd year
scarlet pimpernel	8"	red	all summer
shisho perilla	20"	pink	summer
sweet annie	5'-6'	yellow	late summer
sweet marjoram	15"	white	late summer
tri-color sage	24"	blue/pink	all summer

Biennials

angelica	4'-5'	white	summer
caraway	24"	white	spring
chicory	3'	blue	fall
clary sage	24"	pale pink	summer
dyer's woad	30"	yellow	spring
English daisy	8"	pinks	spring
foxglove	3'	mix	summer
Fuller's teasel	6'	pink	summer
hollyhock	5'-6'	mix	late summer
mullein	5'-6'	yellow	spring-summer
viper's bugloss	2'	blue	summer

Hardy Perennials

aconite	18"	blue	spring
agrimony	3'	yellow	spring
alfalfa	2'-3'	blue	spring
allheal (prunella)	8"	purple	summer
alpine strawberry	12"	white	all summer
American ginger	10"	brown	spring
anise-hyssop	3'	purple	summer
bee balm	3'	mix	summer
betony	20"	pink	spring
bloodroot	12"	white	spring
catnip	3'	white	summer
celandine	24"	yellow	spring
chives	24"	pink	spring
clove pink	12"	pinks	summer
coltsfoot	12"	yellow	spring

Continued on next page

Hardy Perennials	Height	Color	Bloom Time
comfrey	3'	blue	all summer
costmary	3'	yellow	late summer
curly dwarf onion	8"	pink	summer
curly onion	24"	pink	summer
deadnettle	12"-18"	mix	spring-summer
dyer's chamomile	3'	yellow	summer-fall
edelweiss	8"	gray	summer
Egyptian onion	3'	none	summer
elecampane	6'	yellow	late summer
feverfew	20"	white-yellow	summer
flax	20"	blue	all season
Florentine iris	24"	blue/white	spring
garlic chives	20"	white	summer
gipsywort	3'	pink	late summer
gnaphalium	8"	yellow	summer
Good King Henry	26"	green	all season
hop vine	25'	green strobile	late summer
horehound	20"	white	summer
horseradish	3'	white	late summer
hyssop	24"	purple	all season
iris florentine	24"	blue/white	spring
joe-pye weed	6'	mauve	summer
lady's bedstraw	16"	yellow	summer
lady's mantle	24"	green-yellow	spring
lamb's ear	12"	pink	summer
lavender	20"	lavender	summer
lemon balm	24"	white	late summer
lobelia, great	24"	blue	summer
loosestrife	30"	purple	late summer
lovage	5'	white	spring
lungwort	12"	blue	spring
marshmallow	4'-5'	pink	summer
May apple	12"	white	spring
meadowsweet	3'	white/pink	spring
mints	1"-3'	white	late summer
mitsuba	24"	white	summer
motherwort	3'	purple	summer
mugwort	5'	brown	summer
mussinii catnip	10"	purple	spring
oregano	16"	pink	summer
pennyroyal	6"	pink	late summer
restharrow	3'	pink	all summer
Roman chamomile	10"	white	summer
rue	24"	yellow	late summer
rupturewort	1"	green	all summer

Continued on next page

Russian comfrey	24"	lt. blue	spring
sage	24"	blue	spring
St. Johnswort	24"	yellow	summer
salad burnet	24"	pink	summer
scullcap	10"-12"	pink	summer
Solomon's seal	3'	white	spring
silver king	3'	silver	late summer
silver mound	12"	silver	late summer
soapwort	16"	pink	summer
southernwood	3'	yellow	late summer
snakeroot	6'	white	late summer
stinging nettle	3'-4'	green	summer
sweet cicely	2'	white	spring
sweet woodruff	10"	white	spring
tansy	3'	yellow	summer
tarragon	3'	gray	late summer
thymes	1"-12"	pink	summer
valerian	6'	white	summer
vervain	20"	blue	late summer
winter savory	12"	white	summer
wormwood	3'	yellow	late summer
yarrow	6"-3'	mixed	spring-summer

Rhythm

A sense of rhythm can be achieved by using one herb placed in various areas. As you look at the garden as a whole this herb will tie it all together, creating a sense of unity.

At Wormwood Farm we use lady's mantle for spring, dyer's chamomile for summer, and wormwood for late summer. These plants will be seen planted at different points in each of our gardens. In a border, rhythm can be achieved by placing one herb at various points of the border.

Poisonous Herbs

Every now and then, someone asks me which herbs are poisonous; they are usually concerned about a small child or pet. Any book that boasts about all the wonderful qualities of herbs should assume the responsibility for telling about the dangers of the unsafe herbs.

I wonder how many of our ancestors died from their experiments with using plants for medicine and cooking. They learned how to use plants by trial and error and the errors could be fatal.

All parts of some herbs are dangerous. Other herbs will have only certain parts that are dangerous. Elderberry, for instance, has poisonous leaves

Tips from Wormwood Farm

- Plan your color where you want it and when you want it. If you vacation the month of July, the garden color will not be important to you then.
- Time of bloom will be different throughout the New England area. To find out the timetable of the herb bloom in your area, check with a local herbalist. Keep a notebook of bloom dates from your own garden and those you visit.
- As you become more interested in herb gardening you will notice other color combinations in nature as well as in other people's gardens.
- Massing colors can be impressive, but in a small garden there just isn't room. Use a very bright color such as bee balm or dyer's chamomile to brighten even the dullest of corners.
- Cool colors of blue, green and purple will create a feeling of depth and add length to the garden. The warm colors of red, yellow, and orange bring the garden forward.
- White is often used as a contrast color. A bright white will make reds and yellows look even brighter. But a creamy white looks best with blues and purples. Gray and silver foliage will tone down colors that are too harsh.
- In long borders, balance colors so they do not look lopsided in the garden. Different herbs can be used as long as they bloom at the same time.

and bark, yet the flowers and berries are edible. Then there are those herbs that will be unsafe only to persons with sensitive skin or allergies. Correct identification is *absolutely essential* any time an herb will be used internally. There are also unsafe herbs that may look similar to the safe herbs. Take care with old herbals that may contain outdated information about using certain herbs internally. Tansy was once used for cakes, served at church feasts, and also used for medicinal purposes. Today, it has been banned for sale for internal use by the FDA because of its toxicity. *An overdose of tansy can be fatal.*

Classification of Poisonous Herbs

Keep the following safety tips in mind:

- *Label* all poisonous herbs in the garden and in the dried stage.

- A poisonous theme garden should be fenced in for safety and well labeled.
- Keep the telephone number of the local poison treatment center near the phone.
- Do *not* plant poisonous plants near culinary or medicinal plants in the garden. A poisonous leaf could easily be picked, unknown to you, as you harvest the safe herbs.

The following list is divided into two parts. List 1 herbs are *deadly*. List 2 herbs are unsafe in parts or to certain persons. Only herbs usually grown in the New England area are listed. *Know what plants in your particular area are poisonous.*

List 1—Very Dangerous Herbs

Aconite *(Aconitum napellus):* also called monkshood and wolfsbane; all parts are poisonous and improper use can result in death; toxic properties can even be absorbed by the skin.

Arnica *(Arnica montana):* or leopardsbane and mountain tobacco; death possible from internal use; may cause skin rash to some persons.

Belladonna *(Atropa belladonna):* deadly nightshade; has inviting looking poisonous blue berries; all parts very poisonous.

Castor Bean *(Ricinis communis):* grown for its tropical-looking leaves; only the seeds are poisonous; keep red flowers cut off to prevent seeding.

Foxglove *(Digitalis purpureum):* important medicinal herb can be fatal when improper dosage is used; use only under medical supervision.

Henbane *(Hyoscyamus niger):* also called hog bean, poison tobacco, and stinking nightshade; this annual herb is fatal even in small amounts.

Jimson Weed *(Datura stramonium):* fatal in large doses; my usually unsensitive skin will get a burning rash by just handling the fruit.

Lily of the Valley *(Convallaria majalis):* internal use can be fatal; some old and some new herbals will recommend this herb for internal use. Do not use internally!

Larkspur *(Delphinium spp.):* large doses may prove fatal; grown for its dried flowers; a popular herb.

May Apple *(Podophyllum pelatum):* Indians used this herb to commit suicide; will cause death if used improperly. The small, yellow fruit is edible but the leaves, seeds, and root are poisonous.

Angelica

List 2—Unsafe Herbs

Angelica *(Angelica archangelica):* sometimes used in cooking; may prove to be carcinogenic; has several look-alike plants.

Bloodroot *(Sanguinaria canadensis):* contains alkaloids which may be poisonous to some persons.

Celandine *(Chelidonium majus):* reputed to cure warts but may cause rash in some persons. Internal use is not recommended.

Chinese Lantern *(Physalis alkekengi):* ripe fruit is eaten, but the unripe fruit is toxic; large amounts of this herb can cause diarrhea.

Elderberry *(Sambacus candensis):* leaves and bark are poisonous; flowers and berries safe to use.

Epazote *(Chenopodium ambrosiodes):* leaves are eaten but flowering tops and seed heads are toxic.

Figwort *(Scrophularia nodosa):* its aroma befits its other name (stinking Christopher). Used externally for medicine; internally, it is a poison.

Rue *(Ruta graveolens):* causes rash in some people; causes photosensitization when the herb touches wet skin exposed to sunlight, it often makes a rash on the skin. Do not weed when it is wet.

St. Johnswort *(Hypericum perforatum):* may cause a rash on some persons; animals eating this herb may become sensitive to light. Internal use is banned by the FDA.

Figwort

Tansy *(Tanacetum vulgare):* large doses may be fatal.

Wallflower *(Cheiranthus cheiri):* internal use can cause heart failure.

Wormwood *(Artemisia absinthium):* banned by FDA for sale for internal use; this bitter herb may cause insomnia.

Invasive Herbs

When I began my study of herbs, I made two mistakes: their names are horseradish and Fuller's teasel, two very invasive herbs. Invasive herbs are those plants that spread rapidly by underground roots or self-seeding, very generously, becoming pests in the garden.

Horseradish still plagues my garden, traveling quickly by roots. Even though it is excellent in the kitchen, it is a pest outdoors. Fuller's teasel, a biennial, is invasive because it self-seeds, scattering seeds everywhere.

Here is a partial list of invasive herbs:

Herb	Invasive Method
gipsywort	roots
horseradish	roots
lady's bedstraw	roots
mints	roots
motherwort	seeds
pearl yarrow	roots
red yarrow	roots
Roman wormwood	roots
tansy	roots
teasel	seeds
valerian	seeds

Tips from Wormwood Farm

- Plant invasive herbs in their own spot, away from the regular garden.
- Invasive root plants can be grown in containers, to prevent their roots from spreading. Wine half-barrels are popular and attractive.
- Roots can be contained by sinking metal or plastic two feet into the ground, enclosing the herb.
- Self-seeders can be contained by keeping the flower heads cut off to prevent seeds from developing.

Special Problems with Herbs

Dampening-off disease: Discussed in Chapter 2.

Mint Rust: Orange spots will appear on leaves. Immediately cut back to ground level, and burn or properly discard all cuttings. (Do not put diseased material in the compost pile.) If the rust reappears, dig up the mint and discard. Replant with a new strain of mint in a new garden area.

Crown Rot: This will occur if the gardener plants the herbs too deeply. The crown of the plant then has no air and will rot off, killing the plant. Also, keep mulch away from the stem as decomposing material can also rot the crown of the plant.

Powdery mildew: A grayish-white, powder-like substance covering the leaves or flowers. To prevent this, avoid crowding the plants too closely together. Keep plants out of damp, shady areas when they prefer full sun; and keep planted areas well weeded. If mildew gets on an herb, spray with a mixture of warm water and baking soda (2 cups water with cup baking soda). If this does not work, cut the plant back to ground. Herbs often attacked by mildew are bee balm, valerian, mallows, tansy, roses, and turtlehead. Mildew will not kill the plant; it just looks unattractive.

Plant Profiles

Sage *(Salvia officinalis)*

Family—Labiatae (mint)

Synonyms—Garden or common sage

Description—Perennial to 24 inches, coarse, slightly wrinkled, gray-green leaves, lavender blossoms in late June. Saying from ancient herbalist: "Why should a man die while sage grows in his garden." The sage plant provided a choice beverage of the Chinese. They often traded triple the amount of their black tea for the sage leaves. Its name salvia means *to save*, probably because of its many uses as a medicinal herb.

Cultivation—Enjoys full sun, good drainage, and alkaline, slightly lean soil; overly rich soil will produce less essential oil content in the leaves. I prefer to replant the sage plant every three years as it tends to become woody after that time and produces fewer of the succulent leaves. Keep pinched back to make a bushy plant.

Propagation—Easy from seed; start inside six weeks before last frost date. Cuttings or layering of mature herb will add to your supply.

Part Used—Leaf

Harvest—All season; for drying, harvest just before it comes into flower; fresh all season. Do not microwave because sage loses its color if dried too quickly; hang or screen dry.

Uses—Culinary: What would turkey be without sage in the stuffing? Also compatable with chicken, duck, goose, pork, sausage, and onion dishes.
Medicinal: Sage is my favorite herb for gargling to treat a sore throat. Sage tea is for pleasure as well as for medicinal uses for colds, fevers, and spring tonic. For an herbal toothpowder, try the following recipe:

> *1 ounce baking soda*
> *1 ounce sea salt*
> *1 ounce dried sage leaves,* well crushed

Mix and let age 10 days before using. Store in an air-tight container.

Cosmetic: Astringent for skin; use in bath water; a hair rinse for dark-colored hair.
Crafting: Use in culinary wreath; the leaves have good texture when pressed for use in art work.

Dyer's Woad *(Isatis tinctoria)*

Family—Cruciferae (mustard)

Synonyms—None

Description—Hardy biennial to 3 feet by the second year. Yellow flowers followed by black pendulous seeds. The earliest dye known to mankind, but replaced by the easier and more reliable indigo herb in the 1930s. Early

Englishmen dyed their skins with the blue dye for wars and religious rituals, which caused the invading Romans to refuse them as slaves.

Cultivation—Full sun, good drainage, rich soil, and a lot of fertilizer; it will deplete the soil if not fed regularly.

Propagation—Easy by seeds; will self-seed after second year. Start inside six weeks before last frost date.

Part Used—Leaf

Harvest—Leaf just before it comes into flower. Leaves are dried slightly in the sun then ground into a paste with mortar and pestle and formed into a ball by kneading. Balls are dried and then powdered and set to ferment for nine weeks. While they are fermenting, they are sprinkled with water and turned. The dark clay substance that results is used for the dye.

Uses—Primarily used as a dye plant.

Goat's Rue

Goat's Rue *(Galega officinalis)*

Family—Leguminosae (pea)

Synonyms—Herba ruta, caprarine

Description—Herbaceous perennial to 3 to 4 feet tall. Looks like the New England beach pea; the pea-like foliage has white and blue flowers. No scent unless injured, then smells goat-like, hence its name.

Cultivation—Full sun to partial shade. Likes any soil with good drainage. Needs water during drought periods.

Propagation—Seeds or division of root in spring, self-seeds

Part Used—Leaves

Harvest—Leaves and flowering tops all season. Dry on screens.

Uses—Medicinal: tea for fevers. The whole herb is fed to cows to increase milk secretion.
  Cosmetic: In bath water for tired muscles.

Rupturewort *(Herniaria glabra)*

Family—Caryophyllaceae (pink family)

Synonyms—Burstwort

Description—A creeping hardy perennial only one inch tall. The odorless herb has tiny green leaves and insignificant yellow-green flowers. Will grow in the leanest of soils. Good for cracks and crevices.

Cultivation—Full sun to partial shade (grows taller in the shade). Keep well weeded the first year and it will choke out the weeds.

Propagation—Start by seeds, 6 weeks before last frost date, or by division anytime.

Part Used—Leaves

Harvest—All season, dry on paper towels on screens.

Uses—Medicinal: In tea form, has been used for bladder problems since ancient times.

Hop Vine *(Humulus lupulus)*

Family—Urticaceae (stinging nettle)

Synonyms—None

Description—A perennial vine to 25 to 30 feet; takes two years to get well established; will need trellis to grow on, vine is aggressive and strong. Likes rich soil and good air circulation. Cut down vine after frost kills it.

Part Used—Strobiles (little green, conelike flowers).

The hop vine makes an excellent trellis in the garden; it grows to 30 feet in one season and then dies back in the winter.

Harvest—Strobile (individually) for dream pillow or tea; vine for use in wreath making. Green strobiles will fade to a light tan in about 6 months. Dry on screens or hang dry.

Uses—Culinary: used to brew beers and tea (very bitter).

Medicinal: calms nerves, tonic, stimulates appetite. *Caution*—Persons with depression should not use.

Crafting: Pillows filled with hops are reputed to induce sleep and give good dreams; supplement with aromatic scents such as lavender, rose, or mints.

Thymes (*Thymus vulgare and spp.*)

Family—Labiatae (mint)

Synonyms—Common thyme, mother of thyme

Description—Over 25 common available varieties for the New England gardener, all from 1 to 12 inches, vigorous spreaders, many branched leaves; flower colors from white to pink to purple. The symbol of courage; women in Europe embroidered a bee hovering over a thyme plant on scarves to give to their knights as they went off to the Crusades.

Cultivation—Likes a lean soil with excellent drainage; full sun to partial shade. Good for walkways and rock gardens.

Propagation—some species by seed, not always true to species. Division of plant any time.

Part Used—Leaf

Harvest—Best essential oils are obtained just before the herb comes into bloom. Dry in microwave or on screens in warm area.

Uses—Culinary: This is my favorite culinary herb: when in doubt, use thyme. Goes well with just about all foods; tea for pleasure; excellent with chowders, soups, vegetables, meats, salads, and egg and rice dishes.

Medicinal: antiseptic for external use on wounds; internally, a tea for flatulence, diarrhea, or worms. *Caution*—excessive use can cause symptoms of poisoning and over-stimulate the thyroid gland.

Cosmetic: hair rinse, mouth wash, and in bath water.

Craft: potpourri, flowers for wreaths.

Stuffing

Using day-old bread, break bread into pieces. Mix together:

4 cups bread pieces
3 medium eggs, beaten
2 medium onions, finely diced
2 tbsps crushed sage leaves (4 tbsps if fresh)
2 tbsps crushed parsley
½ tsp black pepper, freshly ground
½ tsp crushed thyme

Use to stuff turkey or other fowl, and bake as usual.

FIVE

My Rosemary Wears Pantyhose

(How to Care for your Container Garden)

IN ORDER TO keep their tender perennials alive and safe from freezing, the early settlers brought them into their dimly lit cabins. They hoped the plants would survive the cold, harsh winter so they could be replanted outside in spring. Today's homes have more windows, providing much better sunlight conditions inside. Glass sun rooms are gaining in popularity, as are small affordable greenhouses. Fluorescent lighting has made it possible to have a living garden in any room or apartment.

Here is a summary of those herbs which make good houseplants:

Aloe: The plant for treating burns; every home should have one for just this purpose. Aloe can spend the summer outside in the shade; north window for winter inside. Don't overwater.

Bay leaf: A slow grower. Do not plant directly in the ground outside in the New England area. It can summer outside in a container in shady area; inside, give bright light. If using leaves for cooking, dry them first.

Cardamom: An evergreen spice herb for low-light areas. Fragrant leaves can be clipped for potpourri. It rarely flowers inside, giving us those pods for cooking. Low-water requirement makes this an easy plant to care for.

Curry: Put your curry outside for the summer and bring it in for winter. Highly aromatic curry scent will be supplemented with bright yellow flowers. Put in south or east facing window. This is not the culinary curry. The culinary curry is actually a blend of several different herbs and spices.

Dittany of Crete: A rare herb that is becoming better known, dittany makes an excellent hanging-basket specimen. It has a bi-leaf system; the woolly gray-green leaves have terminal, papery bracts ending with pink flowers. Full sun inside winter, shade outside in summer. Do not let plant dry out completely.

Eucalyptus naturally deodor-
izes a home and provides
material for dried flower craft.

Eucalyptus: Even though more common out west, eucalyptus makes an interesting houseplant for New England homes. Use a large container; keep outside in summer and bring inside for winter. Likes good light or sun. There are several varieties available. Those that do well in my home include: eucalyptus globulus, the blue gum, used for cold medicine; eucalyptus cinerea, the one that crafters love for its round, bluish foliage used in arrangements and wreaths; eucalyptus citriodora, a nice, lemon-scented herb. Do not add lime to these plants. They will also tolerate the dry atmosphere of winter homes, adding natural scent as a bonus.

Lemon Grass: Not a beautiful herb, but the leaves are very fragrant and a good addition to potpourri as well as for making a delicious tea. Keep out of direct sunlight.

Lavenders: There are many varieties of lavenders, many of which are not winter-hardy in New England. Keep them inside in a sunny window and they will usually bloom for you. Fernleaf and spike lavender are just two good varieties for indoor use.

Mexican Oregano: Hot and spicy; if that's your taste, you will want one of these oreganos. Happy in eastern or southern window exposure for winter and can go right in the ground in summer.

Pineapple Sage: It can summer outside, and will become very large; take cuttings in August for growing as a winter herb in a container. Keep it pinched back to produce a good, bushy herb. Nice in tea and potpourri.

Rosemary: Can be put in ground in spring and then brought into the house in winter. Does not need full sun. Do not let it dry out completely; it likes a good supply of water. Rosemary likes to be in a large pot which it will quickly fill with roots.

Scented Geraniums: Plant directly outside in spring and take cuttings in August for winter; or leave in containers and use on patio. Cuttings are very easy.

Santolina: Both the grey and green variety make nice houseplants, emitting a good aroma. Put the gray santolina in sunny south window. Green santolina prefers less sun.

Outside Care of Tender Perennials

After all danger of frost has passed, the tender perennial can be planted outside. Here are a few suggestions:

- Take them out of the containers and plant directly in the soil. If the herb becomes too large by August to bring back inside, take cuttings for winter plants.
- Place containers on the patio, porch, deck, etc., for decoration. Remember, containers set in hot, dry, full sun will dry out quickly. You may need to water (deeply) several times a day.
- Plant the herb in a pot in the ground. Here is where the "pantyhose gardening" comes in. Follow these steps:

  1. Dig a hole to accommodate pot size.
  2. Stretch pantyhose over entire pot. This will prevent worms and insects from coming through the drainage holes into the container.

3. Place container dressed in pantyhose in hole.
4. Fill in around container right to the rim.
5. Cover top of container with a mulch of crushed rocks or wood chips to hide the pantyhose and the rim of container.
6. Be sure to water well during dry spells.
7. In fall when danger of frost threatens, just pull container out of ground and clean off for use as an inside plant.

Inside Care of Tender Perennials

Tender perennials are basically given the same care as any house plant. Here is what to consider:

Light—Each plant will tolerate a different range of light. Fluorescent lights provide adequate lighting for all herbs mentioned in this chapter. These lights should be from 2 to 6 inches away from the plant's top. Be sure the tops do not come in contact with bulbs. With fluorescent lighting, you can have a garden in any room where you have the space.

Commercially manufactured tiers of lights are available or you can build your own.

Heat—Herbs will tolerate the warmer, dryer atmosphere of modern homes. Ideal temperature is from 50 to 60 degrees. Good air circulation is important; don't push plants together, overcrowding them. Bottom circulation can be accomplished by setting containers on bricks, elevating them off the floor. Do not plant where they receive a constant draft from opening and closing doors.

Humidity—Herbs will tolerate lower humidity than the more tropical-type plants. However, I am a firm believer in misting all plants. This helps keep them clean and raises humidity, even if only temporarily.

Spider mites love a hot, dry area, so misting will discourage them. A bath of liquid soap and water will keep plants from becoming polluted by dust and dirt and also wash off any insect larvae.

Water—Clay pots are porous, drying out quickly in the hot sun. Herbs in clay pots need more watering than those in plastic pots. Leave a depression in the soil at the top of all containers to serve as a basin for water. Do not let any pot dry out to the point where the plant wilts. If this happens too many times, it will kill the plant's roots. Certain plants are thirstier than others, so learn from watching them which prefers the most water. Once you have a feel for this, watering will be easy. Use room-temperature water on your plants. If you have chlorine and fluorides in your water, let the water sit exposed to the air overnight to dispel some of the gases. Or, you can use rainwater if you wish.

Soil—Soil in a container needs to be a little richer than outside soil, since this will be the entire life-support system of the plant. Here is a recipe for a rich mix:

> 6 parts good loam
> 4 parts peat moss
> 1 part perlite
> 2 parts vermiculite

For each one gallon of mix add 2 tablespoons bone meal and 1 teaspoon fertilizer (5-10-10 combination). Fill container loosely with soil mix, put plant in and firm gently. Water by capillary action if possible.

Soil Medium—Use a soilless medium for your hanging baskets to keep the container light in weight unless you are using a very secure holding device, plastic or wire baskets as opposed to the heavier wood or clay pots. With a soilless medium, you will need to provide a weekly fertilizing program. I use 2 to 3 inches of those little styrofoam "peanuts," which often come as packing material, on the bottom of my baskets for drainage and then fill with soilless medium.

A final word about hanging-basket containers. They bring a person's eye up and thus provide a nice visual balance to containers on the floor. By hanging at various lengths, you can create a colorful wall display.

Fertilizer—A good fertilizer program is necessary for most plants grown in the limited space of a container. Those herbs that like a lean soil with limited fertilizer include scented geraniums, rue, lemon grass, rosemary and cardamom. With these herbs, I fertilize once a month from January to October, letting them rest the other two months. For other plants, I prefer to fertilize every two weeks with a mild solution. Use one half the recommended dosage suggested by the manufacturer. Most herbs would prefer to be under-fertilized than over-fertilized. Too much fertilizer will produce weak stems that will break easily, and you will have less of the desired essential oils in over-fertilized herbs.

Containers—There is a wide variety of colors, shapes, and sizes to match every decor you have. Remember, this is the life support of the plant so the container should be large enough to hold the plant and have available growing room. When you see the roots coming out through the bottom drainage holes, that is the time to repot into a larger container.

Annual Herbs
as Container Plants

When using annual plants in containers for your patio or windowsill gardening, remember that they will die at the end of their annual cycle. Keeping flowers cut off will help to prolong the life of the plant. However, once it flowers and goes to seed it has completed its natural life cycle. Annuals generally prefer the sunniest windows, but also do very well under fluorescent lights. Fertilize every two weeks during the growing cycle. Start cuttings before the plant dies to keep a steady supply of herbs.

Here is an overview of annuals that grow well inside containers:

Basil: The small leaf basils do best in containers; they prefer a rich, moisture-holding soil, set in the sunniest windows.

Scarlet Pimpernel: This attractive little herb, too often ignored in the herb garden, is called "poor man's weatherglass" because it will not open its tiny red heads when the weather is bad. Inside, it likes a sunny window and is excellent in a hanging basket. Its sister, the blue pimpernel, which has slightly larger flowers, makes a good basket companion to the red.

Summer Savory: The bean herb; its peppery taste is excellent with bean dishes. Full sun and a lean soil will suit summer savory just fine. Keep pinched for a good bushy plant.

Sweet Marjoram: Another good basket herb. Grow in full sun with a little lime added to the soil.

Parsley: Actually a biennial, it will live out its two-year cycle in an indoor container. Both the flat leaf, stronger-tasting, Italian parsley and the favorite curly, garnish parsley do well in containers. Just be sure to use it frequently, as it loves to be cut.

Care for these annuals in the container as you would tender perennials.

Perennial Herbs
for a Container Garden

Hardy perennial herbs are brought inside the house to provide freshly grown herbs all winter long or because there is insufficient outside space for a garden. The care of these plants is the same as for the tender perennials covered earlier.

Some perennial plants need a cold dormant period each year in order to retain health. Examples of these are members of the allium family (the onions), which includes chives, garlic chives, and Welsh bunching onions. Here is the cold dormancy process for chives:

1. Dig up the herb and pot in an appropriate container.
2. Cut stems back to within 3 inches of the root.
3. Place outside in an area where it won't be forgotten.
4. Water if rainfall is insufficient.
5. Leave outside for 3 to 6 weeks of cold, freezing weather.

If this cold process is not followed, the chives will be weak and wimpy-looking, and possibly will die before spring comes. In addition to the onion family, another herb that likes this cold dormancy period is the horehound, an interesting-looking houseplant with grey-green leaves. It needs a good draining pot and a lean soil with a little lime added. Keep it clipped to prevent its flowering.

Here is a brief profile of other perennial herbs which grow well inside in containers.

Mints: Mints are not exactly beautiful, but the reward of fresh leaves makes growing them worthwhile. Use as large a container as possible. Likes a medium soil with a little bone meal and full sun. Those that do best in containers are the orange mint (bergamot), peppermint, spearmint, and ginger mint.

French Tarragon: Doesn't dry as well as some herbs, so it is nice to include it among your houseplants for the winter. Needs a three-week, cold dormancy period before coming inside. Keeping it pinched back will keep it looking good. Full sun and a fair soil are required.

Thymes: Almost all thymes will tolerate inside conditions; from full sun to a bright north window. Looks nice in a hanging basket.

Winter Savory: A small, shrubby herb that lends itself to the possibilities of bonsai gardening. Likes full sun and a little lime. Slow grower.

Lemon Balm: Full sun and medium soil. Keep clipped in any shape you want. Don't let it completely dry out. Gives fragrance to stale rooms. If leaves start getting yellow, give less light and more water.

Rue: An interesting blue-green foliage herb, grows well inside. Caution is advised: Some persons are allergic to rue and may develop a rash from it, so keep it out of the reach of children and pets. Full sun and a lean soil are required.

Catnip Mussinii: There's a fifty-fifty chance on whether your cat will like it or not. Has pretty, blue-purple flowers and is very fragrant. Trim off flowers and it will rebloom for you. Full sun and medium soil.

Roman Chamomile: A nice, refreshing, apple scent; makes a very good tea. Keep in sunniest window; use medium to lean soil.

Alpine Strawberry: A little herb that is excellent in a basket, blooming and producing small strawberries all year long. Full sun, good soil, and fertilizer programs are needed.

Herbs on the Patio

Not everyone has a large amount of land for gardening. However, by using containers you can have the pleasure of gardening on a patio, deck, porch or in a windowbox. Using containers places each individual herb in a special environment of its own. It no longer blends in with other plants but is a unique specimen. Containers planted with herbs can be moved wherever you want color or handy culinary herbs. You can use anything that will hold dirt and support drainage holes. Any plant will grow one season in a contained condition, so if you do not have any wintering-over space, you would treat all the herbs as annuals for one season's growth.

Plant Profiles

(All plants described in this section are tender perennials.)

Bay Leaf *(Laurus nobilis)*

Family—Lauraceae (laurel)

Synonyms—Sweet bay, bay laurel

Description—An ancient evergreen tree, average 3 feet tall, with thick, shiny, aromatic leaves; small, greenish flowers in fall on mature plant. This slow grower is an ideal houseplant. It has been used for protection down through history; the Greeks and Romans honored their warriors, athletes, and scholars with a chaplet of bayleaf (a chaplet is a wreath worn on the head).

Cultivation—Good soil for container; do not overwater or overfertilize the bay plant. Inside, give bright light but not full sun. Occasionally plagued by the "scale" insect. Outside, keep in shady area. Repot when you see roots in drainage holes.

Rose Bay Potpourri

Mix together:

> 2 quarts rose petals
> 1 cup bay leaf
> 1 cup lavender buds
> 1 cup orange blossoms
> 1 cup clove pink flowers
> ½ cup cut orris root
> ¼ cup crushed nutmeg pieces
> ¹/₈ cup cinnamon chips
> 6 drops sweet orange oil

Let mixture age 3 weeks before using. A nice bedroom potpourri.

Propagation—Slow and poor germination by seed. Cuttings also slow but usual way of propagation.

Part Used—Leaf (dried only)

Harvest—All season

Uses—Culinary: Used for long simmering in soups, stews, chowders and sauces. One of the herbs in bouquet garni (see Chapter 9). One leaf in a dish is usually enough; remove before serving and *do not eat.*

A bay leaf in flours and grains will keep the weevil out.

Crafting: Use in potpourri.

Curry Plant *(Helichrysum augustifolia)*

Family—Compositae (daisy)

Synonyms—None

Description—Slow-growing tender perennial reaching 18 in. Narrow gray leaves with a curry scent; small yellow flowers in summer. This plant makes a lovely houseplant and lends itself to bonsai training.

Cultivation—For inside growing, provide a sunny window or fluorescent lights. Prefers a lean soil with some lime or bone meal added. For outside, treat as an annual, or bring inside when there is a danger of frost.

Propagation—Seeds or stem cuttings

Part Used—Leaf and flower

Harvest—All season. Dry on screens

Uses—Miscellaneous: Dried flowers for wreath making; potpourri for scent and color. Leaf is added to moth bags because of its insect-repellent qualities. Using it as a houseplant will help to keep away musty aromas as it acts as a natural deodorizer.

Dittany of Crete *(Origanum dictamnus)*

Family—Labiatae (mint)

Synonyms—Pepperwort, righte dittany

Description—This tender perennial makes an excellent hanging-basket specimen. A bi-leaf herb; at the end of the small, round, woolly leaves appears a light, very delicate-looking, apple-green, papery bract ending with small pink flowers. Dittany of Crete is just becoming well known to the general public, although it was introduced to America in the 1930s. But this is not a new herb, having been used in Europe since 1500 B.C. Native only to the island of Crete, where folklore says that if a deer was shot with an arrow and then ate the dittany herb, the arrow would fall out.

Cultivation—Inside for winter, give full sun and plenty of water. For outside growing use in less sun, use hanging basket on porch or deck. Does not do well planted in the ground in New England. Provide light, well-drained soil with lime or bone meal added. Feed all year with a good fertilizer. If leaves turn yellow it is getting too much sun.

Propagation—Cuttings in the spring

Part Used—Leaf

Uses—Medicinal: tea for women in labor; antiseptic for wounds.
   Miscellaneous: often used as an ornamental.

Lemon Grass *(Cymbopogon citratus)*

Family—Grass

Synonyms—Sweet rush

Description—Broad, grass-like foliage with a very aromatic lemon scent. Holds its scent better than most other lemon-scented herbs. Tender perennial in New England area.

Cultivation—As a houseplant, it will grow to 2 feet. Inside, keep in low-light area; outside, keep in shade. Provide a light soil and feed monthly. One problem we have with lemon grass is our big, fat, black tom cat; he will eat the plant right down to the root whenever he finds it.

Lemon Mint Tea

Mix together:

> 2 tbsps fresh lemon grass leaf
> 2 tbsps fresh spearmint

Steep in 1½ cups boiling water for 5 minutes. Serve with a dash of honey.

Propagation—Seed germination is poor; division of roots anytime

Part Used—Leaf

Harvest—All season; dry on screens

Uses—Culinary: to flavor soups, stews, and desserts; excellent in tea.
   Miscellaneous: Potpourri—adds texture and scent. Commercial—used in perfumes and shampoos.

Lemon Verbena (*Aloysia triphylla* and/or *Lippia citriodora*)

Family—Verbenaceae (verbena)

Synonyms—Herb Louisa

Description—Tender deciduous shrub; rough-textured, lance-shaped, highly aromatic leaves; pale lavender flowers in August.

Cultivation—Can be treated as an annual, planted outside for summer, taking cuttings in July for planting the following year; can also be set in the ground (pot and all) using the pantyhose method. It will become very large outside and will need to be repotted. Likes full sun, good drainage, and an alkaline soil; fertilize from March to August with one half the recommended strength of fertilizer. Keep pinched back for a bushier plant. High humidity surrounding this herb will keep away red spiders, which seem to like it.

Winter care—Since lemon verbena is a deciduous shrub, it will automatically drop its leaves in the fall. When you bring the pot inside, cut the plant back to half its original size (saving the leaves to dry); keep in a low-light area, just barely watering enough so it doesn't dry out completely. In January, introduce to more light (gradually) until you have it in full sun. Start fertilizer program and pinch constantly to prevent it from becoming leggy. If all this is too much work, treat it as an annual.

Lemon Verbena Jelly

1 cup lemon verbena leaves
3 cups apple juice
1 package powdered pectin
4 cups sugar

In a large kettle, combine apple juice, lemon verbena leaves, and pectin. Bring to a full rolling boil (a boil that cannot be stirred down). Strain out leaves, add sugar, and bring back to a full rolling boil. Stir constantly for 1 minute. Remove from heat. Skim off any foam on top with a wooden spoon. Fill sterilized jars, leaving ¼ inch head space. Seal with hot paraffin wax. Makes approximately 7 half-pints of jelly.

Propagation—Cuttings in spring

Part Used—Leaves

Harvest—All summer, dry on screens

Uses—Culinary: Tea, jelly
   Medicinal: tea is used for fevers and digestive problems, as a sedative, and for flatulence.
   Cosmetic: refreshing scent for bath water.
   Crafting: adds lemon scent to potpourri.

Mexican Oregano (*Lippia graveolens*)

Family—Verbenaceae (verbena)

Synonyms—Mexican sage

Description—I must confess I was not a lover of oregano until I met the Mexican oregano, with its hot, spicy flavor. The pungent leaves are lance shaped with cream-colored flowers. A tender perennial in New England.

Cultivation—Can be treated as an annual in the summer or set in the ground in a pot using the pantyhose method. Likes full sun, good drainage, and a little bone meal or lime added to the soil. Keep pinched back all year for a good, fat, bushy plant.

Propagation—Seeds or summer cuttings

Part Used—Leaves

Harvest—All season, screen dry or microwave

Use—Culinary: in chili, soups, stews, spaghetti sauces, and meats. An herb worth experimenting with.

Rosemary

Rosemary *(Rosmarinus officinalis)*

Family—Labiatae (mint)

Synonyms—Herb of remembrance

Description—An aromatic evergreen that's a tender perennial in New England. Highly-scented leaves are spiky and lance shaped. Flowers are blue, white, and occasionally pink. One of the better known and more popular herbs; the symbol of remembrance, it is used in wedding ceremonies and at funerals. Once used in the preservation of bodies during the winter, when they could not be buried outside.

Cultivation—Full sun to partial shade. Do not let your rosemary dry out completely or the leaves will turn brown and die. Biggest reason people lose their rosemarys during the winter is underwatering them and placing them in too warm an area. They prefer 50-60°F temperature. Feed a weak fertilizer all year round. Outside, sink pot right into the ground using the pantyhose method. Rosemarys like large pots; they will quickly grow to fit the pot. Keep lower leaves cut off to grow as a standard.

Propagation—Easy from seed but not always true to species; cuttings in spring and summer.

Part Used—Leaves

Harvest—All season, dry in middle of summer when at fullest growth (screen dry).

Uses—Culinary: A good, refreshing cup of tea, can be used alone or blended with most other herbs. Lay a sprig of rosemary under your meats, fish, and poultry. Use in scented sugars, butters, breads, and desserts.

Medicinal: Tea is antiseptic, diuretic, and good for digestive problems. For aching muscles, use rosemary steeped in olive oil as a massage. A gargle for bad breath, it is said that if you drink rosemary tea in the morning your breath will be fresh all day long.

Cosmetic: Used continuously for dark hair, it will highlight it. Helps get rid of dandruff and dry scalp. Queen Elizabeth used it in her famous "Hungary Water," made by steeping rosemary in white wine for a week and then straining into bottles.

Crafting: a very popular ingredient in potpourri; sprigs can be used (fresh or dried) for wreaths.

Rosemary Jelly

Add 8 four-inch-long sprigs of rosemary to 5 cups of cranberry juice. Add 1 twelve-inch-long broken cinnamon stick and 8 whole clove buds. Bring to a boil, remove from heat. Cover and let steep for 15 minutes. Strain. To liquid add:

2 tbsps grated lemon peel
1 package fruit pectin

Bring to boil, stir constantly and boil one minute. Remove from heat, skim off foam with wooden spoon. Pour into sterilized jars, leaving ¼ inch head space. Seal with paraffin wax.

Three popular scented geraniums are (left to right) rose, nutmeg, and lemon.

Scented Geranium *(Pelargonium)*

Family—Geraniaceae (geranium)

Synonyms—None

Description—These aromatic, tender plants are perennials from South Africa. They were very popular during the Victorian age. The various species are available in about 100 varieties. However, don't expect gaudy flowers like those found on annual geraniums. Most scented geraniums have small, delicate, flowers, and the foliage often mimics other herb or fruit scents. The following list includes some of the more popular varieties available:

Common Name	Botanical Name
almond	P. Quercifolium
apple	P. Odoratissimum
apricot	P. Scabrum
chocolate mint	P. Tomentosum spp.
cinnamon	P. Gratum
coconut prostrate	P. Grossulariodes
coconut upright	P. Parviflorum
ginger	P. Nervosum torento
gooseberry	P. Grossulariodes spp.

Continued on next page

Pink Peppermint Potpourri

Mix together:

2 cups peppermint geranium leaves
1 cup flowering pink thyme tops
1 cup pink rose petals
1 cup assorted pink flowers
1 tbsp crushed coriander seed
1 tbsp crushed cloves
2 tbsps caraway seed
1 tbsp cut orris root
2 drops peppermint oil

Let age for two weeks before using; good potpourri for a den or man's room.

lemon	P. Crispum
lime	P. x nervousum
nutmeg	P. x fragans
old fashioned rose	P. Graveolens
old spice	P. Logeei
orange	P. Citriodorum
peppermint	P. Tomentosum
pine	P. x Fragans tupentha
prince rupert (lemon)	P. Crispum prince rupert
southernwood	P. Abrotanifolium
strawberry	P. Scarboroviae

Cultivation—Scented geraniums can be potted year round, repotting as they outgrow their pots, i.e., when the roots come out at the bottom of the drainholes.

SIX

Birds, Bees, and Butterflies

(How to Attract and Use Nature's Helpers)

I LEARNED EARLY in my gardening career that the more birds around the gardens the fewer insects we have. We are as organic as possible here at the farm. For man and nature to co-exist, we must use fewer chemicals that can pollute our land and ground water. Chemicals are upsetting the natural balance of our world. Every year more and more chemicals are being banned (going the way of DDT) because of toxicity to man and nature. Why aren't these chemicals thoroughly tested *before* they are released to the public?

Organic gardening can be our small part in helping to preserve the natural order of things. Birds, bees, and butterflies have a role to play in this order, as we shall see in this chapter.

Birds in the Garden

Birds have always been associated with gardens. In the gardens of the kings and aristocrats of olden times, aviaries, fishponds, dovecotes, beehives, and even some small zoos were included. Aviaries were especially popular in the 1700s and 1800s. They were built near dining areas so the birds could serenade the people as they dined. Today, lunch in the garden is no less pleasurable with singing birds.

In the 1700s a "ha-ha" was introduced to gardens. This was a large ditch dug between the lawn area and the pasture area. It was deep enough that the cows and sheep could not cross, giving an open look so that visitors to the garden could enjoy the grazing animals. With our smaller gardens of today, the use of real animals has given way to animal statues.

The Bird Garden

One reason to attract birds is for the pleasure of enjoying their song, beauty, and sometimes funny antics. But more important is their enormous appetite for insects. Of the 700 bird species of North America, about one half of these are insectivorous, aiding us in keeping down the insect population in the garden.

In late spring I know when the insects have arrived even before the first mosquito bite. Every year when the barn swallows return they dive-bomb me to let me know they are 'home.' These birds follow the insect population which is their main diet. It's hilarious watching them swooping down over the fields and pond, scooping up insects. They nest on the front of our garage not because that's where we want them, but because *they* decided it was the best spot.

For the bird watcher, making a garden of herbs and flowers just to attract birds will be fun. This garden will be enclosed with evergreen trees for shelter and nesting sites. The water supply will be a bird bath or small water garden. A bench for observing the birds will add a nice touch. Feeders will be placed throughout the area. This garden should be where you can enjoy it from a window of your house. Birds will quickly know what to expect from the occupants and can become very bossy when the feeder is empty.

Feeding the Birds

The three necessary requirements for attracting birds to your garden are food, water, and shelter. You should feed the birds during their hard times in the cold winter months. However, some of us prefer to have feed available year round. The birds will visit the summer feeder for an occasional lunch, especially in bad weather. But most often they forage on their own. If you are starting a new feeding station, put it up in July or August since it does take time for word to get around that you are offering winter accommodation. The only rule is *once you start feeding, don't stop!* No running off to Bermuda for a vacation unless you leave a bird-feeder sitter. Once the birds stay and depend on you for food supply, stopping feeding can cause them serious problems. At the first sign of a big storm, they will eat earlier and heavier. They are good weather forecasters, so watch them. During storms go out and clear away the snow cover so they can get at the food easily. There is every possible kind of bird feeder available; these include large martin house condominiums, smaller plastic or wood, even a windowsill feeder with a two-way window so you can observe the birds closely but they can't see you. Plans for making your own feeders can be found in books in the library or any book store. You can even grow gourds to make your own birdhouses.

Feeders hung in trees will attract chickadees, titmice, and nuthatches. Ground feeders attract mourning doves, juncos, cardinals, sparrows, and thrushes. Do not use metal on your feeders since it will injure tiny feet in winter. Keep your feeders clean and remove any feed that becomes mildewed from rain; bad feed can make birds sick or even kill them.

Because bird watching and feeding is a popular hobby, food for feeders can be found in many different types of stores. Foods available are commercial mixes, sunflower seeds, special seeds of millet or teasel, and thistle seed. Cracked corn, found at feed stores, is inexpensive and a good winter feed because it warms the body.

Robins, starlings, cedar waxwings, and orioles enjoy eating fruit. Most birds enjoy white bread, donuts, and popcorn. Provide suet balls for woodpeckers, juncos, and chickadees. Here is a mix we use:

> Save *bacon fat* until you have 1 cup. Melt to soften, add ½ cup *peanut butter* and 2 cups of *commercial bird seed mix*. Pour into small containers (I use the plastic dishes that oleo comes in). Set dish on ground or put holes in sides and tie on strong string for hanging on branches. (Holes can be punched in plastic by heating a large needle over a candle flame.) Place where you can enjoy it from a window; have a perching area nearby where the birds can watch for their enemies.

Water

A bird bath or water garden will provide the birds with their water supply. In winter, supply water daily or invest in a heating system for the bird baths. Water gardening is coming into its own these days, adding a new dimension to gardening. Inexpensive plastic tubs and sturdy plastic sheeting are making it easy to design your own small water garden.

To Make a Basic Water Garden
1. Dig hole to desired depth; a good simple size to start with would be ½ ft. deep by 3 ft. long. Remove all sharp objects and stones.
2. Line bed with damp sand for good, solid, even base. Don't leave any holes in base. Tamp it down firmly.
3. Gently spray water over bed. Do not disturb sand as you water.

4. Drape plastic liner over excavation (or insert commercially made plastic container). To determine plastic liner size:
   - Measure depth, length, and width of hole.
   - The liner length will be twice the depth of the hole added to the length of the hole.
   - The liner width will be twice the depth of the hole plus the width of the hole.
   - Add 12 inches onto the width and length of the liner so the ends will be secure under the rim of bricks or rocks.
5. Fill pool with water slowly, making sure plastic is tight and not folding over.
6. Let set for a couple of days before finishing the top rim. Then add your decorative rims, rocks, or bricks.
7. If a large pool is made, you will need pumps and water circulators. In a small pool, run hose in pool once a week to keep debris out and water fresh. There are many small pumps and fountains for small gardens available in garden centers or local nurseries.
8. Add decorative plantings around the pool.

We were fortunate enough to have a farm pond dug a few years ago. This has been one of the best investments we have made in the landscape; not only has it provided added fire insurance, water for gardens in dry seasons, and a place to swim, but it has brought in new species of birds and wildlife. Blue heron, yellow legs, wild mallards, and the bossy little killdeer have all become yearly residents. Every evening we enjoy a serenade from the large amphibian population.

Shelter

Old hedgerows are slowly disappearing under the blade of the bull-dozer and new developments. Hedgerows are favorite nesting sites and feeding areas of birds and small animals. It is our responsibility to plant this type of covering for our bird friends. Hedgerow coverings consist of:

- Canopy cover = tall trees
- Undershrubs = medium-size shrubs
- Ground covers = assorted herbs and flowers

An example would be a cedar tree, an elderberry shrub, and spearmint with daisies.

Evergreen trees provide shelter from the blizzards of winter as well as food and nesting areas. Deciduous trees such as oak, beech, and horse chestnut are especially appealing to many species for nesting and food. Generally speaking, the more you plant, the more bird species you will see. Field areas, no matter how small, will provide nesting areas for the bobolink and meadowlark; just don't mow the field until the end of summer when babies are out on their own.

Dust Baths and Other Attractions

Birds clean themselves relentlessly, spreading their wings and laying in awkward positions to sunbathe. They also enjoy a dust bath, which can be provided for in the bird garden. Dig out a 3 ft.-square area, fill with an 8-inch mixture of wood ashes, sand, and light loam. The dust bath helps the birds remove excess oil from their feathers and skin, along with eliminating feather lice. Cats will also find this dust bath appealing to roll in.

Fruit trees and berries will always attract birds. Other plantings to include in your herbal bird garden are:

Flowers	Trees	Vines
alpine strawberry	elderberry	bittersweet
alyssum	mountain ash	honeysuckle
anise-hyssop	mulberry	morning glory
bee balm	snowberry	Virginia creeper
butterfly weed		
columbine		
coral bells		
dahlia		
foxglove		
hollyhock		
mallows		
nasturtiums		
red salvias		
sage		
snapdragons		
teasel		
thistle		

Hummingbirds and Other Friends

"Don't move, listen very carefully," I said to my grandson as he weeded the garden. He froze, listened, then slowly turned his head towards the whizzing sound. His eyes met five hummingbirds gathering the sweet nectar from their favorite herb, bee balm, the birds uncaring of our presence. It's moments like this that make life in the garden all worthwhile.

The ruby-throated hummingbird is the only species found in New England. It arrives in April and leaves in September for warmer climates and fresher flowers. The hummingbird is a favorite of many people. Wear a bright red bandana or sweater in the garden and they may check you out as a nectar source. Bright red and orange are their favorites. Although hummingbirds have a sweet tooth, their main diet consists of insects and spiders; they even use the spider web in their tiny nests. If you have room for more than one family, spread your colorful flowers around your property as hummingbirds are very territorial, often fighting other birds as well as each other for their special area. Plant herbs and flowers so there is continuous bloom all season long. Hummingbirds are huge feeders, needing food every fifteen minutes. They will aid in the destruction of the insect population in return for your generosity.

Let me introduce you to some other bird friends at Wormwood Farm:

Chickadees: Our Maine State bird; abundant here and very friendly, often sitting as close as two feet to us as we fill the feeder, chattering their thanks.

Barn swallows: These acrobats have been with us since we moved here. I really enjoy watching their crazy antics as they swoop low over the pond, almost diving into the water yet just skimming the surface.

Robins: Spring has officially arrived when you see your first robin pulling a fat earthworm out of the front lawn. They will eat their share of ants, beetles, and caterpillars (unfortunately, my blueberries too).

Baltimore orioles: These colorful orange birds nest high in our huge maple tree, consuming a good number of gypsy moths and bag worms, which are very real pests in New England.

Sparrows: We have several species of sparrows flying happily around our farm eating those pesty little aphids.

American goldfinches: I love to watch their bouncy little flight pattern as they flitter from teasel to thistle, often dispelling seeds in unwanted areas.

Starlings and Grackles: Usually considered pests by some bird watchers but they do consume a large amount of insects and will eat the Japanese beetle, which other birds overlook.

Purple martins: The purple martin will consume a large amount of flying insects. They have adapted to suburban living where man has provided elaborate condominium housing. If you make your own birdhouses be sure to paint the martin house white to reflect the sun, making for cooler rooms inside.

Phoebes: A shy bird who enjoys singing from afar, she often talks to me in the garden from a hiding place. As soon as I spot where she is, she flies away to a new location. Phoebes enjoy gypsy moths, ants, grasshoppers, and ticks.

Juncos: Slate-colored ground feeders who eat ants and grasshoppers; they prefer the hedgerows of our woods.

Woodpeckers: Will keep tree insect larvae population down. If available, an old dead tree on the property will provide nesting sites for the woodpecker.

Owls: More often heard in the evening than seen. If you have an area large enough, provide a wooden house for barn owls. They will help clear out mice, moles and rats.

Ravens: A family of ravens nest in a large stand of pine trees across the road from us. Two years ago, a lone raven adopted me, often sitting in the maple and talking to me. He becomes very bossy when there is no bread or popcorn out for him. The smaller birds relentlessly attack him when he comes near their nesting areas.

Other Garden Inhabitants

Squirrels, Chipmunks, and Cats

These frisky little guys can be a problem in some areas by raiding the bird feeders. Metal disks put on the feeders or putting the feeders in areas where they can't get to them often discourage them. But beware because they are very ingenious little guys. We do not have a problem with them as we have a dog in an open area to scare them away.

Cats and birds do coexist. The birds are always on the lookout for predators. Putting bird feeders where cats can't climb or where cats can't hide under bushes will keep the birds protected. Our birds are very aggressive, dive-bombing the cats when they come near any nesting areas.

The reason cats bring dead mice and birds home to you is to contribute their share to the food supply. When pussy brings you a mouse, take it and praise her highly. Dispose of the mouse (she will think you ate it). But when she brings a bird home to you, do not take it; scold her severely, shaking your finger and saying "no-no." She will eventually bring you only mice or moles.

Bees in the Garden

The Romans said the best honey came from Mount Hymettus in Athens where the fields were covered with wild thyme. Virgil wrote of bees and herbs, both of which he kept.

Bees are the only insects that provide man with food. Down through history bees have given us honey, wax for candles, and ingredients for

Scott checks on his bee hive. The bees pollinate our herbs, vegetables, and flowers.

beauty creams. Early settlers brought the honey bee and herbs to North America in the 17th century and they have been very important to us ever since.

Ninety percent of our agricultural crops benefit from insect pollination. Because of chemical sprays and one-crop farming, many farmers now truck in beehives when the crop needs pollination.

A bee sting is not welcomed by most people; some persons are very allergic to the bee venom and must carry special bee-sting kits with them for the immediate attention they need when stung by a bee or wasp. However, on the other side of the coin there exists in Europe a school of medicine called apitherapy, which treats diseases—especially arthritis and rheumatoid diseases—with bee venom.

For those who enjoy working with bees, it can be a profitable sideline. Your state agriculture department can put you in contact with local beekeepers and provide you with information on keeping bees.

Facts Concerning Bees

- Herbs to apply to bee stings: calendula, lamb's ear, comfrey, hyssop.
- To condition the beehive, rub with lemon balm.
- To rid your hands of the human odor when working with bees, rub them with wormwood.

- Do not plant southernwood near the hives as bees do not like this plant.
- To keep ants away from the hives, lay pennyroyal or mint on top of inner cover and plant these herbs near the bottom of the hives.
- Plant willow trees for early pollination, not too far away from the hive as early spring bees will not travel far from their hive.
- Maine's state insect is the honey bee.
- Beeswax is used to make candles (expensive) or as a softening agent in beauty cream.

Bee Theme Garden—Let's talk about some herbs and flowers to plant in a bee garden. The white turtlehead (chelone) is a must; the puffy white flowers host bees. Be careful smelling this pretty flower because the bees go right inside the flower, unseen. My list also includes:

alyssum	mignonette
anise-hyssop	mints
alfalfa	motherwort
basil	purple loosestrife
bee balm	red clover
borage	sage
catnip	savories
chamomile	showy marjoram
foxglove	snapdragons
horehound	thyme
hyssop	valerian
lavender	veronica
lemon balm	yellow centaurea

Other Small Wildlife in the Garden

Amphibians are also helpful in devouring insects; nature's food chain again at work. We know spring has truly arrived at the first sound of an evening serenade of frogs. I always put several toads in the greenhouse to help keep bugs away. Some will spend the summer and others leave as soon as the doors are left open overnight. They need a shaded, protected, moist area for protection from the hot sun during the day. In return, they will patrol the greenhouse at night, consuming a variety of insects. One day I picked up a pot of geraniums to water them and a little toad poked its head out of the soil. Toads will eat slugs, whereas most birds won't touch them. They can consume over 15,000 insects in one season, so it is well worth providing for their needs to keep them around. An upside-down clay pot, with a piece cut out for a door, and a pan of shaded water will provide a mini living area for them.

Another night-hunting insect eater is the salamander. They will hide under rocks during the day and you probably will not see them at all. Box turtles and lizards also will make good greenhouse pets, eating their share of insects. A box turtle will enjoy an occasional dish of lettuce as a reward for his help in clearing out insects. Do introduce natural helpers to your greenhouse provided you don't spray with harmful chemicals.

I suppose it's only fair to tell you that snakes are also beneficial to the garden; they eat moles and mice, but they also eat my frogs and toads. I dislike them very much. I have a gardening friend who has a lovely garden and the last time I visited I saw seven snakes, but she likes them and I don't.

For more information on attracting wildlife and birds to your garden, visit your local library or extension service. They both have many wonderful booklets and books on the subject.

Butterflies

Organic gardeners will be blessed with the fluttering of butterflies in their gardens; those who cover everything in sight with chemical sprays, however, will not. Lepidoptera is the second-largest order of insects with over 700 species found in North America. Butterflies fly during the day and when at rest hold their wings erect. Their antennae are club-like and end in a large curved point. Butterflies are different from the moth, which flies mostly at night and has over 8,000 species. When at rest, moths fold their wings flat or roof-like over their bodies, and they have feathery antennae.

Butterfly Garden—A butterfly garden will be quiet and enclosed for privacy, suitable for meditation and reading. A bench is necessary to sit and watch the butterflies and to rest. Place the garden out of the wind and in full sun for the butterflies. A focal point could be a sundial or a bird bath. Finally, it is a garden for those who prefer sitting to weeding. Butterflies prefer a weedy area, so fill the butterfly garden with lots of herbs and flowers and do minimal weeding. A butterfly puddle is needed; so scoop out an area to keep it slightly muddy. I once had the pleasure of seeing a butterfly "drinking party." Over one hundred swallowtails were gathered at a moist area in the ground, sticking their tongues in and out of the moisture. They covered a two-foot square area. I sat down beside them and put my hand in the middle. They would fly onto my arm, literally covering it, and then down again. They repeated this action every time I put my hand in amidst them. It was a very exciting experience that led to my reading more about butterflies and enjoying them even more. If you are lucky you may see one of these "drinking parties" in your butterfly garden. In our butterfly garden there can be no chemical sprays, fungicides, or germicides.

The butterfly has four stages in its life cycle: the egg, the larva, the pupa, and the butterfly. All stages are very sensitive to chemicals. Even though butterflies are beautiful they do have a taste for rotten fruit and dead fish. Fruit trees can be added to the herb butterfly garden.

Certain butterflies do prefer a particular flower:

- *Red Admiral* needs nettles to breed on.
- *Monarch* needs the milkweed plant, which has very fragrant pink flowers and should be grown more often in the herb garden.
- *Swallowtail* is happy with any member of the umbelliferae family, which includes parsely, fennel, dill, and anise.
- *Fritillaries* will make visits to your violets.
- *Sulphurs* enjoy all clover-type herbs.
- *Painted Ladies* have a hunger for all thistle-type plants.
- *Coppers* feed on dock and sorrel.

For the herbs and flowers for your butterfly garden, select from the bird and bee gardens but DO NOT include wormwood or southernwood; for some reason butterflies dislike their strong aromas. Make this garden chock full of plants.

Plant Profiles

Anise-Hyssop *(Agastache foeniculum)*

Family—Labiatae (mint)

Synonyms—Honey plant

Description—A herbaceous perennial to 3½ feet tall. Licorice scented; appears in spring with purplish leaves; as it matures leaves become gray-green with purple overtones. Simple spike flowers of lavender color are highly fragrant and attract thousands of bees. Birds eat the seeds in the fall.

Cultivation—Easy to grow in any soil with good drainage, even through the cracks in cement.

Propagation—Easy by seed and once planted will self-seed abundantly; or from division in spring.

Part Used—Flowers and leaf

Harvest—Leaf all growing season, flowers in full bloom with lavender color. After frost has turned them brown, you can harvest and spray paint.

Anise-Hyssop

Uses—Culinary: The American Indians used anise-hyssop as a tea and it is just as good for a pleasure tea today. Leaves can be used in cooking desserts (try the Peachy Good Cobbler I developed one year after a bumper crop on our peach trees).

Bee Balm *(Monarda didyma)*

Family—Labiatae (mint)

Synonyms—Bergamot, Oswego tea

Description—Dark, oval, sawtooth-edged, green leaves appearing opposite each other on the stem. Fragrant, bright red, shaggy flowers in July and August (other colors of bee balm come in white, pink, lavender, and mahogany). Its synonym *bergamot* comes from the orange bergamot, which it faintly smells like. *Oswego* is from the Oswego Indians that used this American native herb as a tea. They introduced it to the early settlers and it became a favorite tea during the American Revolution era. Its botanical name comes from a botanist named Nicholas Monardes, who published the first known American Herbal in 1569 called *Joyfull News Out of the New Found World*. He also introduced the herb to Europe.

Cultivation—Full sun or partial shade. Likes a fairly moist but not wet soil. Roots are creeping and shallow so should be hand weeded. Medium soil with lime, bone meal, or wood ashes added yearly. Bee balm is often affected by a mildew problem; cut back after flowering and destroy the cuttings to help prevent the mildew from spreading to other plants. Bee balm will 'middle out,' which means the middle or original plant will die

Peachy Good Cobbler

Sift together:

> 1 cup white flour
> ¾ cup whole wheat flour
> 1 tbsp baking powder

Mix in:

> ½ cup white sugar
> 1 large egg
> ¾ cup milk
> 2 tbsps coffee brandy
> 1 tbsp dried or 2 tbsps fresh anise-hyssop

Mix well and add:

> 1½ cups fresh or canned peaches
> ½ cup sweet cherries
> ½ cup walnuts

Put in 2-quart buttered casserole dish. Bake at 350° oven for 25 to 30 minutes or until firm in center.

Sauce for Peachy Good Cobbler

Mix 1 cup sugar and 3 tbsps cornstarch in saucepan. Stir in (gradually) 2 cups of water. Boil for 1 minute or until mix thickens. Then stir in:

> ¼ cup butter
> 2 tbsps coffee brandy
> 2 tbsps anise-hyssop leaf
> 2 tbsps grated nutmeg

Pour over cobbler to serve.

out in a year or two, leaving a space in the clump of plants. Simply clean out the dead portion, apply some compost, and take divisions from the outer part of the plant to fill in the center.

Propagation—Root cuttings in spring

Part Used—Leaf and flowers

Harvest—Leaf in early spring before mildew strikes; flowers in full bloom.

Uses—Culinary: Flower or leaf in salads, punches, and teas. Leaf in pork or chicken dishes.

Medicinal: Infusions were once used for colds, sore throat, and insomnia. When mixed with equal amounts of peppermint and spearmint in a pillow, it may help to eliminate headaches.

Miscellaneous: An herb for the bird, bee, and butterfly garden. If a bee stings you, mix the leaf or flower with your own saliva and apply to the sting; I have used this several times when stung in the garden and it works. Flowers and leaves are both used in potpourri; flowers are pretty in wreaths.

Caraway *(Carum carvi)*

Family—Umbelliferae (carrot)

Synonyms—Carry ways

Description—A biennial to 30 inches that has feathery leaves; terminal white flowers are white in spring; seeds are green, turning brown. Caraway is an ancient herb, being called karawya by the Arabs. Mentioned in all the old herbals, reputed to help pale women get some face color.

Cultivation—Full sun to partial shade; likes limed, well-drained, fairly good soil.

Propagation—Direct seed in garden or start inside for early crop. Dislikes being transplanted when over a foot high because it has a large tap root. Once planted, will self-seed yearly.

Part Used—Seeds, leaf, and small root part (eaten like parsnips in early spring).

Beets Caraway

1 cup beets in ¼ cup vinegar
½ cup diced apple
1 cup cold, boiled potato, diced
1 tsp horseradish
1 tbsp caraway seed
pinch of black pepper
¼ tsp grated nutmeg
pinch of grated coriander seed

Mix well and serve with a dab of sour cream.

Beer and Caraway Cracker Spread

Melt over low heat in saucepan (or heat in microwave):

½ lb sharp cheddar cheese
1½ tbsps butter

When melted, mix in:

1 tbsp dry mustard
½ tsp garlic powder
½ tsp grated onion
1 tbsp caraway seed
pinch of black pepper
½ cup beer

Blend all ingredients together over low heat. Serve on whole wheat crackers or in a fondue dish as a dip for vegetables.

Harvest—Leaf all season, root in early spring, and seeds as they start to turn brown. Cut off entire umbel and put in brown paper bag that has holes punched in it for air circulation. Hang bag up to dry. Seeds will fall off, dropping to the bottom of the bag.

Uses—Culinary: Custom in Scotland in the early 1900s was to dip buttered side of bread into a dish of caraway seeds; people called it salt-water jelly. Cheddar cheese is also good dipped in caraway. These seeds are very good added to potato salad, cole slaw, breads, cakes, cookies, goulash, cabbage, or sauerkraut.

Dill *(Anethum graveolens)*

Family—Umbellifeae (carrot)

Synonym—None

Description—Hardy annual to 3 feet tall; feathery leaves with terminal umbel yellow flowers, which are followed by green seeds turning brown for those dill pickles. This herb is over 5,000 years old and ancient folklore held that it protected people against witches and evil spirits when hung over doors and windows.

Cultivation—Full sun in medium-rich soil, good drainage, and some lime or bone meal. Likes to be kept weed free. Plant extra if you want the leaf part for cooking. Taking the weed part will slow down the seed production. Also, if you want the black swallowtail butterfly in your garden, plant extra for its caterpillar. Dill can be potted for winter weed.

Propagation—Direct seed early spring after the soil warms up. For earlier weed, can be started inside four weeks before last frost date.

Part Used—Leaf and seeds

Harvest—Weed all season; seed when begins to turn brown. Dry same way as for caraway.

Uses—Culinary: When most people think of dill they think of dill pickles. Both the weed and seed can be used with fish, meats, poultry, potato dishes, vegetables, breads, and cheeses. Very nice as a mild vinegar. As a tea it is best combined with other herbs such as rosemary or mints. Our Sleepy Kee Kee tea may help you sleep when taken just before bedtime.

Fennel *(Foeniculum vulgare)*

Family—Umbelliferae (carrot)

Synonyms—Sweet fennel

Description—Sweet fennel is tall (to 6 feet) and treated as an annual in most of the New England area, although it is a perennial. It has licorice-scented, feathery foliage with yellow flowers if the season is long enough. In Maine we rarely see the flowers or the seed of fennel because a frost usually takes it first. Bronze fennel is the same as the sweet except for its coloring of a reddish-bronze foliage.

Cultivation—Sweet fennel and bronze fennel like a lean, well-drained soil with no compost or manure added.

Part Used—Leaf and seeds of sweet and bronze fennel

Propagation—Start by seed inside; transplant after all danger of frost is past.

Harvest—Leaf all season, seeds in fall; leaf does not dry well

Sleepy Kee Kee Tea

1 part dill seed
1 part fennel seed
1 part peppermint
½ part scullcap

Mix together and age one week before using.

Fennel Seed Muffins

Sift together:

> 2 cups flour
> ¾ cup bran
> ¼ cup sugar
> 1 tbsp baking powder

Blend in:

> 2 tbsps fennel seed
> ¼ cup melted butter
> 1 beaten egg
> 1 cup skim milk

Mix together just until well blended (do not overblend). Bake in well-buttered muffin pans (or use cupcake papers) in 400° oven for 25 minutes or until done.

Uses—Culinary: Leaf and seeds are good in soups, salads, with fish, breads, cookies, and cakes; good vinegar for salads and in the bath.

Medicinal: Fennel seeds are reputed to stimulate milk flow in pregnant women; said to help those on diets, bitten by serpents, or people who have eaten poisonous herbs or mushrooms.

Parsley *(Petroselinum crispum)*

Family—Umbelliferae (carrot)

Synonyms—None

Description—Curly parsley has tight, curled leaves with dark green color. Italian parsley has lighter flat leaves. Both are biennials to 15 inches and are high in vitamins A and C. In ancient Greece parsley was worn as chaplets for sports, games, and funerals; also adorned graves of their loved ones. Greek gardens were often bordered with parsley. The black swallowtail butterfly enjoys lunching on this herb.

Cultivation—Full sun to partial shade with good drainage; likes moist, but not wet, medium-rich soil. Usually treated as an annual, but in pot (inside) will complete its two-year life cycle. If stalks get too tough, cut back to within two inches of base.

Propagation—Seeds

Fennel

Parsley

Part Used—Leaf

Harvest—All season fresh; pick outer leaves as they grow from center out. Microwaving will hold the color nicely, or put in freezer because when dried they lose most of their color and flavor.

Uses—Culinary: Curly is excellent garnish. Both parsleys are compatable with most foods; can be fried (using any good batter you normally fry with).

Medicinal: The reason parsley is served as a garnish is because it aids digestion and acts as a breath deodorizer. So don't leave that parsley on the plate; eat it at the end of your meal. Also acts as a diuretic, antiflatulent, and calmative.

Crafting: Dried stems are used as a dye; makes a natural green dye for Easter eggs; boil the parsley in water with eggs.

Parsley Cracker Spread

Cut finely one large bunch (about 2 cups) of *parsley* into bowl. Add 2 tablespoons of finely diced *onion*. Mix with *salad dressing* or *mayonnaise,* just enough to moisten. Do not add too much; it may even look like it needs more, but once it sets overnight in the refrigerator it will be all right. Refrigerate overnight. Serve with whole wheat crackers. This spread is very popular at my workshops.

SEVEN

Ants, Aphids, and Tansy

(How to Deal with Insects)

WHEN GROWING ANY kind of herb, you will sooner or later have to deal with the insect problem.

One reason herbs are popular is because many of them are fairly insect free and some actually repel or poison insects. These herbs give us a natural material to help fight the insect world.

Healthy, well-grown plants will help keep the insects at bay as they eat the weak ones first. But just because you have insects on your plants does not mean you have sick plants. Constant monitoring of your plants will keep the bugs in check. There are usually more insect problems in enclosed parts of homes and greenhouses due to the poor air circulation. Plants grown outside have the benefit of rain washing them off, fresh air, and good air circulation.

There are good guys and bad guys in the garden world of insects. Knowing which insects you are dealing with will make your job easier. By now you know that I detest using chemical sprays. This chapter deals with how to slow down the insect population using *organic* methods.

Keeping Your Herbs Healthy

Basic good care of your plants will aid in preventing insect and disease infestation. Here are some ideas to help you do this:

- Pick off all spent flower heads and yellowing leaves. Put in compost piles.
- Pinch back plants that benefit from this, for example basil, oreganos, and summer savory. This pinching will make short, strong stems which will produce more of the leaf part you want.
- Do not overcrowd your plants when setting them in the garden. Air circulation is important.
- Do not overwater or underwater; both will cause plant stress.
- Fertilize properly. Too little is even better than too much. Too much fertilizer, especially at the seedling stage, can produce weak stems that break easily. This does not apply to good compost, which you can add regularly in large quantities.
- Misting, especially with herbal waters such as chamomile and yarrow, will discourage red spider mites.
- At first signs of aphids and white flies, give your plants a liquid soap and water bath. A regular bath schedule for plants will aid in keeping them insect and dust free.

Insect-repellent Herbs

These herbs are plants that actually repel certain species of insects. Herbs then become our organic pesticides for use on other plants and in

Tansy, sweet annie, and lavender (left to right) will naturally repel insects; use in pomander balls and sachets.

moth bags. When homes in the ancient times had dirt floors, herbs were strewn on the floor and walked upon, repelling insects and giving off a wonderful scent: What a bonus in those days of little sanitation! Some herbs to consider for repellent uses include:

alliums	pennyroyal
ambrosia	pyrethrum
bay leaf	sage
chamomile	santolinas
costmary	southernwood
eucalyptus	sweet annie
hyssop	sweet woodruff
lavender	tansy
mints	thyme
mugwort	wormwood

The Bad Guys

If I have left out below an insect you think should be included, it is because I have not personally had to deal with it. I am not a trained entomologist, just a garden lover who wants to know and understand the strange little creatures in my garden space. Here is an analysis of some common garden insects that present special problems:

Ants—Undesirable in the garden because they will loosen the soil around the plant roots, causing the plant to wilt. Ants love the honeydew, a sweet substance produced from the anus of aphids, mealybugs, scale, and whiteflies. The ants will protect these insects and move them to other plants. Herbs that ants *dislike* are southernwood, wormwood, pennyroyal, mint, and tansy. Plant these herbs where you have an ant problem. Also, use the cuttings from these herbs as a mulch where there is an ant problem or in your vegetable rows to repel ants.

For a spray to pour into ant hills, try red hot pepper and garlic mixed in water and borax. For the area under the sink, mix wormwood with cream of tartar; this discourages silverfish as well as ants.

Aphids—These soft-bodied, sucking plant lice come in many colors, white, green, pink, yellow, and black. An infestation of aphids will always be seen somewhere during the growing season. Aphids cause loss of plant vigor, stunting plants if the infestation is not taken care of. In addition, they will cause the leaves to curl up. If by carefully observing your plants you catch them early, a soap-and-water bath will probably get rid of them.

Aphid Spray

To a gallon of boiling water add:

¼ cup wormwood
¼ cup chamomile
1 tsp garlic powder
1 tsp onion powder
1 tsp red hot pepper

Steep mixture for 2 hours or overnight. Strain through cheesecloth. Then add 2 tablespoons liquid dish soap. Put in a mister bottle and spray infected plants. Be sure to spray under leaves where aphids usually hide.

Inside, give the plant a bath three days in a row to be sure the eggs are gone. Outside, wash plants off with a hose spray.

Insects are attracted to the color yellow. Yellow sticky strips can be purchased (expensive) and really work well. Or you can make your own. Paint a board (any size) with bright yellow paint. Apply *tree tanglewood* (a sticky substance used to catch and kill insects; can be purchased in most garden centers) all over the board. The insects will be caught on it. When it is full, scrape off the tanglewood and re-apply. This board will also catch other insects, such as the annoying black gnat.

Earwigs—These are soft-bodied, beetle-like bugs with pinchers on their back end. They like to hide under boards and in hollow objects. You can catch them in traps. Take a piece of hose, plug one end and put some bran inside. Lay these where there is a problem. In the morning or late evening, empty the hose into a pail of kerosene. Another trap is to roll up a newspaper and secure with an elastic band or tape. Plug one end with a wad of paper and set in the area of earwigs. They will crawl inside the paper in the evening. Dispose of the paper every few days.

Flea Beetles—Tiny fleas, hardly visible to the naked eye. Signs of their visits will be in the form of little perforated holes in the leaves. Plants with large leaves are more susceptible to flea beetles. These include elecampane, comfrey, and horseradish. Keep the area of these plants weed free so the insects can't have a hiding place. A spray of nicotine in water will repel them. Tobacco plants are easy to grow in New England; use the leaves to make your own insecticide spray.

Japanese Beetles—Black, iridescent beetles, about one-half inch long. These bad guys are my arch enemies. Major war is made against these pests when they appear in July and August. Here is how we do it:

- Hand picking works best for me. They are hand picked off flowers and leaves during early morning or late evening hours; this is when they move slowly. During the hot sunny days they fly away before you can catch them. Dispose of them in cans of mixed kerosene and water.
- Use milky spore disease dust, applied in spring or fall. Milky spore disease, from the spores of Bacillus Popilliae, is a disease that affects the Japanese beetle grub. It is mixed with talcum and dusted on the lawn. The spore causes the blood of the grub to turn a milky white, hence its name. Each dead grub produces more spores that stay in the soil, killing new families of grubs. (This spore is harmless to humans and animals.) However, it will not work on lawns that have been sprayed with chemicals as it is a natural disease and will be killed by chemicals. Use according to manufacturer's directions.
- Plant tansy and rue near plants that the Japanese beetles like (such as the mallow family, roses, fruits, and evening primroses).
- Commercial traps can be hung in the area. Traps are baited with geraniol, which attracts and kills the beetles. Since they do attract beetles, put them some distance away from your plants.
- Hydrated lime sprinkled on grape leaves will repel Japanese beetles from your vines.

Mealy Bugs—These are little sap-sucking bugs that look like pieces of sticky cotton. Ants will help spread them to other plants. A cotton swab dipped in rubbing alcohol and applied directly on the mealy bugs is the best way to kill them.

Red Spider Mites—Tiny red spiders that prefer hot, dry, arid conditions. Keeping the plants well misted and the humidity high will prevent any spiders from getting hold of your plants.

Scale—A hard-shell insect that emits a sticky residue which is soon followed by new scale insects. Scrape off scale with your fingernail and then give the plant a bath in soapy water. The only herb I have had a scale problem with is bay. Scale insects seem to like the thicker-leaved plants.

Slugs—This is not really an insect but a member of the mollusk family, which includes delicacies such as clams, oysters, and mussels. They are hardly seen during hot weather but once it rains you'll swear it rained slugs. They need moisture to move around and are night feeders. Slugs are the most common insect problem I hear about from gardeners. Here are some ways to get rid of slugs:

- Put some beer or yeast in a dish of water; it's the yeast part they like. They will crawl in to drink and then drown.
- Sprinkling salt on them makes them curl up and die. But beware of using too much salt in the garden.
- Hand pick them by using a stick with a nail in the bottom to stick in them. Dispose of them in a pail of kerosene mixed with water or thick oil.
- Traps: They hide under boards and leaves during the day to keep cool from the sun. Lay boards down where you have a problem and hand pick them in early morning or before it gets cool in the evening.
- Slugs do not like wood ashes on their bodies, so spread ashes in areas where they are pests. They also do not like to walk on gravel. Use gravel in walkways and around affected plants.

Wasps, Hornets, and Yellow Jackets—Although these flying insects are beneficial because they eat caterpillars, they are my exception to the rule against using chemical sprays. A yellow jacket sting is especially dangerous. If you get into a nest of yellow jackets you can become allergic to all bee stings or have serious medical problems. Find a good commercial spray and eliminate any nest. Just follow the manufacturer's directions.

White Flies—Very tiny flies that suck juices from plants. When you touch the infected plant, the flies flutter up and then back down again. They are usually present in great numbers resting on the undersides of the plant leaf. They are found on houseplants and in greenhouses. They die outside in New England's cold winters. If natural sprays do not work you may have to try a pyrethrum or rotonone-based mild plant insecticide spray. A recipe for two *natural* sprays appears here.

White Fly Spray No. 1

In one gallon of water add:

> *1 cup dried pyrethrum heads*
> *1 cup elderberry leaves*
> *½ cup chamomile flowers*

Let set overnight. Strain through cheesecloth. Add 2 tablespoons of *liquid soap* and spray on infected plants.

White Fly Spray No. 2

In one gallon of water add:

1 cup rhubarb leaves
1 cup marigold leaves and flowers
1 cup yarrow leaves and flowers
1 tsp garlic water

Let set overnight. Strain through cheesecloth. Add 2 tablespoons *liquid soap*. Spray on infected plants.

All plants can be infested with insects but the following herbs seem to attract certain insect species more often than others. This does not mean they will always (or ever) be infected with these insects.

Plant	Insect Problem
agrimony	aphids
aloe	scale and mites
basil	aphids
bay	scale
bee balm	aphids
calendula	aphids
castor bean	spider mites and aphids
Chinese lantern	striped cucumber beetle
elderberry	Japanese beetle
horseradish	flea beetle
mints	aphids
mallow family	Japanese beetle
parsley	aphids
sage	white flies
violets	aphids

The Good Guys

Some insects are actually beneficial to man because of the number of harmful insects they consume. Here is a brief look at some helpful insects:

Ground Beetles—These large brown or black iridescent beetles live underground or under rocks. You will often see them when you cultivate soil. Ground beetles eat wire worms and other soil insects.

Goldeneye Lacewing—This is a small insect with lacelike wings and red-gold eyes. The adult will eat some plants but the benefit of its larvae eating aphids, mites, and mealy bugs outweighs the damage done by the adults.

Praying Mantis—This insect always amazes me as it sits perfectly still, hands folded, waiting for its prey. The larvae eat aphids; later, it eats anything it can catch. Unfortunately, this includes other good bugs.

Lady Bugs—What child does not know of the pretty little lady bug? The larvae of the lady bug will eat up to forty aphids an hour. Mature lady bugs eat aphids and mealy bugs. Many lady bugs will die for lack of food once an area is thoroughly cleaned out of these insects, so if chemical spray is used there may not be enough insects left for them to survive.

Parasitic Wasp—This tiny wasp is hardly visible with the naked eye. It will leave a tiny, hard, gold, scale-like shell on the leaf. They eat aphids and those pesty little white flies.

Dragonflies—Any pond or stream will have dragonflies that live on mosquito and other water-based insects which are flying around. We have identified seven different species of dragonflies at our pond. They often land on our arms and legs as we sit in the gazebo.

Using Herbs to Protect Your Pets Against Insects

English pennyroyal is the herb used mostly in connection with protection for your household cats and dogs. The botanical name pulegium is derived from the Latin word meaning "flea." Indeed, it does help in repelling fleas. Here are some suggestions for using it:

- Use a handful of pennyroyal boiled in 1 quart of water; put this in the water when you bathe your pets.
- Pennyroyal vinegar, diluted with water as a bath rinse, will make the animal's coat shiny.
- Pennyroyal oil is a highly concentrated substance and should *always* be diluted when applying to either animal or human skin. It will burn the skin if applied directly in concentrated form. Only 2 or 3 drops to 1 quart of water is needed.
- Add pennyroyal tea or oil to the water to wash your floors or pet bedding; it makes the house smell nice as well as repelling fleas.
- Rubbing the fresh leaf of the pennyroyal on the skin of animals or people will repel mosquitos.

Other herbs that have flea-repellent properties are: wormwood, south-ernwood, tansy, rosemary, and lavender. Use them in the same way as you use pennyroyal.

Companion Planting with Herbs

Symbiosis is the relationship of two or more dissimilar organisms (such as plants, animals, humans) living in a mutual environment for the benefit of each other. We call the process of taking advantage of this relationship companion planting. There are pros and cons on the issue of whether companion planting really works or not. Much of this information has been passed down from generation to generation. Some of it has been proven scientifically to be true. For example, before man's changing of the environment if a poisonous plant grew in a certain place, then Mother Nature provided its antidote growing nearby.

Most books say that basil and rue dislike each other. This is not actually true. What they dislike is the same soil conditions. Rue prefers a lean, dry, well-drained soil, while basil needs a rich, moist, well-fertilized soil.

Chamomile is said to be the herbal doctor for other plants. Plants growing near it will always do well. I use it as a misting herb for other plants to keep them healthy. I swear by its use. But again, it's not scientific information. It seems many gardeners have some little information they swear by that has been passed down from a long line of gardeners or farmers. Here are some companion partners offering good symbiosis that we use at Wormwood Farm:

- Calendula and marigolds with all plants: will kill nemodes and discourage bean beetles.
- Chives and other allium family members planted near roses and other vegetables help keep them bug free.
- Hyssop: plant under grape arbors and other fruit and berry plants.
- Basil goes well with all the plants it normally goes with in the kitchen; these include tomato, eggplant, peppers, and onions.
- Bee balm and borage both work well as pollination plants for tomatoes and other garden vegetables.
- Winter and summer savory are the "bean" herbs, both in the kitchen and in the garden.
- Chervil planted with radishes helps keep the flea beetle away.
- Dill grows well with cabbage, lettuce, and onions.
- Sage goes with cabbage and carrots, as does sweet marjoram.
- Tansy is good with berries such as blackberries and raspberries.

- Thyme or horseradish near potatoes will help hide the flower scent from the potato beetle.
- Wormwood, planted around the edges of gardens, will repel deer, ground hogs, and rabbits.
- Pyrethrum, planted around the garden, helps repel insects, as well as providing flower heads for your own sprays.

Using Herbs for Household Chores

Herbal recipes have been passed down through the generations for various aspects of household cleaning and scenting the home. "Strewing herbs" are no longer used, but branches of fragrant herbs can be laid under carpets for the scent to be released when walked upon. I use pennyroyal, southernwood, mint, and wormwood, all of which have flea-repellent qualities as well as nice aromas.

Arrangements of herbs hung on beams, or set decoratively in large vases, add beauty as well as scent. Pots of elderberry leaves and basil will help deter flies in a room. Many herbs have antiseptic and germicidal properties, which are found in their highest concentration in the essential oils. Some of those which have a high content of these properties are:

bay	pennyroyal
cinnamon	root of angelica
cloves	root of elecampane
juniper	rosemary
lavender	thyme

Use these oils (or a strong infusion of the leaf) in the following ways:

- In the water you use to wash floors.
- In your simmering pots.
- Diluted in water and added to your final rinse water in the washing machine.
- Drop of oil on polishing cloth for furniture. Beware that some oils will stain plastic or cloth items.
- Drops of oil can be tucked under chair cushions, put in cupboards, or put under the carpet.

Moth Repellents

Little moth bags are made from various shapes of cloth sewn together on three sides, filled with repellent herbs, and then fastened with a ribbon or sewn shut. Use these moth bags to repel insects and prevent that stored-away, musty smell in bureau drawers, closets, and storage areas.

Moth Bags

Recipe 1

1 part southernwood
1 part wormwood
1 part lavender
1 part rosemary

Recipe 2

1 part tansy
1 part santolina
1 part costmary
½ part pyrethrum flowers
¼ part cloves

Recipe 3

1 part mint
1 part rue
½ part southernwood
½ part rosemary
¼ part cinnamon chips

Recipe 4

1 part vetiver root
½ part patchouli
½ part rosemary
½ part tansy

Recipe 5

1 part cedar chips
½ part quassia chips
½ part costmary
½ part thyme

Recipe 6

1 part thyme
1 part pennyroyal
½ part wormwood
½ part sweet woodruff
(this one is good for stored-
    away books and papers)

All moth bags are made with dried herbs. *Parts* are a way to measure relative amounts. For example, 1 part might represent 1 cup, so ½ part would represent ½ cup. Or use quarts, pints, or any other common measure. This way you can make a small or large amount of mixture according to your needs.

Herbs for Moth Bags—Use singly or in a combination of favorite scents.

To Grow

costmary	rue
lavender	santolina
mints	southernwood
mugwort	sweet woodruff
pennyroyal	tansy
pyrethrum	thyme
Roman wormwood	wormwood
rosemary	

To Buy

calamus root	peppercorns
cedarwood chips	quassia chips
cinnamon bark or chips	tonka beans
cloves	vetiver root
patchouli	

Wax Pastilles—Wax pastilles are small round (or any shape) balls of wax, scented with the essential oils of a repellent-scented herb. These pastilles can be placed in bureau drawers or closets. If using for stored-away items, be sure the temperature does not get hot enough to melt the wax. For hanging in a closet, insert a ribbon in a hole made in the hardened wax by using a heated needle.

Always use extreme care when melting wax over the stove. Use a double boiler and keep baking soda handy in case of a wax fire. Do not spill any on the skin; it really burns.

Plant Profiles

English Pennyroyal (*Mentha pulegium*)

Family—Labiatae (mint)

Synonyms—Pudding grass, flea herb

Description—Low-growing creeping perennial. Small, shiny, slightly oval leaves; lilac flowers in late summer; aromatic mint aroma. Sailors used pennyroyal to purify their drinking water on long sea voyages.

Cultivation—Sandy loam with good drainage; full sun to partial shade. Nice between rocks in an area not walked on much. Water during dry spells. Not always winter hardy in zones 3 and 4.

Propagation—Cuttings of leaf or root division in spring

Wax Pastille

In double boiler melt *1 ounce of paraffin wax* over low heat. When melted add *3 drops of oil* (from above list), $^1/_8$ *cup whole cloves*, or $^1/_8$ *cup cinnamon chips*. Candle coloring can be added if desired. Pour into little metal cups, or muffin tins, to harden. When hard, remove and use. (These are not for burning in your simmering pots; the cinnamon or cloves would catch on fire).

Part Used—Leaf and flower

Harvest—All season, best oil content just before it comes into flower. Screen dry.

Uses—No longer recommended for internal use by the FDA. May cause dermatitis or kidney trouble when used internally. Pennyroyal is the famous flea herb, used in pet health, flea collars, and bath water. When rubbed on skin, it will repel mosquitos. A good scent for potpourri and sachets. Flower attractive for wreath making.

Santolina
Gray variety—*Santolina chamaecyparisus*
Green variety—*Santolina virens*

Family—Compositae (daisy)

Synonyms—Gray variety is called lavender cotton. None I know of for green variety.

Description—Both are evergreen perennials, but not always winter hardy in zones 3 and 4; will depend on what kind of shelter it is given and what kind of winter weather we have.

Gray santolina has silver foliage, grows to 20 inches, with yellow flowers in June and July.

Gray santolina

Green santolina has a more delicate, feathery foliage in bright green; yellow flowers same as the gray variety. Both have a nice refreshing scent and act as natural deodorizer for the home.

Cultivation—Both need good drainage, full sun, and a lean soil with bone meal or lime added. Prune foliage only lightly in spring to encourage growth on old wood; cut out any dead stalks. Remove flowers after bloom to keep plant looking neat. If planted outside, mulch in winter with evergreen boughs. Makes a good potted plant for house or patio.

Propagation—Cuttings or root division in spring. Seeds for gray variety available, but germination has been poor for me.

Part Used—Leaf and flowers

Harvest—Foliage all season, flowers when in bloom. Do not harvest large amounts at one time. Remember, on evergreen plants you are *shaping* when you prune. Cut evenly when you harvest the leaves for moth bags.

Uses—As an insect repellent. Potpourri ingredient for scent and color; gray is nice if you are making a pink and silver potpourri. Flowers dry nicely for wreaths and tussie mussies.

Southernwood *(Artemisia arboratum)*

Family—Compositae (daisy)

Synonyms—Old man, lad's love, garderobe

Description—Feathery grey/green evergreen perennial; insignificant yellow-green flowers; rarely blooms in zones 3 and 4. Pungent aroma repels insects when it grows in the garden and also when it's dried later. Name *lad's love* came from the ointment once made from its ashes and applied to young men's faces to encourage growth of the beard. *Old man* comes from the long life of the plant; *garderobe* from the French use of southernwood as an insect repellent in their closets.

Folklore tells us that if a young maiden puts southernwood under her pillow at night, the first man she meets in the morning will be the one she will marry. Was also used in courtrooms to ward off "jail fever" in early English courts.

Varieties of Southernwood:

common southernwood	3-4 feet tall, good hedge herb
tangerine southernwood	5-6 feet tall, good back of border herb, fruit scented
lemon southernwood	3-4 feet tall, nice lemon scent
camphor southernwood	2½ feet tall, stong camphor scent, slow grower

Cultivation—All like full sun to partial shade; lean to good soil with bone meal or lime added. Prune only in the spring to cut out dead branches and encourage new growth; never prune after August as it needs its wood to go through the winter.

Propagation—Layering, cuttings, or root divison spring

Part Used—Leaf

Harvest—All season until August, hang dry.

Uses—Culinary: Early Italians used it to rub on lamb before cooking. Some people enjoy it as a tea herb. *Use internally with caution.*
    Medicinal: as a tea for a spring tonic.
    Cosmetic: used as a hair rinse for dandruff and in the bath water.
    Miscellaneous: Insect repellent; lay in damp cellars and under cupboards to repel ants and give a good scent; plant near doorways and under windows to stop ants from entering the house.

Rue

Rue *(Ruta graveolens)*

Family—Rubiaceae (madder)

Synonyms—Herb of grace

Description—Hardy perennial 2 feet tall; blue-green, pea-like foliage; yellow flowers followed by interesting pods.

Cultivation—Likes a lean soil in a well-drained area with lime or bone meal added; full sun in sheltered area away from high winds. Not always winter hardy in zones 3 and 4; slow to come back in spring. All parts contain a substance called rutin, which is very bitter and may cause a rash in some persons when they touch the plant. Even though old herbals recommend its use in cosmetics and medicine, *it has been banned by the FDA for internal use and it is generally unsafe except for the uses listed below.* Do not weed around this herb when it is wet.

Propagation—Seeds, cuttings in the spring

Part Used—Leaf, root, pods

Harvest—All season, pods at end of summer, screen dry or stand upright in a jar.

Uses—Miscellaneous: insect repellent and disinfectant; roots produce a red dye; pods used in wreaths and arrangements.

Pyrethrum *(Chrysanthemum)*
White variety—*C. cinerarifolium*
Painted variety—*C. coccineum*

Family—Compositae (daisy)

Synonyms—Painted daisy

Description—Ferny dark green leaves. White flowers said to have more insect-repellent qualitites than the painted variety. Herbaceous perennials to 24-30 inches.

Cultivation—Good loam soil with lime or bone meal added. Full sun, good drainage. Keep dead flowers picked off for more blooms.

Propagation—Seeds or root divison of mature plant.

Uses—The flower heads are dried and used as an insecticide to kill mites, aphids, thrips, moths, and caterpillars. Pyrethrum will kill adult lady bugs but not their larvae.
    Never use pyrethrum internally; it is a poison.

Tansy *(Tanacetum vulgare)*

Family—Compositae (daisy)

Synonyms—Butter buttons, scented fern, hindheal.

Description—Herbaceous perennial to 3-4 feet; forms a broad clump of ferny leaves; can be slightly invasive; slight camphor scent; grows wild in New England area. Flowers are yellow and button-like. In William Cole's

Art Of Simpling (1656), the author assures maidens that "tansy, laid to soak in buttermilk for 9 days, would make the complexion fair."

Early English custom was to observe Easter time with tansy cakes. These were thought to purify the humors of the body after the limited fare of lent. *Tansy is now banned by the FDA for internal use due to its toxic properties.*

Cultivation—Full sun to partial shade; any soil will suit this herb; I have mine on the edge of the lawn where we can mow down invading roots.

Propagation—Root division in spring

Part Used—Leaf and flowers

Harvest—All season, hang dry leaf and flowers

Uses—Miscellaneous: leaf as an insect repellent to repel ants, fleas, and flies or as ingredient in moth bags. Plant near fruit trees for protection of fruit. Flowers for arrangements and wreaths or as color for potpourri.

Wormwood *(Artemisia absinthium)*

Family—Compositae (daisy)

Synonyms—Absinthium, common wormwood

Description—Herbaceous perennial to 3 feet, gray-green top leaf, gray underneath. Strongly divided, cut leaf; insignificant flowers at end of summer; pungent aroma. When working with wormwood, keep hands away from eyes, nose, and mouth; the bitter scent will stay on the hands for some time.

Cultivation—Full sun to partial shade; good drainage, lean to medium soil with bone meal or lime added. Keep clipped back for a bushy shrub or it will get tall and weedy by end of summer. If you want material for drying, let it go to flower.

Propagation—Seeds, cuttings, or root divisons

Part Used—Leaf

Harvest—All season, dry by hanging

Uses—Medicinal: commercial use for medicinal and veterinarian preparations. *Banned for internal use by the FDA,* but I have some older customers that use it as a tea, which is extremely bitter to my taste buds. Old medicinal used to expel worms in children.

Crafting: good base for wreaths, but beware that some persons are allergic to the smell of the dried wormwoods, especially the annual wormwood, sweet annie.

EIGHT

Gathering in the Harvest

(How to Process Your Herbs)

A LADY ASKED me one day, "How do you dry your baby's breath, it looks so nice?" "We just throw it in the corner of the attic," I replied, causing her to look at me suspiciously. Sometimes when we are in full swing of summer harvesting, time becomes an expensive commodity and shortcuts are taken. Since baby's breath is almost dry when you pick it, it really needs no special care. Strawflowers are also almost dry when you pick them, but they must be wired when fresh or it is very difficult to get a wire through the dried flower head. The reason for wiring stems of flowers is because some of them may have weak stems that easily break. Old herbals recommend harvesting herbs on St. John's day or the summer solstice, which is around the twenty-third of June. This is compatible with the proper growth stage of the herbs for harvesting, although there are exceptions as noted below.

The oil content and taste of herbs will vary from garden to garden. The variables are based on individual soil texture types, soil pH, amount of fertilizer, and the amount of water the herb receives. Consider also *when* the herb is harvested, *how* it is harvested, and *how* it is dried and stored. It is very disappointing to wait until the herb has gone by and then to try to harvest a good crop. All you get are old, tasteless herbs.

In 800 B.C., Greek priests were the doctors. They employed men, called root diggers, to gather their herbs. Root diggers would spread fantastic stories about the hazards of digging herbs in order to keep the competition down. For example, they said that peony roots could only be harvested in the darkness of night. If done during the daylight, a digger would run the risk of having his eyes plucked out by woodpeckers. Also, if an eagle were seen flying nearby when digging hellebore, the gatherer would die within the year. Another tale was that mandrake root was supposed to resemble the human figure and would cry out as it was being taken from the ground. Dogs needed to be leashed to pull this root so the evil spirits would not harm the human root digger.

Harvesting Procedures

Learning to harvest your own herbs and flowers will come mostly from hands-on experience. You can read and study the tips and how-tos but only by actually doing it will you learn the feel and look of the herbs and when they are just right for harvesting. Harvesting will depend a great deal on the weather and how early or late the herbs grow in the spring. Every year is different. The following hints will aid you in your harvesting of herbs:

General Harvesting Tips

- Leaves with the greatest oil content will be those harvested just before the herbs come into flower. Examples are thyme, oregano, and the mints. Use these choice leaves for cooking, medicine, and teas. Use second and third cuttings for cosmetics and crafting. Exception is sweet marjoram which has its best oil content when in the budded to full flower stage.
- Always cut your herbs with scissors or a knife. Tugging at the plant will disturb the roots, causing the plant to wilt. You may even risk pulling it entirely out of the soil.
  The plant has a vital food life force. The nutrients in the root send food up the stem to the leaves and flowers starting in the morning. The nutrients return in the afternoon so by evening the vital food force has returned to the roots for night storage. I prefer to harvest around ten or eleven A.M. while the herb is full of nutrients and before the sun robs the leaves of essential oils.
- Harvest on a dry day, after the morning dew has evaporated.
- If you must wash your herbs before gathering, wash them down with a hose during very early morning hours and harvest only when thoroughly dried.
- If circumstances make harvesting possible only when herbs are wet, cut and paper towel dry completely, then put them in the

microwave for one minute. This method is not recommended unless there is absolutely no other choice.

- Harvest only that amount of material you can properly take care of immediately. Herbs left standing around will wilt, producing unusable material.
- Label during all steps of harvesting and processing. Some dried herbs will lose aroma and look like all the others. Labeling helps prevent the serious mistake of ingesting unsafe herbs by accident.
- Annual herbs can be harvested as soon as they are about 8 inches tall. Leave at least 5 inches on the stem when harvesting to produce more material, since several cuttings are possible with annuals over the season. In late summer, when there is danger of frost, cut them back to the ground. Basil, for example, needs lots of cutting to produce bushy plants.
- Perennials can be harvested as soon as they have 4 to 6 inches of growth. Do not cut more than one quarter to one third of the entire plant at one time. Herbaceous perennials (those plants that die back to the ground in fall) can be harvested to the ground at the end of the season. Among these are bee balm, lemon balm, chives, comfrey and mints.

Those herbs with woody stems (such as southernwood, lavender, and winter savory) need their woody stalks to go through the winter. Do not cut back severely after August.

Harvesting Herb Flowers

Flowers are cut and dried for use in cooking, teas, cosmetics, medicine, potpourri, and wreath making.

Those that we mention below all belong to the herb kingdom. There is also a large number of everlasting flowers grown just for the purpose of cutting to dry for craft work; included here are strawflowers, statice, baby's breath, ammobium, acrolinium, and ammi majus. One benefit of drying herbs and flowers is the nice aroma the whole house gets as they dry for that special bouquet or wreath.

In general, flowers are harvested when in full bloom. Old, faded flowers will dry even older and more faded looking. Lavender is harvested in the bud stage because that's when it has the best oil content. If you don't pick it at the proper time, let it go to flower and harvest to use in wreaths. Even the leaf has some lavender scent for a wreath.

Pearly everlasting, joe-pye weed, agrimony hemp, and globe thistle have the problem of *fluffing out*. This is my word for the process that happens when certain flowers are picked and, unlike others that stop growing when harvested, these flowers continue to open up to the flower stage. When picked in full flower, they will continue to open up to disperse their seed, thus fluffing out. However, when harvested in the budded stage, they continue to open to the flower stage and stop.

Flowers can be hung to air dry by their stems, microwaved, or in the case of small petals, screen dried. For flower petals such as roses or calendula, lay a paper towel on the screen first and then put the flowers on the paper towel to dry. Plants will shrink during the drying period, some petals as much as one half their original size. The following chart will help you select the correct drying method and use for your herbal flowers:

Flower	Drying Method	Uses
allheal (prunella)	hang	wreaths, tea, medicine
anise-hyssop	hang	cooking, tea, wreaths
basils	hang/screen	cooking, tea, cosmetic, wreaths
bee balm	hang	cooking, tea, medicine, cosmetic, potpourri, wreaths
calendula	screen	cooking, medicine, cosmetic, potpourri
chamomile	screen	tea, medicine, cosmetic, potpourri
chives	hang	cooking, wreaths
clove pinks	microwave/ silica gel	cooking, tea, potpourri
elderberry	screen/ microwave	cooking, tea, medicine, cosmetic
feverfew	hang/screen	tea, medicine, potpourri, wreath
gnaphalium	hang	wreath, potpourri
hollyhock	screen	tea, medicine, potpourri
joe-pye weed	hang	medicine, wreaths
lady's mantle	hang	medicine, wreath
larkspur	hang	wreath, potpourri
lavender	hang/stand	medicine, cosmetic, wreath, potpourri
pearly everlasting	hang	medicine, wreath, potpourri
pyrethrum	screen	insect repellent
roses	screen/ silica gel	cooking, tea, cosmetic, wreath, potpourri
safflower	hang	cooking, wreath, potpourri
showy marjoram	hang	wreath
tansy	hang	wreath, potpourri
violets	screen/ microwave	cooking, tea, medicine, cosmetic, potpourri
yarrows	hang	medicine, cosmetic, wreath

The Herbal Seeds

Seeds are harvested from the following herbs:

Herb	Uses
anise	cooking, tea, medicine
caraway	cooking, tea, medicine, potpourri
coriander	cooking, tea, medicine, potpourri
dill	cooking, tea, medicine, wreath, potpourri
fennel	cooking, tea, medicine, cosmetic

Fennel and anise rarely flower or set seeds in zone 3 or 4, but *the foliage can be substituted in any recipe calling for the seeds.*

Harvest seeds as they begin to turn brown, but remember that all seeds will not mature at the same time. Poke holes in the sides of a brown paper bag for air circulation. Cut off the seeded umbels and put them in the bag; dry in warm, dry room. It takes approximately two weeks for seeds to dry. Then clean away the chaff and stems. If desired, you can heat the seeds in the oven at 350° for one minute to kill any insect larvae. But if you do this, it also kills the germination potential of the seed.

Harvesting Herbal Roots

Most roots are dug in the fall, usually after a frost or two. If roots are harvested too early in the season they will be mushy and soft, shrinking as they dry.

Harvest roots in early morning or early evening, when the vital food nutrients are in the root system.

Drying Method 1—Slice roots, spread on screens, air dry, turn frequently to prevent mildew. They will take several weeks to dry. With this method, and those below, watch for mildew, especially with larger, slower-drying roots.

Drying Method 2—Put in oven on lowest temperature you have (leave door open). Turn frequently. Dry for several hours (about six to nine) and finish with air drying on screens. Will cut drying time down to about a week.

Drying Method 3—Put on screens and cover with cheesecloth, sun dry outside. Bring roots inside during damp or rainy days and in the evening. It will take several weeks for roots to dry, depending on the weather.

Drying Method 4—Dry in a commercial dehydrator (prices range widely). Follow manufacturer's directions for drying.

Tips from Wormwood Farm

- Using a garden fork, carefully dig up the roots, taking care not to break them.
- Wash off the soil; a good hosing usually does the trick.
- Where applicable, peel off the rind.
- Cut into size wanted.
- Dry by one of the four methods described.

The following chart will provide a quick reference for root harvesting time. *Any* of the above methods may be used to dry *any* of these roots. Iris florentine must be cut into small pieces, but all the others can be dried whole, or cut to dry faster.

Herb	Year to Harvest	Season
angelica	first	fall
burdock root	second	fall
comfrey	any	fall
elecampane	second	fall
Florentine iris	end of second	fall
horseradish	second	fall
lovage	any	fall
marshmallow	end of second	late summer
soapwort	any	anytime
valerian	any	late summer

Harvesting Pods

Pods are the seed coverings left after the flower has died and produced seeds. They are useful as art decorations in floral arrangements, wall designs, and wreaths. Some pods can be spray painted or dipped with a liquid dye made especially for flowers and dried material. The following herbs produce attractive pods and are easily grown in the New England garden.

Baptisia: Harvest when pods turn black. This plant is sometimes called the rattlesnake plant because the seeds in the pod rattle like the tail of a rattlesnake.

Elecampane: The yellow daisy flowers leave a brown, daisy-shaped pod. Nice when sprayed with gold or silver.

Fuller's teasel: A favorite pod, the teasel comb can be harvested all season. Spray paint those harvested after a frost.

Hop vine: The hop flowers are called strobiles, which are conelike pods. Harvest early when bright green; they will fade to tan in about six months.

Martynia (the unicorn plant): Forms interesting pods and is good for drying. Harvest at the end of the season, though pods may still be green. Let them set in a warm, dry place for two or three months. The exterior will turn brown and fall off, revealing a black pod with a green stripe.

Martynia (the unicorn plant) with pods.

Purple coneflower: The purple flower petals drop off, leaving a brown to black pod; can be spray painted.

Rue: After the yellow flowers drop, rue will produce small, interesting pods. These can be spray painted and are especially nice done in gold and silver for the holidays.

Turtlehead: A spike of small pods, useful in floral arrangements; can be spray painted.

The Drying Process

Drying should be done as quickly as possible to preserve essential oils and flower color. The basic requirements are warmth, no direct sunlight, and good ventilation. An attic, spare room, garage, or any place that meets these requirements can be used. Here are some of the most common drying methods.

Simple Hanging Method

This is an easy, natural way to dry your material. We use this method whenever possible at Wormwood Farm since we dry a large amount of material. Here is the process:

1. Gather your material in small bunches. Thick bunches will mildew and rot in the center.
2. Fasten an elastic band around the bunch of stems. The elastic will shrink as the material does. Ribbons and string will not shrink and the material will fall out.
3. Fasten a clothespin onto the elastic.
4. Pin the clothespin onto a wire coat hanger. You can put quite a lot of these bunches on the coat hanger, but do not overcrowd because you need good air circulation.
5. Label material.

Length of drying time will depend on thickness of the material, and the termperature of the room used. It should not be less than 50°. If you have cats, put drying catnip high enough so the cats can't pull it down. When your material is dried, strip the leaves off the stems, keeping them as whole as possible. Be absolutely sure all material is well dried. Store in airtight containers, away from heat source, and label. Remember, this dried material is *highly flammable*. Do not store in direct sunlight; it will quickly fade the material.

Screen Drying

The first time I visited the Shaker Village at Sabbathday Lake, I came home and put screens on blocks as they had done. It provides a large area with good air circulation for drying leaves and flowers too small to hang. Spread leaves and flowers lightly over the screens and label. Do not pile too thickly or they may mildew.

Here are some suggestions for screen drying particular herbs:

Comfrey: When drying comfrey, each leaf must be separated: if you overlap the leaves, they will turn black where they touch each other. Try it and see what I mean.

Small flowers: When drying small flowers on screens, place paper towels on the screen to hold the flowers. This makes it easier to retrieve the flowers when dried. Some flowers and leaves tend to shrink to half their original size when dried. Remember this when harvesting and gather a large quantity of material. Those that shrink a lot are calendula, violets, johnny-jump-up, and rose petals.

Microwaving

After years of dealing with faded blue cornflowers, I was rescued by the microwave. Partially drying cornflowers in the microwave sets the color so that it does not fade. There is still a lot of research under way on drying in the microwave. Since there is a wide variety of microwaves with different settings, the best I can do is tell you what I do and hope you will experiment and see how you feel about the taste and color of herbs and flowers. Then let me know what you think and what works best for you. Here are the two methods I use for microwaving:

Microwave Method 1

This is used for culinary herbs; parsley, dillweed, savory, basil, and thyme have all come out very nicely.

1. Put a large cup of water in back of the microwave.
2. Lay several thicknesses of paper towels on the tray.
3. Spread herbs or flowers evenly and not too thickly on towels. Cover with a paper towel.
4. Or you can place a plastic colander in the oven with flowers stuck in the holes. This keeps the heads upright and the stems down.
5. Use a setting of 300 watts or set on defrost. Microwave for 1 minute, then check to see if it needs more time. Do not overmicrowave, or material will fall apart; better to finish off with air drying on the shelf.
6. Remember that food cooked in the microwave will be very hot and will continue cooking for a bit after it shuts, off so take this into consideration when doing the flowers. I take them out damp and let them air dry to finish them off.

Microwave Method 2

This method involves using silica gel to dry flowers. It is *not a safe method* for herbs or flowers that are to be used *internally!* Silica gel is a strong commercial product that can absorb the moisture from your flowers, drying them very quickly. Here is the process:

1. Using about 4 cups of silica gel, lay 2 inches of the gel on the bottom of a cardboard box of plastic container.
2. Set flowers in, not overcrowding. Cover gently with silica gel, being to

keep the petals from separating. They will dry in whatever position you place them.

3. Place the container in microwave at 350° or on defrost.
4. Place a cup of water in back of the microwave.
5. Dry for about 3 minutes.
6. Remove and let set for 15 minutes. Flowers should be dry. Gently shake off the silica gel and store the flowers in a cardboard box in a dry area.

Oven Drying

If your oven can hold an even temperature that is less that 95° then you can dry your herbs in the oven. If the temperature is too high or an overly long period of time is used, the herbs will be robbed of their essential oils. Leave the oven door open to let the moisture out. Watch carefully, turning occasionally to prevent burning. (This is also good for root drying.)

Other Processes

Freezing

Frozen herbs will last up to six months. For soups and stews put herbs in a blender with chicken or beef stock; blend with setting on high. Freeze in ice cube trays, then put in plastic bags when frozen. Take out just the amount you need for a soup or stew.

Another freezing method is to fill a container with boiling water. Dip whole bunches of herbs into the water, count to ten and remove, dry and cool on a paper towel. Freeze uncovered on cookie sheets and then pack in individual bags. Try combinations such as parsley, thyme, and tarragon, or chervil, basil, and oregano. Most culinary herbs will freeze well.

Sugar or Salt Pack

Sugar and salt packs will produce two products, an herb product and a scented, flavored salt or sugar for cooking. Here is how to make a sugar or a salt pack.

1. Put a layer of salt or sugar in an airtight container.
2. Layer fresh herbs on top.
3. Layer with salt or sugar; continue until container is full.

The sugar and salt will absorb the moisture from the herbs as they dry, making the sugar and salt hard. Herbs will dry nicely. Both products can be used in any recipes.

Herbs for salt pack include any of the culinary herbs such as chervil, dillweed, basil, marjoram, or parsley. Herbs for sugar are good with the sweet herbs of mints, anise-hyssop, scented geraniums, borage, pineapple sage, costmary, and bee balm.

Drying with Silica Gel

Silica gel is for drying *only* those products used for crafting. It is unsafe to use on herbs to be taken internally. Silica gel is good for drying those herbs and flowers that do not dry well by hanging or laying on screens. The expensive silica gel will last virtually forever. After drying a selection of flowers, put the gel in the oven (on low) and dry it out; then reuse. Here is my method for drying whole herbs with silica gel:

1. Put one-half inch silica gel into an airtight container with a cover.
2. Layer your herbs or flowers on the gel. Cover slowly with the gel by letting it flow over and around the herbs.
3. Do not overcrowd the herbs and keep flower heads intact.
4. Seal container and check every three days for dryness. When dry, remove the herbs or flowers.
5. Store in airtight container until ready to use.

You can put some of the gel in the storage box to keep undried material from absorbing any moisture. Some plants which lend themselves to the silica gel method are rose buds and flowers, clove-pinks, adonis, edelweiss, and red yarrow.

A few final thoughts on drying herbs:

- Length of drying time will depend on the water content of the individual herb or flower, the method used, atmospheric conditions, room temperature, and the thickness of the plant material.
- Be sure all material is well dried no matter what method you use or you will end up with mildewed, unusable material.
- Hanging herbs on the kitchen beams is decorative, but they will become dusty and dirty; don't use them internally.
- Finally, experiment with different methods to dry your herbs and flowers to see what suits you best.

Storing

Once herbs are dried, strip the leaves from the stems. Clean away any debris or foreign objects. Dried herbs can be stored in large, uncut pieces, crumbled in small pieces with the hand, or made into a powder with a mortar and pestle.

Keeping the leaves as large as possible will help retain the essential oils longer. Store in airtight containers only (plastic or glass is the best material to use). Store these herbs away from heat sources, direct sunlight, and in a dry area.

To store herbs and flowers for craft work, you can put them in cardboard boxes, separated by tissue paper or newspapers, or gently wrap them in tissue paper. Do not lay them so they crush each other.

Herbal Vinegar

A good way to store your herbs is in vinegar. The vinegars will pick up the flavor and aroma of the herbs, preserving them for a long period of time. Cider vinegar has some nutritional properties, so I prefer using it. White vinegar has no nutritional value, but is useful in making pink vinegar from flowers of the chive plant and the opal basil herb. Wine vinegar is often used by the gourmet cook and it makes a nice gift.

Herbal vinegars have many uses:

- Cooking with fish, poultry, stews and vegetables
- Marinades for meats
- In the bath water to help keep the acid mantle of the skin normal
- Diluted with water for a hair rinse to give you shiny hair
- In wash water for floors and walls
- In the last rinse cycle of the washing machine

Herbal vinegar bottles are dipped in hot wax to coat the top.

Making Herbal Vinegar

1. Fill wide-mouth glass container with whatever amount of herbs you want to use.
2. Pour enough vinegar over the herbs of your choice to cover them.
3. Cover container (no metal covers).
4. Set on counter for ten days.
5. Strain herbs out of vinegar.
6. Pour into attractive sterilized bottles; wine bottles or salad dressing bottles work well.
7. If desired, add fresh herb stalk to vinegar; this is nice if you're giving as a gift, but if you plan on long-time storage, do not use.
8. Seal cap on tight (again, *not* metal)
9. For gift giving, dip your vinegar bottle top (with the cap on securely) into scented wax. Here is the procedure:

   - melt ½ lb. wax
   - stir in 1 tbsp cinnamon or cloves
   - check cap to be sure it is secure. If the cap comes off during this process you could be badly burned.
   - hold bottle upside down and dip cap and top of bottle into the wax (make sure the bottle is not very cold or it may break).
   - dip only for a second to put a coat of wax on it; then take it out, let set a second, re-dip; repeat this process until the wax builds up to the desired thickness. Six to ten dips will usually do it.

10. Label the bottle and add a pretty ribbon.

Tips from Wormwood Farm

- Do not use metal during this process as it causes a reaction with the vinegar.
- Crush the herbs and pound the seeds for better saturation.
- You can warm the vinegar (but never boil) for faster steeping time. Steep for five days when warmed.
- The basic recipe for all vinegars is 2 cups of fresh herbs or 3 tablespoons of dried herbs to 2 cups of vinegar.
- Do not add water to vinegar; it will make it cloudy.
- Use one herb or a combination of several herbs.
- Combine antiseptic herbs with vinegar to use for cleaning, among these thyme, rosemary, and pennyroyal. Find new ways to use your herbs in your everyday living.

Herbal Vinegar Recipes—During the haying season at my grandfather's farm, my grandmother would bring out a drink called switchel for the workers. This was made with vinegar, water, and molasses. It really quenched our thirst. To make switchel, mix 2 cups of boiled water with 2 tablespoons cider vinegar and 1½ tablespoons of molasses; cool and serve with ice cubes.

Twelve Herb Vinegar

To *one gallon of vinegar*, add the following fresh herbs:

> *4 large basil leaves*
> *1 six-inch piece rosemary*
> *1 three-inch winter savory leaf*
> *3 good-sized parsley heads*
> *3 large mitsuba heads*
> *4 dried bay leaves*
> *1 six-inch sweet marjoram head*
> *4 four-inch thyme pieces*
> *1 large dill seed head (or several pieces of dillweed)*
> *1 large lovage leaf*
> *3 whole clove buds*
> *4 whole peppercorns*

Pour vinegar over the herbs, steep for ten days, strain, and bottle.

Spearmint Vinegar

Warm 1 quart of *cider vinegar* (never boil the vinegar). Add 1 cup of *white sugar* and 2 cups of *minced spearmint leaves*. Simmer for 5 minutes, then let steep for one half hour. Strain and bottle.

Orange Vinegar

Peel rind from one *orange* (use only the rind and not the white pith). Add to:

> *1 cup dry vermouth*
> *1 cup white wine vinegar*
> *1 clove bud*
> *1 tbsp dried orange-scented geranium leaves*
> *½ tsp sugar*

Let the mixture steep for eight days, then strain and use with fish or poultry.

Steak Marinade with Herbal Vinegar

Mix together:

¼ cup Worcestershire sauce
½ cup herbal vinegar (sweet marjoram, thyme, or salad burnet).
1 tsp garlic powder
1½ tsps summer savory
1 tsp thyme

This recipe makes enough marinade for two pounds of steak for a barbecue.

Plant Profiles

Catnip *(Nepeta cataria)*

Family—Labiatae (mint)

Synonyms—Kitty nip

Description—Herbaceous perennial to 4 feet tall has typical square stems that are characteristic of members of the mint family. Gray-green leaf on top with downy undersides, toothed-edged leaf, white flowers on stalk from July to frost, with a slightly minty aroma. Well known as a cat herb, because cats get a euphoric feeling from eating and rolling in it, and usually follow this by a long nap. Some cats like fresh catnip only, others dried only, and some both ways; however, there are cats that dislike all catnip. Rats dislike catnip; I'm not sure if it's the herb they dislike or the fact that it's a kitty hangout.

Cultivation—Grow in full sun or partial shade. Prefers lean soil with good drainage and some lime or bone meal added. Cut back severely as it comes into flower; it will keep producing leaves all season.

Propagation—Seeds or spring root division. Will self-seed. There is an old saying:

> *If you set it, the cats will eat it,*
> *If you sow it, the cats won't know it.*

If cats bother your young seedlings, they can be protected by putting a wire cage over the seedlings until the herb becomes well established.

Part Used—Leaf

Harvest—All season. Hang dry or gather just the leaves and screen dry. Save first cuttings for your tea and let the cats have the later cuttings.

Uses—Medicinal: Well known as a cat herb, but will make a good cup of tea for pleasure. I often enjoy a cup just before bedtime as it seems to help relax me. It's reputed to be good for colds, diarrhea, and irritability when used in the form of a tea; not more than two cups a day is recommended. Externally, make as a salve or oil preperation for cuts and other wounds.

Horseradish *(Armoracia rusticana)*

Family—Cruciferae (mustard)

Synonyms—Mountain radish

Description—A herbaceous perennial with large strap-like leaves to 3 feet tall. Flowers are an attractive, creamy, fragrant white. Invasive, fleshy root high in vitamin C and potassium. Its first use was as a medicine when it was soaked in vinegar and used to remove freckles.

Cultivation—Likes a rich soil in the full sun. Feed with compost and well-aged manure for large roots. Difficult to eradicate once planted so put in area where it is to stay; even a small piece of root will start a new bed of horseradish.

Propagation—Slow growing from seed; usually root cuttings are taken.

Part Used—Leaf and roots

Harvest—Leaf in early spring, used fresh; roots in fall after a few frosts.

Uses—Culinary: Leaves can be eaten raw in salads or boiled as a vegetable green. Root is preserved in vinegar and used as a condiment to accompany baked beans, fish, and meats.

Horseradish Canapes

Mix a jelly sauce in your blender as follows:

> *1 10-ounce jar of apple jelly*
> *1 10-ounce jar of pineapple preserves*
> *1 tbsp horseradish preserves*
> *1 tsp dry mustard*

Spread Ritz crackers with softened cream cheese, then top with a teaspoon of horseradish jelly sauce.

Medicinal: Horseradish is a stimulant and a diuretic. William Coles says, "horseradish fed to children with worms, will soon killeth the worms."

Preservation—Harvest the root in the fall after a few frosts. Wash dirt off and peel the hard outer skin off. It must be processed immediately after it is harvested, as it soon loses its potency. Cut in small pieces with a grinder or blender (an old hand grinder provides the best texture). Pack in sterilized jars and pour cider vinegar over it (just to cover). Seal with a cover and keep refrigerated once the seal is broken.

Silver King *(Artemisia albula)*

Family—Compositae (daisy)

Synonyms—Artemisia

Description—Herbaceous perennial to 3 feet with gray-silver, deeply toothed foliage; white-silver flowers in late summer. Slight scent, quite invasive.

Cultivation—Full sun to partial shade, medium-rich soil with bone meal or lime added. Beautiful massed in a garden but soon takes over the other plants.

Propagation—Root division

Part Used—Leaves and flowering tops

Harvest—All season and before the flowering tops turn brown. Harvest several times a year to get different-sized textured leaves for wreaths. Dry by hanging.

Uses—Crafting: popular among floral arrangers and wreath makers.

Silver Mound *(Artemisia schmidtiana)*

Family—Compositae (daisy)

Synonyms—None

Description—Shimmering mound of silver-gray foliage and white-silver flowers. Even though a member of the herb family, it is sold by greenhouses as a herbaceous perennial; grows into a mound shape, making it a good specimen for the border. Height is one foot.

Cultivation—Full sun or partial shade; must have good drainage; grows in most soils with bone meal or lime added.

Propagation—Root division or stem cuttings

Part Used—Leaves

Harvest—All season, hang dry or lay on screens

Uses—Miscellaneous: Has some insect-repellent properties, as do all members of the artemisia family, but is used mostly as an ornamental, with the foliage cuttings used in wreath making and potpourri.

Pearly Everlasting *(Anaphalis margaritacea)*

Family—compositae (daisy)

Synonyms—Everlasting

Description—Herbaceous perennial to 20 inches tall. Gray-green foliage is topped by terminal, woolly, white flowers from July on. Very slight scent. Native to New England area, especially the northern wilderness. From Josselyn's *Voyages to New England* (1663) "the fishermen, when they want tobacco, take of this herb." The Indians used it in ceremonies to drive away evil spirits.

Cultivation—Lean, sandy soil with good drainage in full sun to partial shade. Will be plagued by the caterpillar of the painted lady butterfly.

Propagation—Seeds or root division, will spread quickly once established.

Part Used—Leaf and flowers

Harvest—Leaf in early season; flowers in budded stage before they fluff out. Hang flowers and screen dry the foliage.

Uses—Medicinal: Leaves were once used for tobacco and medicinally for colds, burns, and asthma. As a child, I remember my father smoking and using incense from an herbal concoction for his severe case of asthma; pearly everlasting was one of the ingredients used.

Crafting: Flowers make excellent additions to a wreath and a good white color for potpourri.

Roses *(Rosa spp.)*

Family—Rosaceae (rose)

Synonyms—None

Description—A description of a rose is unnecessary, it being one of America's favorite flowers. In the world of herbalism, we are interested mostly in those highly fragrant, old-fashioned rose species. The history of the rose goes back to the writing of *The Iliad*. Many customs and folklore have evolved over the years concerning the rose. One of those: It was thought

Rose Cake

Mix your favorite white cake mix or use a commercial cake mix. Divide the batter into three parts:

In part one—add 4 tsps grated walnuts
In part two—add ½ cup clean rose petals
In part three—add ½ tsp red food coloring

In 9 by 9 inch, buttered cake pan, pour first part, then part two, and then part three. Do not mix. Bake for 30 minutes or until done in 350° oven. Frost with confectionary sugar frosting, sprinkle on white coconut, and decorate with fresh rose buds.

Rose Petal Salad

To 1 cup of *cottage cheese* add:

½ cup rose petals
½ cup pineapple chunks
½ cup walnuts

Serve on a bed of fresh lettuce.

Also: Freeze your rose buds in a tray of ice cubes to float on punch bowls. Fill trays of ice cubes with pink lemonade and rose petals. Roses are edible, so use them to decorate your deserts and salads.

Rose Water

Fill a glass or stainless steel pan with clean *rose petals*. Cover with boiling-hot *distilled water* and simmer for one hour. Let steep for four hours, then strain out the petals and repeat the process with new petals, simmering and steeping. Strain, bottle, and refrigerate.

Rose Vinegar

Fill a glass container with your *rose petals*; cover with *cider vinegar*. Set aside on counter for ten days. Strain and bottle. Use diluted as a hair rinse or on skin as an astringent in your bath water (test first for skin sensitivity).

that if a rose hung over the dinner table, all secrets would be held in confidence, or *sub rosa*. Maybe this is where the rose arrangement on the center of the table came from. There is a wide variety of roses available to the herbalist to grow in the New England garden; here are some I enjoy.

Cabbage rose (rosa centifolia)
Damask rose (rosa damascena)
Dog rose (rosa canina)
French rose (rosa gallica)
Musk rose (rosa muscosa)
Sweet brier (rosa eglantine)

Cultivation—Shelter from harsh winds but ensure good air circulation. Give full sun with good drainage and water in dry spells. Likes a rich, well-composted soil. Feed during the growing months with a good fertilizer. Keep flower heads picked off and prune dead stems in early spring. Roses are subject to rose slugs, aphids, lead hoppers and mildew. I hate to say some species may need a chemical spray, but do not spray unless absolutely necessary to save the plant. Most old-fashioned species are winter hardy but for added insurance pull soil up around the base of plant for protection during snow-covered winters. Remove in early spring before growth starts.

Propagation—Cuttings and suckers

Part Used—Flowers and hips (the seed pod)

Harvest—When in budded or full bloom stage; best way to preserve is in silica gel. Hips are harvested when they turn red in the fall. Not all roses will produce hips.

Uses—Roses have been used for centuries in cooking, cosmetics, and just on the table to uplift the spirits.

NINE

Good King Henry and Other Culinary Herbs

(How to Use Herbs in Cooking)

ONCE YOU GROW and use your own fresh herbs and dry them for winter use, you will no longer be satisfied with those tasteless, adulterated herbs from the store shelf. A large percentage of the herbs we purchase from the store are imported from foreign countries. They come in bales, like hay, and often include weeds and other herbs. They are fumigated and processed; by the time they get to the store they are already almost past their prime. Your dried herbs should be replaced every year for good taste and aroma. Seeds will last longer, up to three years. Growing your own herbs will provide the necessary material to replace them yearly.

Herbs used in commercial foods are usually in the form of the essential oils. Basically, this is because it's easier to control the amount used and many people do not like to see the green leaves in their food.

Herbs for the Culinary Garden

See Chapter 3 for designing your culinary garden. The following herbs are those that can be grown in the culinary garden, whether you are an "everyday" or a gourmet cook. The chart below will suggest some of the foods that are compatible with the herbs. Any of the culinary herbs can be used in making vinegars, oils, and butter. Because everyone has individual taste buds, it's difficult to recommend what you will enjoy; experiment

157

to find your favorites. When adding herbs in your foods, crush them in your hand and inhale their wonderful scent. To learn the taste of herbs, use them in butters and test them on bread or crackers.

Hardy Perennial Culinary Herbs

Herb	Part Used	Goes Well With
alliums (onions)	bulb, stalk	breads, soups, salads, fish, meats, poultry, rice, pickles, vegetables
alpine strawberry	fruit	beverages, sauces, cakes, desserts, fruits, garnish
anise-hyssop	leaf	beverages, salads, jellies, cakes, cookies, desserts, fruits
costmary	leaf	fish, meats, poultry
French tarragon	leaf	fish, meats, poultry, vegetables
Good King Henry	leaf	soups, salads, fish, meats, poultry, rice, vegetables
horseradish	leaf, root	leaf: vegetables, salads root: condiments, meats, beans
lemon balm	leaf	beverages, breads, salads, fish, meats, poultry, rice, sauces, vegetables, jellies, cakes, desserts, fruits
lovage	leaf	soups, salads, meats, poultry, rice, vegetables
mints	leaf	beverages, soups, salads, fish, jellies, cakes, cookies, desserts
mitsuba	leaf	soups, salads, fish, meats, poultry, rice, vegetables
oregano	leaf	soups, salads, fish, meats, poultry, rice, vegetables
sage	leaf	breads, poultry, stuffings, fish
salad burnet	leaf	soups, salads, poultry, rice, sauces, vegetables, fruits, garnish
sorrel	leaf	soups, salads, vegetables
sweet cicely	leaf	beverages, breads, salads, cakes, desserts, fruits
thyme	leaf	soups, salads, meats, fish, poultry, rice, sauces, vegetables, jellies, fruits
winter savory	leaf	soups, salads, fish, meats, poultry, rice, beans, vegetables

Tender Perennial Culinary Herbs

Herb	Part Used	Goes Well With
bay	leaf (dried)	soups, fish, meats, poultry, pickles
Mexican oregano	leaf	soups, salads, fish, meats, poultry, vegetables, jellies, cakes, desserts, fruits
rosemary	leaf	beverages, breads, soups, salads, fish, meats, poultry, sauces, cakes, desserts, fruits
scented geraniums	leaf	beverages, salads, sauces, jellies, cakes, desserts, garnish

Annual and Biennial Culinary Herbs

anise	seeds, leaf	cakes, cookies, fruits, desserts
basil	leaf	breads, soups, salads, meats, eggplant, tomato dishes, egg and cheese dishes
borage	leaf, flower	beverages, soups, salads, cakes, fruits
calendula	petals	soups, salads, rice, cakes, desserts, or as a substitute for saffron
caraway	seed	breads, salads, rice, cabbage dishes, goulash, cake, cookies, desserts
chervil	leaf	soups, salads, fish, rice, vegetables, garnish
coriander/cilantro	seed, leaf	breads, soups, salads, meats, pickles, vegetables, cakes, desserts
dillweed	seed, leaf	breads, soups, salads, fish, poultry, pickles
epazote	leaf (flowers may be *toxic*)	rice, beans
fennel	seed, leaf	bread, salads, fish, vegetables, desserts
parsley	leaf	breads, soups, salads, fish, meats, poultry, rice, sauces, vegetables
shisho perilla	leaf	soups, salads, rice, sauces, garnish
summer savory	leaf	breads, salads, fish, meats, beans, sauces, vegetables
sweet marjoram	leaf	breads, soups, salads, fish, meats, poultry, rice, vegetables

Using Culinary Herbs

Herbs are used in seasoning foods exactly as you would use salt and pepper. Herbs can be put in salt shakers with large holes and sprinkled on foods. If you're new at using herbs in your cooking, start with a small amount until you determine your special favorites. Because I have been using herbs in my cooking for over ten years, I add more than the averge person does.

- Don't season every dish with the same herb. It will become boring after a while.
- It's fun to have an herb dinner with every dish flavored with a different herb, but as a general rule for everyday meals, it would become confusing.
- Start by adding small amounts of herbs until you develop a taste for herbs. It's much easier to add more of an ingredient than to remove it.
- *Cold Foods*—When mixing herbs into cold foods, they must be allowed to set at least two hours and preferably overnight. This gives the herb and food a chance to blend together.
- *Hot Foods*—You have been taught all your life to add your herbs and spices at the start of cooking spaghetti sauces and simmering sauces and stews. Now I have come along to tell you that is all wrong. *Hot foods should have their herbs added during the last fifteen minutes of simmering.* The reason is that some herbs will become bitter during long simmering and others will lose their flavor altogether. The next time you make spaghetti sauce try it this way and see what a difference it makes.
- Don't be afraid to experiment with your herbs.
- Keep your herbs in airtight containers.

Seasoning with Herbs

> *To be a good cook means the economy of your great grandmother and the science of a modern chemist. It means much tasting and no wasting. It means English thoroughness, French art, and Arabian hospitality. It means, in fine, that you are to see that everyone has something nice to eat.*
>
> —Ruskin

The recipes in this chapter are all from Wormwood Farm. Some are old family recipes passed down from generation to generation. Some are new concoctions. I had to make some of them over and write down exact measurements of this and that, as most of my cooking is more art than science.

During the growing season, you will have an abundance of herbs to use in your cooking, but don't forget to dry some for winter use. See Chapter 8 for information on how to dry and store your herbs.

The following recipes can be used with either fresh or dried herbs. Remember, when using fresh herbs *double* the amount of herbs called for in the recipe. Lovage, celery leaf (called smallage), celery seed, and mitsuba can be used interchangeably. For licorice flavor, anise-hyssop, fennel, and anise can be used interchangeably.

Favorite Culinary Herb Recipes

Wormwood Farms No Salt Blend

Mix together, keep in airtight containers, and use as a substitute for salt:

¼ cup sweet marjoram	⅛ cup sage
¼ cup thyme	⅛ cup spearmint
¼ cup parsley	¼ cup paprika
¼ cup winter savory	1 tbsp onion powder
¼ cup Mexican oregano	1 tbsp garlic powder
¼ cup basil	1 tbsp ground black pepper
¼ cup lovage	¼ tsp dillweed

New England Seafood Spice

Great served with lobster, crabs, oysters, clams, and mussels. Use to sprinkle on casseroles or in stuffings for seafood. Mix well and store in an airtight container:

1 tsp allspice	½ tsp clove, ground
1 tsp thyme	1 tsp Mexican oregano
1 tsp celery	4 bay leaves
1 tsp black pepper	2 dried chile peppers

Bouquet Garni

A popular herb used with soups, stews, and goulashes. You can put this blend in cheesebags, or tie together a small bouquet of fresh herbs for flavor in soups and stews.

1 bay leaf	1 tsp rosemary
1 tbsp parsley	1 tsp thyme
1 tbsp sweet marjoram	

Fines Herbes

A nice blend with meats, soups, stews, and vegetables. Mix and store in airtight container:

1 tbsp sweet marjoram	*1 tbsp thyme*
1 tbsp parsley	*1 tbsp celery seed*
1 tbsp sage	*1 tbsp lemon balm*
1 tbsp summer savory	*½ tsp black pepper*

Spiced Pepper Mix

Will add flavor to meats, fish, poultry, vegetables, and sauces. Mix together and store in an airtight container:

¼ cup black pepper	*1 tbsp mitsuba*
2 tbsps lemon thyme	*1 tbsp garlic powder*
1 tbsp caraway seed, ground	*1 tbsp Mexican oregano*
1 tbsp paprika	

Poultry Blend

Excellent used in stuffings or any dish using poultry.

2 tbsps sage	*1 tbsp sweet marjoram*
2 tbsps parsley	*1 tbsp Greek oregano*
2 tbsps celery leaf	*½ tbsp thyme*
1 tbsp summer savory	

Herb Blend for Beef

Use this blend for any beef dish, for example, in meat loaf, hamburgers, steak sauce.

1 tbsp winter savory	*1 tbsp parsley*
1 tbsp basil	*1 tbsp chervil*
½ tbsp sweet marjoram	

Herb Blend for Pork

Use this in stuffed pork chops, goulash, or any pork dish.

1 tbsp lemon basil	*1 tbsp chives*
1 tbsp rosemary	*½ tbsp sage*
1 tbsp chives	

Herb Blend for Soups and Stews

1 tbsp winter savory   *1 tsp rosemary*
2 tbsp sweet marjoram   *1 tbsp lovage*
1 tsp thyme   *1 tbsp chives*

Seasoned Flours

Mix the following herbs in 6 cups of flour, store in an airtight container. Sift to use in biscuits, fried foods, gravy and sauces.

1½ tbsps garlic powder   *2 tsps oregano*
3 tsps black pepper   *1 tbsp celery leaf or seed*
2 tsps thyme   *1½ tbsps paprika*

Seasoned Sugars

Made the same way as seasoned flours; use for pies, cakes, puddings, desserts, or to sweeten teas.

1 vanilla bean   *1 tbsp rosemary*
1 tbsp lemon balm   *1 tbsp sweet cicely*

Herbal Teasers (Appetizers)

Clam Dip

Mix all ingredients together and serve with chips.

1 cup sour cream
1 small can minced clams
1 tsp minced chives
½ tsp garlic powder
1 tsp minced opal basil
1 tsp lemon basil
1 tbsp chili sauce

Nutty Devil Spread

Mix *1 large can of deviled ham* with *1 tablespoon salad dressing or mayonnaise*. Add:

1 tbsp chopped parsley
2 tbsps chopped Egyptian onion tops

Mix well and serve on crackers.

Greek Devil Spread

Boil *6 eggs* until hard. Grate finely and add *1 small can of deviled ham* and *1 tablespoon of salad dressing or mayonnaise*. Add:

¼ tsp garlic powder
½ tsp thyme
½ cup minced olives

Spread on wheat crackers and top with an olive.

Havarti Melt

In fondue dish or double boiler over low heat, melt *1 pound havarti cheese*. When half melted, add:

1 tbsp caraway seed
1 tbsp chopped parsley

Serve by dipping crackers, broccoli, or cauliflower into melt.

Bread and Butter

Who can resist the aroma of hot, freshly baked bread, right out of the oven and buttered with your own special, herbal butter blend? Make these butters to learn the different tastes of your culinary herbs. Test it on plain white bread or crackers. Do not try to taste a lot of different blends at one time; your taste buds need a break between tastings to be sufficiently sensitive.

Herbal Butter Recipe

Add to *½ cup butter or margarine:*

1 tsp lemon juice
2 tsps dried or 4 tsps fresh herbs

Use your herbal butters on breads, meats, fish, poultry, eggs, vegetables, or for sauteeing and basting.

Whipped Butter

In blender on low speed mix *1 pound of butter*; add *1 tablespoon of lemon juice* and *1 beaten egg*. Gradually add *¼ cup of heavy whipping cream*, blending until fluffy. Then fold in by hand *½ cup of minced fresh herbs* or *2 tablespoons of dried herbs* of your choice.

Your herbal butters will last one week in the refrigerator or one month in the freezer. For a different taste, try herb butters on your fresh garden corn on the cob. Herbs that are compatible with corn are thyme, dillweed, chives, and sweet marjoram. To make these Wormwood Farm favorites, mix ingredients together and let set for 2 to 3 hours to blend the flavors.

Chive Butter

½ cup butter
1 tbsp chives
1 tbsp parsley
¼ tsp fresh rosemary

Bacon-Sage Butter

½ cup butter
4 strips crisp bacon, crumbled
1 tsp fresh chervil
½ tsp fresh sage leaf

Butter for Fish and Meats

2 cups butter
1 tbsp parsley
1 tbsp chives
2 tsps dry mustard
1 tsp horseradish
½ tsp black pepper

Paprika Butter

Melt 2 tablespoons of butter. Add 1 teaspoon minced onion and ½ teaspoon minced garlic; for 10 seconds. In another bowl mix:

4 tbsps butter
1 tsp salad burnet
1 tsp paprika

Combine the two butters, mixing well; serve on meats, poultry, or vegetables.

Mint Butter

Mix:

> ¹/₃ *cup butter*
> *¼ cup mint leaves*
> *2 tbsps lemon juice*
> *1 tsp bee balm flowers*

Lemon Butter

Mix together:

> *½ cup butter*
> *2 tbsps lemon balm*
> *1 tsp parsley*
> *1 tsp calendula flower petals*
> *1 tsp lemon juice*

Good on fish, salads, or desserts.

Dilly Butter for Fish

(This is also good on bread.)

> *½ cup butter*
> *1 tsp oregano*
> *1 tsp dill seed*
> *1 tsp dillweed*

Herbal Bread Recipes

Do not use your herbal butters on breads that contain herbs; it would be too much of a good thing. Use plain butter or margarine. Here are some herbal bread recipes:

Rosemary Biscuits

Mix together:

> *4 cups flour*
> *4 tsps cream of tartar*
> *2 tsps baking soda*
> *¼ cup crushed rosemary leaves (use mortar and pestle to crush).*

Cut in with knife: *½ cup shortening.* Add and mix well: *1½ cups of milk.* Knead until soft. Roll out, cut into circles and bake at 450° for about 6 minutes or until slightly brown on top.

Dilly Casserole Bread

Butter a 2-quart casserole dish and set aside; mix *1 pkg. of yeast* into
¼ cup of hot water. Stir. Heat *1 cup of cottage cheese* to lukewarm.
Add two together; then add the following:

1 tbsp melted margarine	*2 tbsps minced dill weed*
2½ tbsps sugar	*2 tsps dill seed*
1 tsp salt	*1 tsp minced parsley*
¼ tsp baking soda	*1 beaten egg*

Stir in: *2¼ cups of flour*, mixing well; cover and let rise until double,
about one and a half hours. Stir dough down. Place in buttered
casserole dish. Let rise for 40 minutes. Bake in 350° oven for about
35 minutes or until crust is golden brown. Remove and brush top
with butter. Cool in dish for 5 minutes and move to cooling rack.

Salad Recipes

The 17th-century gardener of James II thought that at least thirty-five ingredients were necessary for a good "sallet." Made not only to please the
palate but the eyes as well, salads were decorated with flowers such as
clove pinks and roses. Here are some of my favorite salad recipes:

Broccoli Salad

Mix the following ingredients together:

1 medium onion, diced	*2 hard-boiled eggs, diced*
2 cups broccoli, diced	*1 cup mushrooms, diced*
1 cup raisins	*¼ cup parsley, minced*
6 slices crisp bacon, broken	*1 tbsp pickle relish*

Add and mix in the following dressing.

Pat's Creamy Dressing

Mix well:

1 cup salad dressing (or mayonnaise)
3 tbsps sugar
¼ cup milk
1 tbsp salad burnet
1 tbsp caraway seed

Add to broccoli salad or cole slaw.

Herby Croutons

In saucepan melt *¼ cup of butter*. Stir in rest of ingredients slowly:

> *1 tsp powdered garlic*
> *¼ tsp powdered onion*
> *¼ tsp Tabasco sauce*
> *½ tsp parsley, finely minced*
> *½ tsp thyme, finely minced*
> *½ tsp paprika*

Add *3 cups of stale bread* cut into cubes. Coat them evenly, sautee-ing until slightly brown. Dry on shelf in open air. Use within a week. Croutons can be added to broccoli salad just before serving, or used wth a tossed green salad.

Maine Potato Salad

Cook *5 medium Maine potatoes* cut into cubes, until done. Cook 4 *medium fresh eggs* until hard-boiled; mix together with:

> *2 tbsps prepared yellow mustard*
> *3 tbsps pickle relish*
> *2 tbsps caraway seed*
> *1 tbsp Mexican oregano*
> *1 tsp black pepper*
> *1 tsp salt*

Mix with enough *salad dressing or mayonnaise* to moisten (about 1 cup). Sprinkle with *paprika* and garnish with *parsley sprigs*.

Soup Recipes

Cabbage Soup

Cook *1 pound of hamburger*, drain and mix with:

> *1 large can of V-8 juice*
> *1 package dehydrated onion soup*
> *1 can whole corn*
> *1 small head (about 4 cups) diced cabbage*

Cook over low heat, until cabbage is cooked. Stir occasionally. 10 minutes before serving, add:

> *1 tbsp chervil*
> *1 tsp basil*

New England Seafood Chowder

Peel and dice *4 medium Maine potatoes*. Cook in small amount of water with *1 medium onion, diced*. When done add:

1 pound boneless haddock or pollack
1 pound scallops
½ pound oysters
½ pound shrimp
½ pound lobster meat
¼ pound real butter

Cook over low heat until fish is done, about 5-10 minutes. Add *3 quarts whole milk*; simmer until warm (or add milk already warmed). Set aside, keeping warm. Fry salt pork pieces, about ½ cup, until crispy, drain and set aside. Ten minutes before serving add:

salt pork
1 pint real cream
1 tbsp minced parsley
1 tbsp minced thyme
1 tsp black pepper
¼ tsp garlic powder

Vegetable Recipes

Herbs compliment vegetables very well; experiment with your favorites and find some exciting surprises. Here are two ways we use herbs with vegetables.

Chived Corn

In frying pan heat *2 tablespoons of olive oil*. Saute *1 cup of chives (or broadleaf chives)*. Remove chives; saute *½ cup of diced peppers*. Add:

sauteed chives
1 can whole corn
1 can stewed tomatoes

Warm these up and add:

½ tsp garlic
½ tsp salt
½ tsp oregano
½ tsp basil

Serve plain or over shrimp or scallops.

Honey of a Carrot

Cook and slice *1 pound of carrots (or use 2 cans)*. Add and set aside:

> *3 tbsps honey*
> *1 tbsp sweet cicely*
> *2 tbsp broadleaf chives*
> *¼ cup slivered onions*

In sauce pan, saute *1 diced medium onion* until golden brown, then add rest of ingredients and cook until well coated.

Chicken and Rice Recipes

Orange Chicken

Clean and cut up *chicken*, roll in coating mix and bake in oven on broiler pan for 15 minutes; turn, cook an additional 15 minutes, or until done. Baste chicken while cooking with basting mix (given below). For the coating, mix together:

> *2 tbsps finely diced Egyptian onion*
> *1 tsp paprika*
> *½ tsp rosemary leaf, crushed*
> *¼ cup cornmeal*
> *1½ cups flour*

For basting mix, mix together *1 cup of orange juice* and *¼ cup of marmalade*. Serve Orange Chicken with Calendula Rice (given below).

Calendula Rice

Cook and set aside *1 cup of rice*. Saute:

> *¼ cup diced onion*
> *¼ cup diced celery*
> *1 tbsp butter*

Slowly add and mix in:

> *¼ cup mushrooms*
> *½ cup green peas*
> *1 tbsp calendula petals*
> *¼ cup sliced almonds*
> *1 cup chicken broth*

Add to rice and serve.

Pasta Recipe

It's easy to get some free help on weekends when we serve our spaghetti sauce à la Wormwood Farm. Try it with spaghetti or macaroni.

Wormwood Farm Meat Sauce

Brown *3 pounds of lean hamburger* and *1 pound of hot sausage* in frying pan.
Add to large kettle with:

1½ large cans of V-8 juice
2 large cans of whole tomatoes
½ pound diced mushrooms
1½ cups raisins
2 bay leaves
2 cloves garlic

Simmer these ingredients for 4 hours over low heat, stirring occasionally. 15 minutes before ready to serve add:

1 tbsp paprika
1 tbsp basil
1 tsp Mexican oregano

Dessert Recipes

Many herbs are compatible with dessert-type foods such as cakes, cookies, puddings, etc. Two of our favorites are:

Herb Jelly Roll Cake

Mix cake batter of:

3 eggs
1 cup sugar
1 tbsp butter
1 tsp milk
1 cup sugar
1 tsp baking powder

Spread thinly over a cookie sheet that has been oiled and lined with parchment paper. Bake 10 minutes at 375° or until done; because of thinness, it will cook quickly. Turn cake out on wax paper and spread with your favorite *herbal jelly*. Roll cake. Sprinkle top with confectionary sugar. Decorate with fresh flowers and leaves.

Frosted Spicy Carob Cookies

Mix together:

> ½ cup shortening
> ½ cup brown sugar
> ½ cup molasses
> 1 beaten egg
> 2 tsps baking soda dissolved in 8 tbsps hot water

Set aside; mix the following dry ingredients:

> 2¼ cups flour
> 4 tbsps carob powder
> 1 tsp ground ginger
> 1 tsp ground cinnamon
> 1 tbsp ground coriander
> 1 tsp ground cloves

Combine the two mixes; stir in *1 cup of walnuts*. If cookies seem too thin, add more flour. Bake in 350° oven for 10 minutes (do not overcook). Mix and frost with:

> 2 cups confectionary sugar
> 1 tbsp melted butter
> maple syrup for consistency desired

Pineapple Sage Jelly

Mix *¾ cup of water* and *1 box of Sure-Jell pectin* in saucepan. Bring to a full rolling boil. Stir continuously to prevent burning. Boil for 1 minute. Stir in:

> 5 cups sugar
> 3 cups herb apple juice (see below)

Stir for about 3 minutes. Scoop off any foam. Ladle into sterilized jars and seal with wax. To prepare the juice, steep chosen herbs in warmed apple juice overnight; strain and use in jelly recipe.

Plant Profiles

Alliums (Botanical names below)

Family—Liliaceae (lily)

Description—The following varieties grow in New England gardens:

Egyptian onion is an unusual looking herb; the top bulbs and scape are used in cooking.

- Common Chives—Allium schoenoprasm: pink to purple flowers in spring, clumps enlarging every year.
- Broadleaf Chives—Allium schoenoprasm spp: a solid, flat, wide scape; good texture for soups and stews.
- Welsh Bunching Onion—Allium fistulosum: the bulb in the ground is usually not eaten, but the large, round, hollow scapes are eaten. White flowers dry well for wreaths.
- Egyptian Onion—(also called multiplier, walking onion, the pregnant onion) Allium cepa: little onions form at the end of the scape. Either the top bulbs or the scape can be eaten; the bottom bulb is not eaten. Top bulbs will fall to the ground and start new plants.
- Garlic Chives—Allium tuberosum: also called Chinese chives; flowers are fragrant, white and dry well for arrangements.

Cultivation—Sun or partial shade. All alliums enjoy a good soil and like to be weed free.

Propagation—Chives and garlic chives are easy by seed but take two years to flower; all are quicker to maturity by root division in spring.

Part Used—Bulbs, scapes

Harvest—All season. They lose a lot of flavor when dried. Freeze or preserve in vinegar oil. Harvest flowers when in full bloom to dry for wreaths and arrangements.

Herb Quiche

Butter a 10-inch pie plate. Sprinkle on a mixture of:

>   *3 tbsps bread crumbs*
>   *2 tbsps minced parsley*
>   *2 tbsps grated parmesan cheese*
>   *½ tsp dry mustard*

Mix in bowl and pour onto bread crumb mix:

>   *2 cups whole corn*
>   *1 cup French-cut green beans*
>   *½ cup chopped Welsh bunching onion scapes*
>   *½ tsp dried thyme*

In blender, mix the following and pour over vegetable mix:

>   *3 eggs*
>   *¹/₃ cup flour*
>   *2 cups milk*
>   *4 tbsps parmesan cheese*

Bake in 375° oven for about 40 minutes or until center is done.
Remove from oven and sprinkle on top a mixture of:

>   *2 tbsps parsley*
>   *3 calendula flower petals*
>   *1 cup slivered onions*
>   *1 cup grated cheddar cheese*

Broil under broiler until cheese is melted.

Uses—Culinary: All can be used interchangeably in the herb quiche recipe above.

French Tarragon (*Artemisia drancunculus*)

Family—Compositae (daisy)

Synonyms—Little dragon

Description—Herbaceous perennial to 3 feet tall; yellowish-green stem with alternate long, slender leaves; flowers greenish-yellow in July and August. Drancunculus means little dragon. This herb was once considered a cure for the bite of dragons and other serpents. Russian tarragon (Artemisia dracunculoides) is considered by some to be inferior to the French variety; leaves are more hairy and it spreads quickly in the garden.

Cultivation—Full sun to partial shade in light, well-drained soil. Do not add much fertilizer. Not hardy in zone 3 in New England. For winter, mound base with wood ashes or sand.

Propagation—Russian tarragon by seeds, but the French tarragon does not set viable seed and therefore must be propagated by root division or cuttings.

Part Used—Leaves

Harvest—Leaves all season. Loses its flavor when dried so preserve in vinegar or oils, or freeze.

Uses—Culinary: Use in small amounts until you get used to its taste: use too much and it has a bitter taste. Use with chicken, veal, fish, cheese, and egg dishes.
  Decoration: Flowers are insignificant but can be dried for interesting use in wreaths.

Good King Henry (*Chenopodium bonus henricus*)

Family—Chenopodiaceae (goosefoot)

Synonyms—Lincolnshire asparagus (from where it was grown in England), mercury, smiddy leaves, fat hen, smearwort.

Description—Dark green, arrow-shaped leaves with homely green flowers; the herbaceous perennial grows to 2 feet. The name is said to come from King Henry, who loved the herb. Other herbalists say it was named Good King Henry to distinguish it from the poisonous goosefoot plant, bad henry.

Cultivation—Likes a rich, composted soil with manure and loam; full sun with good drainage, but not dry soil. Keep those homely, flowering tops cut off for a good bushy plant with lots of leaves for eating.

Propagation—Seeds are slow to germinate and reach maturity; divide the plants in early spring.

Part Used—Leaf

Harvest—Leaves all season; freeze for winter soups

Uses—Culinary: Use any way you use spinach; good in salads, soups, quiche, and with other cooked greens.

Salad Burnet *(Poterium sanguisorba or Sanguisorba officinalis)*

Family—Rosaceae (rose)

Synonyms—Common burnet, garden burnet

Description—A herbaceous perennial, very hardy to 2 feet tall with serrated leaves. Pretty, rose, spike flower if left to flower.

Cultivation—Will tolerate good to lean soil with good drainage. One of the first herbs in spring and one of last to succumb in fall. I have even picked some in December, until the snow cover made it too difficult to get at. Has a long tap root and dislikes being transplanted after its first year.

Propagation—Easy by seed, will self-seed in the following years

Part Used—Leaves

Harvest—Leaves all season. Keep flowers cut off for more leaves. Does not dry well. Good when preserved in vinegar and oil for winter use.

Uses—Culinary: Has a cucumber flavor, making it excellent for fresh salads and soups. Compatible with most foods, meats, poultry, fish, vegetables.
  Medicinal: Old herbalists believed it aided digestion.
  Cosmetic: Softens skin when used in facials and skin rinses.

Savory
(Winter savory-*Satureja montana*)
(Summer savory-*Satureja hortensis*)

Family—Labiatae (mint)

Synonyms—None

Description—Winter savory is a woody perennial with small stiff leaves and white flowers in midsummer; 12 inches tall, it is a good specimen for bonsai training. Summer savory is an annual to 18 inches; has a spicy fragrance, leaves turn purplish if cold weather occurs. Makes a good potted plant for the windowsill.

Cultivation—Both want full sun and good drainage. Add lime or bone meal to your sandy or medium-loam soil.

Propagation—Both easy by seed or cuttings. Winter savory's mature plants can be divided in spring.

Part Used—Leaf

Harvest—Summer savory all season; winter savory just before it comes into bloom; dry leaves on screens.

Uses—Culinary: Winter savory has a stronger flavor than the summer savory. It is called the bean herb, because of its affinity to bean dishes, both baked or green beans. Good with soups, rice, vegetables, gravies, sauces, meats, fish, and poultry. Often suggested as a substitute for pepper.

Medicinal: Said to be beneficial when used as a gargle for a sore throat. A good herb for the beekeeper as the bees love its spicy nectar. When stung by a bee, chew the leaf and apply it to the sting.

Miscellaneous: Spicy aroma makes it useful in potpourri or sachet.

TEN

Tea for Two and Flowers, Too

(Eating Flowers and Drinking Herbal Teas)

NOT ALL THE FLOWERS growing in your garden are just pretty. Many of them can be used in your everyday cooking; use them to decorate salads and cakes or to make wines, vinegars, and syrups. Freeze them in ice cube trays to decorate beverages and punch bowls. Some flowers can be dipped in batter and fried like tempura.

Let me summarize again some of the basic safety rules for the consumption of herbal flowers. I suggest you follow them religiously.

- Correctly identify the flower to be used.
- Do not eat any flower you do not know for sure is safe. Many flowers are poisonous.
- Do not harvest flowers in unfamiliar areas; they may have been chemically sprayed. The state of Maine does spray beside the roadways.
- In your own garden, do not spray those flowers you will be using for cooking or teas, medicine, or cosmetics.

Edible Flowers from the Herb Garden

Borage: Blue, 5-pointed stars to decorate cakes, salads, and puddings. Float in punch bowls or freeze in ice cube trays.

Calendula: Most of the older herbals call this herb "pot marigold" so when marigold is recommended for teas or cooking, it is the calendula they mean. The hybrid marigold, popular as a bedding plant, is very bitter. Pull the petals off the orange or yellow calendula, discarding the green calyx as it is very bitter also. Calendula is often substituted for the very expensive saffron herb. Use in cakes, soups, salads, butters, puddings, and rice dishes.

Calendula is a hardy annual.

Clove Pink (Dianthus): Spicy, clove-scented, pink flowers can decorate your cakes and salads. Float in punch bowl or freeze in ice cubes. Can be packed in sugar for winter use.

Elderflowers: Harvest the white flowers as they come into full bloom; they go by very quickly and turn brown. Their duty is not to add beauty to the landscape but to produce the elderberries. Fry in batter.

Violets: Wild blue violets and johnny-jump-ups are used to decorate cakes and salads. Float in punch bowls or freeze for drinks. Violet syrup gives a new taste to pancakes, waffles, French toast, and vanilla ice cream.

Nasturtiums: Spicy flowers which add color to salads. Nice in a sandwich with cream cheese.

Violet Syrup

Fill a glass jar with *blue violet flowers*. Cover with *boiling water*, then cover jars. Steep for 24 hours. Strain out flowers. You will have what looks like a jar of ugly, gray, dishwater. Then the magic comes in. Measure violet water into a saucepan. For each cup of liquid add *2 cups of sugar* and *2 tablespoons of lemon juice*. The magic takes place as you add the lemon juice, turning that ugly-looking water to a lovely, light, lavender. Bring liquid to a boil. Boil 1 minute. Pour into airtight containers. Will last 9 months in refrigerator.

Roses: Use to decorate cakes, salads, and desserts. Freeze in ice cubes for beverages.

Herbal Teas

People all over the world, from the most primitive to the most sophisticated, have for centuries steeped herbs and flowers in boiling water to make a tea for pleasure or medicine. Tea has played a role in our own New England history. During the American Revolution, the Boston Tea Party completed the change from drinking black, imported teas to the native American herbal teas. But before the Boston Tea Party, colonial housewives were already preparing native teas because living in the wilderness made getting black tea difficult and expensive. The housewife learned from Indians and trappers what herbs to use. Although these herbal teas antedated the revolution, many were called "liberty teas" after the Boston Tea Party.

In 1774, the *Virginia Gazette* listed some herbs to be used in place of the black tea; among them were:

betony	Oswego (bee balm)
blue mountain tea (sweet goldenrod)	raspberry leaves
chamomile	sage
clover	sassafras root
dog rose	sweet marjoram
melissa tea (lemon balm)	thyme
mints	

The taste for certain herbal teas is often an acquired taste. If you find you are not really pleased with the taste, try a little honey to sweeten up the tea. I always used honey when I first started drinking herbal teas but now I seldom do.

How Safe Are Herbal Teas?

When using any food product for tea, you must be responsible for knowing just how safe that product is. Commercially labeled products often have incomplete information, only to meet the necessary legal requirements. Those herbs you grow yourself may or may not have proper information available on using them safely. Most of our information has been handed down through the years and many of the old herbals recommend herbs that have now been designated unsafe to use internally.

The FDA compiled an analysis of herbs in 1976 due to growing production of commercially made herbal teas. The analysis has three categories:

1. Unsafe herbs—these may be poisonous because of various toxins produced by the plant.
2. Undefined safety—words used to label herbs that have not been researched by the FDA.
3. Safe herbs—This labels herbs but does not imply that they are safe. It just says that they are not known to be unsafe. How's that for bureaucratic jargon?

These listings are incomplete, confusing, and often just a lot of paperwork. Some herbs labeled unsafe are subsequently approved for flavoring in alcoholic beverages. Just because an herb is listed as safe does not mean it is safe in every use. Some herbs, when used in excess, can cause symptoms of poisoning. To list all the exact conditions of safety would mean another book. Use all herbs internally in moderation; for example, the overuse of sage or nutmeg can cause symptoms of poisoning, yet they are safe in small amounts. The following is a partial list of FDA recommendations:

Those listed as banned for sale for internal use include:

calamus root	southernwood
lobelia inflata (Indian tobacco)	sweet woodruff
mandrake	tansy
mugwort	tonka beans
St. Johnswort	wormwood
sassafras root	

Those approved only for flavoring alcoholic beverages:

elecampane	vervain
hibiscus flowers	vetiver
lemon verbena	violet leaf

I personally use some herbs that are banned by the FDA, such as mugwort. Yet those not banned, such as rue and pennyroyal, I would not use internally. *You must take the responsibility to learn all you can about the herbs you want to use internally.* Check several sources before using any you are not familiar with. For more information of the FDA Compliance Policy Guide, contact the FDA in Washington, D.C.

Making Herbal Teas

You will find a big difference when growing and making your own herbal teas. You will be assured of a pure, high-quality, unadulterated product. Herbal teas can be made with either fresh or dried herbs. Because the dried is a concentrated product, use less of the dried than you would of the fresh. The basic amount for one cup of tea:

1 cup of hot water
1 tsp dried herb or 2 tsps fresh herb.

Most herb teas are made by the infusion method, used for leaves, flowers, and seeds:

1. Boil your water
2. Pour over leaf in cup
3. Steep for 5 to 15 minutes, depending on how strong you like your tea.

The decoction method is used with hard seeds, roots, or barks:

1. Put root or bark in saucepan with hot water
2. Bring to a rolling boil
3. Boil for 5 minutes
4. Strain

Teas can be made loose and strained with a strainer, enclosed in special tea strainers, or put in commercially available tea bags. Here are some other suggestions for herbal tea making.

- Chlorine and flouride may affect the taste of the herbal tea.
- Store your herbal teas in airtight containers, away from heat and sunlight.
- Do not use aluminum when making herbal teas; use glass, porcelain, or stainless steel pots.
- Do not use herbal teas in excess. Some are medicinal herbs which may cause side effects if used excessively.
- Make teas from a single herb or a blend of many different herbs.
- Because every person is unique and has different sensitivities, allergies, and medical problems, experiment carefully and in moderation.

The following list includes herbal teas that we have at Wormwood Farm for our own personal use:

Seeds Used as Tea

Alfalfa: High in vitamin K. For some people it may provide relief from arthritis. Do not use if taking anticoagulant drugs.

Anise: Reputed to be gentle for children; relaxing just before bedtime.

Caraway Seed: Good for children when used in moderation. Some herbalists believe it aids the digestive system and eases coughs.

Dill Seed: Used throughout history as a tea for children with colic; a calmative just before bedtime.

Fennel Seed: Also was used for children's colic. The herbalist Culpepper said fennel seed tea was good for obese persons.

Flowers for Tea

Chamomile: The tea given to Peter Rabbit for his bellyache when he ate too much from Mr. McGreggor's garden. Since it is a member of the ragweed family, it may cause reactions to those who have hay fever.

Clover: Can be picked from your unsprayed fields to add to your cultivated herbs; nice with thyme and chamomile.

Elderflower: Bland alone; add to rosemary, sage, or alfalfa.

Calendula: Usually added to other herbs.

Lavender: A sweet tea, some herbalists believe it relieves a headache.

Leaves for Tea

Agrimony: An herb used more in the past than today; I enjoy it mixed with alfalfa and rosemary.

Alfalfa Leaf: Same as for the alfalfa seeds.

Basil: Spicy taste may be helpful to relax a person before retiring.

Borage: Use young leaves or flowers; said to be a laxative. Do not overuse.

Bee Balm: The Oswego tea so popular for its minty taste during the early colonial days.

Costmary: A minty taste with the aroma of bubble gum. Good combined with the mints.

Catnip: High in vitamin C. Reputed to give you a good night's sleep because it is a calmative.

Hyssop: Has an unusual taste that I enjoy, but my son hates it.

Lemon Balm: Called melissa tea during the revolution; combines with every herb except lavender.

Lemon Grass: Good combined with costmary, a good strong lemon flavor; plant can be grown on the windowsill for winter tea cuttings.

Lemon Thyme: Add to cider for a new taste.

Sweet Marjoram: Use leaves and flowers; may provide relief from a headache.

Mugwort: I enjoy it with agrimony or chamomile tea, but be aware, it has been banned for sale for internal use by the FDA.

Parsley: Not often thought of as a tea; has a mild flavor that blends very well with other herbs.

Mints: There are several different varieties of mints; all are good in teas.

Raspberry or Blackberry Leaves: Picked wild or cultivated in your garden; these are old herbal teas.

Rosemary: I often serve this mild herbal tea at beginner herb workshops; most people enjoy it.

Sage: The Chinese love sage tea. Try sweetening it with maple syrup. Do not overuse as it may cause symptoms of poisoning.

Scullcap: A friend of mine, in her eighties, swears scullcap tea is what keeps her going. Relaxing before bedtime.

Thyme: A spicy flavored tea; mixes well with other herbs.

Tea Recipes

Note: All blends in the following recipes are made with dried herbs. You can substitute fresh herbs by doubling the amount used. Mix your teas and let blend in airtight container for 2 weeks before using.

Rhode Island Tea Thyme

1 cup thyme
1 cup rosemary leaf
1 cup mint

Red Sunset in Connecticut

1 cup hibiscus flowers
½ cup rose hips
1 cup lemon balm
1 cup peppermint
¾ cup orange flower petals
¾ cup wild cherry bark

New Hampshire Nobel Adventure Tea

1 cup bee balm flower and leaf
1 cup alfalfa
½ cup rose hips
½ cup anise seed
¼ cup peppermint

Massachusetts Strawberry Pink Tea

In *3 cups of water* steep for 20 minutes:

½ cup lemon balm
½ cup lemon basil
½ cup lemon-scented geranium

Strain and add *1 cup strawberry juice* and *1 tablespoon honey*. Serve with ice.

Vermont Arthritis Tea

1 cup alfalfa leaf
1 cup rosemary
¾ cup scullcap
½ cup parsley
½ cup chamomile
½ cup sage

Shakespeare Tea

"Here's flowers for you, hot lavender, sweet mints, savory, and marjoram."

—The Winter's Tale

2 cups mints
½ cup sweet marjoram
½ cup summer savory
¼ cup lavender

Plant Profiles

Basil *(Ocimum basilicum)*

Family—Labiatae (mint)

Synonyms—None

Description—These tender annual herbs are probably the most used for cooking by the general public. The word basil comes from the Greek *basilikor* meaning royal or king and it has many legends associated with it. The Hindus regarded basil as sacred and cultivated it near their temples for protection against misfortunes and as a guide into heaven when they died. In Rumania it was thought that if a young girl gave basil to her lover it would make him hers forever. And another legend tells us that if we carry basil in our pocket it will attract money to us.

Some of the most popular varieties are:

- Sweet Basil: to 20 inches, medium-size basil leaves; most frequently grown variety.
- Mammoth Basil: has large-size leaves, some the size of your hand; to 20 inches tall.
- Spicy Globe Basil: small leaves growing to 12 inches in the shape of a round globe.
- Opal Basil: a pretty, purple-leaved basil; makes an attractive-colored vinegar when made with white vinegar; to 20 inches tall.
- Lemon Basil: small leaves with a distinct lemon-flavored scent and taste; grows to 15 inches; nice in tea.
- Cinnamon Basil: cinnamon flavor, spicy basil, good in tea; flowers nice dried and used in wreaths; 20 inches tall.
- Ruffle Basils: a hybrid basil in either green or purple; ruffle-edged leaves make an attractive addition to the garden; used as you would any basil for cooking; 20 inches tall.
- Genovese Basil: said by some herbalists to be the true basil; looks the same as the sweet basil; 20 inches tall.

Cultivation—Basil is the most tender of all the herbs. It is the last to be planted in the ground in spring and the first to succumb to frost in the fall. Enjoys full sun and a rich, moist soil. Feed every three weeks during the growing season. Pinch back to keep it bushy and producing lots of leaves. Basil makes a good potted herb for the windowsill.

Propagation—By seeds, start 4 to 6 weeks before you're ready to plant outside. Basil, started too early, will become leggy. For winter, start in early August in large pots.

Part Used—Leaf

Pesto Pizza

My son developed this recipe, a green pizza that tastes great. Have your homemade pizza crust ready (or you can buy the frozen ones). Fill with the following pesto sauce:

In blender mix:

> *2 cups fresh basil leaf*
> *½ cup parsley leaf*
> *¾ cup olive oil*
> *4 tbsps chopped walnuts*
> *2 tsps garlic powder*
> *1 tsp salt*

Blend this mixture and then put into a bowl and add:

> *½ cup grated parmesan cheese*
> *½ cup freshly grated romano cheese*
> *2½ tbsps melted butter*
> *2 tbsps hot water*

Mix well and spread on pizza crust; top with *mushrooms, green peppers, onions, and pepperoni.* Sprinkle the top with parmesan cheese. Bake in 350° oven until done. (Toppings can vary with your likes and dislikes, just as with any pizza.)

Harvest—All season; does not dry well; store in salt pack or vinegar.

Uses—Culinary: Compatible with tomato dishes, eggplant, pasta, zucchini, meats, fish, and poultry.

Sweet Marjoram *(Marjorana hortense)*

Family—Labiatae (mint)

Synonyms—Annual marjoram

Description—Spicy scented annual. Bushy, gray-green leaves with white flowers. Greeks used marjoram in crowns (or chaplets) for the bride and groom to assure them of happiness.

Cultivation—Full sun in well-drained, light soil. Add lime or bone meal. Will do well on the windowsill.

Propagation—Seeds early spring, cuttings midsummer.

Part Used—Flowering tops

Sweet Marjoram Italian Dressing

Mix well together in blender:

> *½ cup olive oil*
> *½ cup cider vinegar*
> *1 tsp dried sweet marjoram*
> *½ tsp garlic powder*
> *½ tsp Italian parsley*
> *½ tsp paprika*

Serve on a chef's salad.

Harvest—It has the best oil concentration when in flower but it can be used all season. Hang or screen dry.

Uses—Culinary: Sweet marjoram has an affinity for most foods; use in butter, salads, soups, meats, poultry, vegetables, and in tea or vinegar.
  Medicinal: Herbalists believe that sweet marjoram, taken in the form of a tea, will aid digestion, relieve headaches, and be a good general tonic.
  Potpourri: Often called for in potpourri recipes for its spicy aroma.

Hyssop *(Hyssopus officinalis)*

Family—Labiatae (mint)

Synonyms—None

Description—A deciduous, evergreen, shrub-type herb; will lose its leaves in fall for winter. The purple spike flowers are attractive; you can use hyssop clipped in a hedge shape for the formal garden or walkway.

Cultivation—Likes full sun to partial shade, light to medium soil with good drainage, and lime or bone meal added to make the soil alkaline

Propagation—By seeds or root division in the spring

Part Used—Leaves and flowers

Harvest—Leaves all season; flowers for fresh arrangments

Uses—Culinary: Used by old-time herbalists to season vegetable dishes. A tea for pleasure, use in moderation. As a tea, it may help those with rheumatism and stomachaches. Externally, it was used in bath waters for pleasure and to soothe aching muscles.

Agrimony *(Agrimonia eupatoria)*

Family—Rosaceae (rose)

Synonyms—Church steeples, sticklewort, cockburr

Description—Herbaceous perennial growing to 3 to 4 feet with rough, hairy leaves in toothed leaflets. Flowers are on yellow spikes (this is where the name *church steeples* came from). The yellow flowers are followed by burrs. The plant has a faint aroma of apricots.

Cultivation—Full sun to partial shade, good loam soil with good drainage, and a little bone meal or lime added. Keep well weeded; it does not like competition from weeds.

Propagation—Seed is easy for beginners. Will self-seed once established in the garden; root division in spring.

Part Used—Leaf, flower, root

Harvest—Leaf all season (best oil content just before it flowers); flowers when in full bloom, and root in fall. Hang dry.

Uses—Culinary: as a tea for pleasure.
   Medicinal: According to old herbals, agrimony is a mild astringent; used for a spring tonic tea and as a gargle for sore throats and colds. In the form of an ointment, it was used on external wounds and sores.
   Cosmetics: Because of its astringent properties, it was used for the skin and it may help eliminate pimples and the redness of acne by using it as a skin wash. Make herbal water and keep in refrigerator.
   Miscellaneous: As a dye plant: one of the herbs grown in the dye theme garden, agrimony flowers, leaves, and stems are used with a mordant of chrome to give a fawn color, and with iron to produce a darker gray color.

Violets *(Viola odorata)*

Family—Violaceae (violet)

Synonyms—Sweet violets

Description—8 to 10 inch herb with heart-shaped leaf; early spring brings forth blue flowers. A favorite flower of Napoleon and Josephine.

Cultivation—Full sun to shade; medium-good soil with good drainage. Overcrowding causes more leaves than flowers; simply thin out the herb.

Propagation—Root division in spring. It will self-seed once established.

Part Used—Leaves and flowers.

Violet Orange Ice

Put a scoop of orange sherbert on a bed of lettuce. Surround with fresh orange slices and decorate with violets.

Harvest—Leaves before it comes into bloom for best essential oil content; flowers when in full bloom. Screen dry.

Uses—Culinary: Flowers are used to decorate cakes, salads, and desserts. Float in punch bowl or freeze in ice cubes.

Medicinal: A gargle for a sore throat. As a tea, it is reputed to be laxative and help relax you for a good night's sleep.

ELEVEN

Making Scents Out of the Garden

(Using Scented Herbs and Crafting)

THE USE OF fragrance dates back six-thousand years, when crocks of roses and other fragrant herbs and flowers were buried in tombs. Herbs and spices were also used in embalming the dead. It's hard to tell when the first fragrant bouquet of flowers was set in water on a table to decorate a home. Did cavewomen enjoy herbs and flowers for their beauty as well as for their usefulness in cooking and medicine?

Religions have used herbs, spices, and flowers throughout history. Pagan rituals used decorative flowers and fragrant herbs during ceremonies. Early Christian religions banned the use of flowers and herbs because of this pagan association. In later years they began to use them in their own rituals, rededicating them to their own special saints and the Virgin Mary. The layman was discouraged from using herbs and flowers in everyday life because they were to be used for religious purposes only. However, it wasn't long before nobility was knee-deep in fragrant rose petals; Nero was famous for his indulgence in roses and other fragrant herbs, spices, and flowers. Secret fountains were hidden in order to spray fragrance upon people as they walked past. Cleopatra even had the sails of her ships sprayed with the fragrance of violets. The nobility employed persons just for the purpose of strewing fragrant herbs and flowers on the dirt or stone floors; remember, those were times of unsanitary conditions.

Later, fragrances became even more useful. During the era of the plague, "little tussie mussies" were carried to ward off diseases. These are little bouquets of fragrant herbs and flowers tied with a ribbon and held in a doily. The people at that time thought that if bad smells caused disease then good smells would prevent it: It's true that some of those herbs and flowers do contain antiseptic and fumigant properties. Judges kept bunches of rue and lavender on their benches to prevent them from getting "jail fever."

Our ancestors boiled fragrant herbs on the stove and then carried the smoke from room to room. Later on, pots of simmering herbs, spices, and flowers were left on the back of the wood stove to scent the home. Modern practice has fragrances contained in ceramic pots or electric simmering pots, as well as simmering on the wood stove.

The Fragrant Garden

In Chapter 3 we listed many of the fragrant herbs to plant in your garden. Now we will be more specific about how to use these herbs. It's hard to grow a garden of any kind without including some fragrant plants. Gardens of fragrance can be just for the pleasure of sitting and enjoying the fresh aromas or they can have a purpose, such as the making of potpourri, sachets, wreaths, or fresh arrangements for the home.

The scent of fragrant plants is released in various ways. Valerian throws off its sweet scent to those as far away as twenty feet. Costmary, on the other hand, sits demurely and waits to be caressed before emitting her lovely, spicy scent. The little ground cover, sweet woodruff, will not give scent as it grows. However, when dried it produces a vanilla, hay-like scent which makes it valuable for potpourri making. Not all herbs and flowers have a pleasant scent. Coriander, for example, is affectionately called "stinky." As it grows it has a terrible smell, similar to dirty socks, yet as the seed dries it becomes more and more fragrant. Unlike some seeds, it does not lose its fragrance with age; it only becomes more fragrant, probably one of the reasons it was used in ancient tombs. Hyssop has a smell that many of us enjoy, but some will turn up their noses and say it smells like a skunk. Everyone has a different preference in aromas as well as tastes in foods. One way to test the scent of a plant is to pick a leaf or flower and gently crush it into the palm of the hand, releasing its essential oils.

Using Fragrant Herbs in the Home

There are many ways to add fragrance to your home naturally, without the use of those expensive chemicals. Why buy a can of instant scent that is just that? Spray it and the scent lasts an instant and then disappears. Instead, you can put a fragrant bowl of potpourri on the table and have it deodorize your home for several months. Rosemary, santolina, eucalyptus, and lavender, when grown in pots inside the home, naturally deodorize your rooms. Recently, scientific evidence has proven that plants remove pollutants from the home. Use several plants for best results.

Several herbs have antiseptic properties; add these herbs to your water when you wash floors and walls. No need to use strong, harsh chemicals to clean today's easy-care materials. My recipe for a cleaning solution is:

> Steep *1 cup of herbs* in *3 cups of boiled water* overnight (see list below); in the morning, strain out the herbs and add to *1 gallon of hot water*:
>
> *1 cup cider vinegar*
> *2 tbsps liquid soap*

Herbs containing antiseptic properties are:

agrimony	lavender
angelica	pennyroyal
bay (use with other herbs)	peppermint
cinnamon	rosemary
cloves (use ½ cup in above)	thyme
coriander seed	

Herbal Rug Freshener

To keep your rugs smelling nice between shampoos. Mix together:

> *1 box baking soda*
> *2 cups crushed lavender*
> *1 cup pennyroyal*
> *1 tbsp crushed coriander seed*

With mortar and pestle, crush dried herbs as fine as possible. Let age for 2 weeks so scents will blend with baking soda. Sprinkle on rug and let set overnight. Vacuum in the morning. You can substitute your favorite scent for the lavender. Beware of using cloves or cinnamon on your rug as they may stain it. Check the type of material in your rug and test a small portion first.

Vacuum Cleaner Scent

Vacuum cleaners can get a musty smell after a long period of use. This can be eliminated and you can produce a pleasant aroma as you vacuum by using this vacuum cleaner scent. Mix together:

1 cup kitty litter (unused, of course)
1 cup crushed lemon balm
1½ cups crushed white peppermint
1 cup lemon basil
½ cup pennyroyal

Let age two weeks. Use ¼ cup of scent in your vacuum bag; change every time you change the bag.

Herbal Waters

Herbal waters can be added to the last rinse cycle of your washing machine and used to clean cupboards and closets. Herbal waters are made the same way as tea (boil water and pour over herbs, let steep, and strain). Use 1 cup of herbs to 2 cups of water. Keep refrigerated if not used within two days. Herbs to be used in the machine to make your clothes smell nice include:

basil	mints
chamomile	rosemary
clove pinks	roses
costmary	scented geraniums
lavender	sweet marjoram
lemon herbs	thyme

Use any scented herb of your choice in your herbal waters.

Potpourri

The art of making potpourri is really very simple; all the ingredients are put in a bowl and mixed together. The secret is to know the ingredients and what makes a good blend. You can collect fragrant and colorful material from your gardens but you will need to buy oils, most fixatives, and spices.

When making potpourri, you will need the following equipment:

- Mortar and pestle for crushing herbs, flowers, seeds, spices, barks, and resins.
- Large bowl, glass or stainless steel is preferred. Plastic and wood will hold scent and may spoil other potpourri mixes.

Use stainless steel for making potpourri. Mortar and pestle come in handy for grinding herbs and seeds.

- Large spoon (optional); most of us use our hands to mix the potpourri, but if your skin is very sensitive you may want to use plastic gloves or the spoon.
- Measuring cups and spoons.
- Eye dropper to measure oil.
- Air-tight containers for aging and storing potpourri. Glass and plastic bags are suitable.

The Ingredients of Potpourri

Potpourri is a mixture of leaves, flowers, seeds, roots, barks, and resins in any combination. A wide variety of ingredients can be used.

Main scent—This will be the scent that predominates. Normally, it is the primary ingredient. I have divided the basic scents into five categories:

Spicy: Examples are clove, cinnamon, ginger, star anise, and nutmeg.

Flowery: Examples are rose, lavender, rosemary, violet, lilac, jasmine, and gardenia.

Citrus: Examples are orange, lemon, lime, strawberry, and peach.

Herb: Examples are mint, sage, costmary, tansy, thyme, marjoram, and lemon verbena.

Woodsy: Examples are pine, spruce, bayberry, cedar, oak moss, and fir.

Blender and Bulk—A blender is a compatible scent that enhances the main scent. It may consist of one other scent, a small combination, or a dozen other scents. Roses, lavender, and rosemary are all very compatible with most other herbs and flowers. However, lavender and lemon-scented herbs are not compatible with each other. Bulk (also called fillers) consists of herbs or flowers which are added to the potpourri to give more body to the mixture and save on the expensive main ingredient. Bulk also has another purpose: to add texture, color, and sometimes scent.

Texture and Color—Texture and color are especially important if you are displaying your potpourri in open baskets or other open containers. They become less important in sachets or closed containers. Colorful flowers from your own garden can be gathered for your potpourri. Some will retain a small amount of fragrance, but are basically used to add color. Examples of some flowers to collect and dry for potpourri color are:

- roses and bee balm (red)
- bee balm, acrolinium, clove pinks (pink)
- pearly everlasting, pearly yarrow (white)
- cornflowers, violets, delphiniums (blue)
- calendula, dyer's chamomile, gnaphalium (yellow)
- calendula, butterfly weed, wallflower (orange)
- allheal, anise-hyssop (purple)
- tansy (yellow tansy becomes brown after frosts)
- mignonette, hops (green)
- silver mound, silver king, Roman wormwood (silver)

The 1980s saw the introduction of dyed wood chips for color and bulk in potpourri. Some commercial potpourri makers have added a large amount of this bulk to their product, using less of the naturally fragrant ingredients. This brings larger profits to the company because the bulk is less expensive than the main scents; but the potpourri fragrance does not stand the test of time.

Using more of our natural scents will make the best potpourri, but the dyed wood chips will give a good selection of color choices for decorating the home.

Maine woods potpourri (see recipe later in this chapter) is full of texture. This produces a feeling of having part of the woods in a bowl. Maine woods, and other potpourri with a lot of texture materials, is meant to be displayed in open containers. Materials that will give you *good texture* for your potpourri include:

Star anise: star shaped; spicy aroma; will last indefinitely if kept in enclosed container.

Rose hips: Good in strawberry potpourri; look like dried strawberries.

Cones: Gather your own if you can or buy a variety of shapes and sizes at the craft or herb store.

Hawthorn berries: Small, red berries that add color, texture and bulk.

Whole cloves: Spicy aroma.

Cinnamon: Comes in chips especially for potpourri, or you can buy it in sticks and break to desired size; ground cinnamon is best used in sachets.

Bay leaf: Used whole or broken.

Sumac berries: Be sure you know the difference between the poisonous kind and the non-poisonous kind if harvesting from the wild. If you are unsure, buy them. Nice color in Christmas, woods, or strawberry potpourri.

Strawflowers: Nice flowery touch, especially in a Christmas potpourri.

Fixatives—I will be discussing only those fixatives of a botanical nature. There are animal fixatives, but the animal either dies or suffers severe discomfort in the manufacturing process. The little musk deer was almost wiped out because of the killing of the deer for use by the perfume industry. Eventually, the practice was banned and the deer was put on the protected list.

A *fixative* is an ingredient that holds all fragrances together and keeps the various aromas from dropping out individually and thus changing the original aroma. Most fixatives will be purchased. One, orris root, can be grown in your own garden. Here are some examples of fixatives. Most of them can be used interchangeably.

Orris root: From the Florentine iris. The rhizome is the part used. To harvest, dig second-year roots, clean and cut into small pieces. Once it dries, it soon becomes "hard as a rock." Orris root is the most popular fixative, probably because it is the most available one. It comes powdered, granulated, or cut. Some persons may be allergic to orris.

Calamus root: From the wild, sweet flag plant; can be grown in the cultivated garden if you have a very moist area. Softer than the orris root, which it resembles. *Poisonous if ingested.*

Gum benzoin: Comes from various styrax trees; comes in large clumps of material that look like rocks but are easily broken into the size you want; or it can be powdered with mortar and pestle. *Do not use internally.* You may sneeze from the dust particles.

Gum arabic: From the acacia trees. Water soluble, making it valuable in simmering potpourris and scented herbal waters.

Oak moss: Found in the woods, gray-green color; can be purchased in craft stores and herb shops. Has a slightly musky aroma; good in woods–type potpourri.

Vetiver: Dried root of a tropical grass, also called khus-khus; can be grown as a house plant in a large pot; good texture also .

Cedar wood chips: Some fixative properties but are best used in combination with other fixatives; good texture, and can be dyed decorative colors. There is a special dye for dried and wood materials called Dip It; or you can use food coloring to dye the wood chips; soak in dye, then dry on the shelf on paper towels.

Salt: Salt is often called for in older potpourri recipes; use only sea salt or kosher salt. It will help to dry out any moisture.

Other materials which have some fixative properties but should be used in combination with the above are: coriander seeds, sandalwood, balsam of Peru, patchouli, citrus rind, and myrrh.

Oils—There are two kinds of oils on the commercial market, essential oils and fragrant oils. It is important that you know the difference and how to use them safely.

Essential Oils: a volatile (rapidly evaporating) oil possessing the characteristic odor or flavor of the plant from which the oil is obtained. You will probably not be making essential oils at home as a distillery is needed. In the 17th century, every good "still room" had its own distillery equipment to make oils. These oils are highly concentrated. In this concentrated form *caution* must be used as some oils will produce a burning sensation if applied directly to the skin. Essential oils are diluted and used in small amounts. Some oils are used for cooking, medicine, cosmetics, and potpourris. Know which ones are safe and which ones are toxic when taken internally.

Fragrant Oils: These oils are chemically produced to imitate a certain scent. This process creates aromas which are impossible to produce naturally. For example, strawberries have no natural oil so by chemically making it we can have strawberry scent for our potpourris, sachets, and craft work.

Fragrant oils also make available scents that are too expensive to make naturally; for instance, violets, roses, and jasmine all cost hundreds of dollars an ounce to produce because of the large amount of natural

Tips from Wormwood Farm

- Keep all oils out of reach of children and pets. Some oils in concentrated form are toxic and *may cause death if taken internally.*
- Essential oils banned by the FDA for internal use include sweet birch, cedarwood, sassafras, thuja, and wintergreen.
- Some oils will cause skin irritation. If using in perfumes and cosmetics, test for twenty-four hours before using. Those that will burn if applied directly to the skin include bitter almond, pennyroyal, citronella, and patchouli. Always dilute the oils for cosmetic uses.
- Certain oils applied to the skin and then exposed to sunlight may cause a rash or brown spots. Included are bergamot, lavender, cedarwood, rue, and St. Johnswort.
- Store all oils in dark, airtight containers away from heat and direct sunlight.
- An eyedropper is handy to dispense oils as only a drop or two is needed in most cases. Do not leave dropper in bottle, because some oils will eat the rubber. Be sure to recap the bottle.

material that must be used. Also, chemically made scents give us more choices for potpourris, sachets, and other crafted items. They are toxic and should *never* be used internally.

Herbs which produce natural essential oils considered safe by the FDA for *cooking* include: allspice, fennel, lemon, mints, garlic, thyme, basil, ginger, rosemary, clove bud, and sage.

Potpourri, sachets, and other crafted items can use both essential and fragrant oils.

Containers For Potpourri

Once your potpourri is made, you will want to display it in the nicest way possible. Some of the containers we use at Wormwood Farm are:

Baskets: Line a basket with a pretty cloth, Spanish moss, or oak moss. Fill with potpourri. For a gift, you might add a little figurine, wrap the entire basket in saran wrap, and tie on a tussie mussie.

Shells: Seashells are available in the New England area. Fill with your favorite potpourri. They make a nice addition to a bathroom, bedroom or cottage.

Tins: Decorative tin boxes come in all sizes, shapes, and designs. Fill with potpourri. The scent will last longer in covered tins, since the scent can be released only when needed and the tin then recovered.

Glass containers and goblets: A fancy goblet full of potpourri and tied with a bright ribbon makes a nice gift for a hospital patient. Glass containers show off the potpourri best, so use lots of texture and color.

Vases: Fill a vase with potpourri, then add dried flowers and you have a nicely scented arrangement.

Warning: Potpourri is strictly for the purpose of scenting the air and filling sachets; never use internally. Many of your potpourris contain toxic materials which, if ingested, can cause a severe reaction.

Potpourri Recipes

Note: All ingredients must be completely dried. Mix ingredients together and store in an airtight container for 2 to 3 weeks to age. Put in a container of your choice.

Orange Blossom Special

3 cups orange blossom flowers
2 cups orange peel
1 cup lemon peel
1 cup rosemary
1 cup vetiver
½ cup orris root
½ cup cinnamon root
1½ cups orange-colored flowers (e.g. calendula)
4 drops sweet orange oil

Spicy Apple Scent

2 cups apple mint
1 cup rose hips
½ cup sumac berries
½ cup lemon peel
¼ cup star anise
1 tbsp cinnamon chips
1 tbsp whole cloves
1 tbsp caraway seed
6 drops spicy apple fragrant oil

Spicy Rose Potpourri

1 cup rose petals or buds
½ cup rosemary
¼ cup lavender
½ cup crushed bay leaf
½ cup orris root or calamus root
¼ cup coriander seeds
1 tbsp cinnamon chips
1 tbsp whole cloves

Lemon Alive

1 cup lemon grass
1 cup lemon verbena
1 cup lemon basil
1 cup lemon balm
1 cup lemon marigold leaf and flower
1 cup yellow-colored flowers or wood chips
3 drops lemon grass oil

Strawberry Fields

1 cup strawberry leaves
1 cup lemon balm
1 cup rose petals
1 cup rose hips
1 cup hawthorn berries
½ cup orris root, cut to size
1 cup uva ursi leaf (or pinquica leaf)
1 cup cinnamon chips
1 tbsp crushed or grated nutmeg
1 cup star anise
6 drops strawberry oil

Blueberry Cobbler

1 cup blue flowers (cornflowers are nice)
1 cup juniper berries
1 cup uva ursi leaves (or pinquica leaf)
1 cup lemon balm (or lemon grass)
1 cup blue-dyed wood chips
4 drops blueberry oil
½ cup orris root or calamus root

Maine Woods

1 cup cedar tips
1 cup dried green pine needles
1 cup patchouli
1 cup sweet woodruff
½ cup orris root, cut
1 cup sandalwood chips
½ cup uva ursi (or pinquica or bay leaf)
¾ cup summer savory
¾ cup quassia chip
¾ cup juniper berries
¾ cup hawthorn berries
½ cup star anise or allspice
1 cup sumac berries
1 cup small cones
1 cup green dyed wood chips
8 drops green forest oil (or 3 drops pine oil and 3 drops Siberian fir oil)

Sachet Recipes

Sachets will include: a main scent, bulk, fixative, and oil.

Scented Geranium Sachet Mix

1 cup peppermint geranium leaf
½ cup rose geranium leaf
½ cup nutmeg geranium leaf
¼ cup mint leaf
¼ cup orris root, powdered
¼ cup costmary leaf
1 tbsp coriander seed, crushed

Gather all the ingredients in a bowl, with the exception of the orris and coriander seed, then dry it on screens and label it. When dry, make sachet. No need to dry separately if only the amount called for in the above recipe is used.

Rose Sachet

3 cups rose petals
1 cup sandalwood powder
½ cup rose-scented geranium leaves
¼ cup powdered gum arabic

Powder and mix all ingredients; add to sachet bag.

Pillows and Other Uses for Scented Herbs

Pillows can be made and stuffed with scented herbs. If you wish, a separate, small pillow can be made and then stuffed and inserted in a larger pillow for removal when you want to wash the larger pillow. If you have allergies, you may want to use a fixative other than orris root.

During the Victorian days, herbs and flowers had symbolic meanings. A pillow made with herbs, along with a note describing its meaning, would make a welcomed gift. A recipe is included here.

Tussie Mussie

A tussie mussie is a small bouquet of fragrant flowers and herbs wrapped in a doily and tied with a ribbon. During the Victorian era, they were very popular; they were made from handcrafted doilies and held in the hand. Today we usually substitute a paper doily. Tussie mussies can be carried in the hand, used to decorate packages, made as corsages, and used to decorate individual table settings.

Pomander Balls

Pomanders are decorative, scented balls, made from apples, oranges, lemons, or limes studded with whole cloves and sprinkled with a spice mix. They are used in closets, bureau drawers, or stacked in a dish for decoration. To make pomanders:

Take one orange (or other fruit mentioned above), push whole cloves into the skin as close as possible without putting them on top of each other. As the fruit dries the cloves will tighten up also. An average-sized orange will require about 2 cups of cloves to be completely covered. When done, finish by sprinkling with spice mix. Age in open air (until dry) before using, about 2 to 3 weeks.

Loving Pillow

4 parts violet flowers (violets for modesty)
3 parts rose petals (roses for love)
1 part anise seed (for pleasant dreams)
½ part rosemary (for remembrance)
½ part fixative (to hold it all together)

A good combination for a man's pillow.

Spice Mix

Note: Not for internal use. Also good as sachet and potpourri mix.

1 tsp ground cinnamon
1 tsp ground cloves
1 tsp ground nutmeg
½ tsp ground ginger
½ tsp powdered orris root

Tie a pretty ribbon around your pomander and hang it in the closet; it will last up to five years. This is a good project for children.

Wreath Making with Herbs

During the Roman era, wreaths were called chaplets and they were worn on the head. They were also frequently used for table decorations. Wreaths can be designed to fit into your home decoration scheme or designed with a special theme. A few of our *theme wreaths* are as follows:

Culinary Wreath—Can be used for kitchen decoration or the herbs can be cut and used in cooking (remember, if they hang around for very long, they become dusty). Sage can be the main base, decorated with opal basil, parsley (dry by microwave for best color), tri-color sage, dill, rosemary, winter savory, anise-hyssop flowers, bee balm flowers, white peppermint blossoms, and chive blossoms.

Witches Brew Wreath—Made with herbs known for "protection" against witches or evil spirits. Hang on the door to keep evil spirits away. Eucalyptus base is decorated with a selection of bay leaf, betony flowers, cinnamon sticks, dill, elecampane pods, heather, hops, juniper, mugwort, pennyroyal, pine sprigs and cones, lavender, rosemary, rose buds, vervain, wormwood, rue, or yarrow. Of course, not all these herbs need to be used; choose what is available or desired.

Plain Base Wreath—This is made of one material which can then be decorated with different items each month for a different theme. Herbs that make good single bases are: silver king, silver mound, sweet annie, ambrosia, santolina, showy marjoram, pearl yarrow, and lady's mantle.

The Spirit of America—This red, white, and blue wreath has been a popular seller. Made with equal amounts of white pearl yarrow, blue cornflowers (also called bachelor buttons), and red bee balm.

Making a Straw-Based Wreath

Material needed:

> one 10-inch straw-based wreath
> florist pins
> dried herbs and flowers

1. Decide on a particular design. With magic marker, divide base into 4, 5, or 6 equal parts. Lay out dried material to fill all spaces.
2. Cut stems 3 to 4 inches in length.
3. Make small bunches; be sure they are all the same size. You will use less big, thick plants and more small plants to get the same size bunches.
4. Starting with the inner part of the wreath, lay herbs on wreath and secure with one or two push pins. Keep the inner circle tight, making sure the material does not fill the circle, making the hole too small.
5. Put on outer layer and secure with pins.
6. Finish with middle section.
7. When completed, check for any gaps in design and fill in with that particular plant.

Lay material on inner part of circle; secure with pins.

Lay material on outer edge of straw wreath; check for similarity of length.

8. Keep plants all going around circle in same direction. Hang your wreath in an area out of sunlight and away from any heat sources, such as wood stoves or electric heaters. To clean wreath, gently blow with hair dryer set on low.

Center is filled with colorful flowers and herbs.

This wreath includes sweet annie as inner and outer base; the center is hydrangea, joe-pye weed, anise-hyssop, and purple tri-color sage.

Hens and chickens here used in a living wreath.

Plant Profiles

Lavender *(Lavendula spp.)*

Family—Labiatae (mint)

Synonyms—None

Description—Fragrant, gray-green, narrow spike leaves; flowers are very fragrant, from light lavender to a deep lavender in color, including a pink or white variety. In New England, lavender vera (augustifolia) and munstead are hardy when given the proper growing conditions. Lavender (from Latin) means to wash; it was popular in Roman baths and also used as one of the strewing herbs for the floors. Because of its highly scented flowers it has been a popular herb throughout history.

Cultivation—Needs full sun and excellent drainage; it likes a lot of wood ash or bone meal added to make a high alkaline soil. Cut it back in the spring only, as lavender needs its woody stalks to go through the winter months. It dislikes windy areas so plant it where it has protection from any harsh winds. Mulch in winter with a light mulch such as evergreen boughs or straw; heavy materials that mat down on the herb.

Propagation—Seeds (take two years to produce flowers); cuttings during summer, or root division (with care).

Part Used—Flowers

Harvest—Havest flowers for potpourri and tussie mussies when in budded stage as this is when they have the highest oil content. If the flowers get by you and open up, harvest and use in fresh arrangements or in wreath making. Cuttings from the leaf part have some scent also and make nice additions to potpourri or wreaths. Lay on screens to dry or stand upright in a jar.

Uses—Culinary: used in tea mixes for pleasure and in vinegar making.
   Medicinal: tea is reputed to help relieve a headache.
   Crafting: used mostly in the making of wreaths, floral arrangements, sachets, tussie mussies, and other items used for fragrance.
   Cosmetic: highly scented for baths; made into waters or oils for the skin.

Lemon Balm (*Melissa officinalis*)

Family—Labiatae (mint)

Synonyms—Sweet balm

Description—Light green, oval-shaped leaves with a lemon scent. Grows to 3 feet if not clipped; it can be clipped as a hedge for summer, but this herbaceous perennial dies back in winter.

Cultivation—Good drainage, full sun to partial shade. Poor soil produces the best oil content and aroma; likes bone meal and lime.

Propagation—Seeds, root division, cuttings; also self-seeds if not clipped.

Part Used—Leaf

Harvest—Leaves all season; lay on screens or hang dry

Uses—Culinary: good as a tea blended with other herb teas. Use in salads, desserts, or with cheese and mint dishes.
   Medicinal: used for salves or oils since the 1600s for treatment of wounds. According to some herbalists it has anti-depressant qualities, useful for treating depression, stress, anxiety, and tension. Often used in tea form as a tonic to lower high blood pressure.
   Fragrance: its lemony scent is welcomed in potpourri and sachets.

Costmary (*Chrysanthemum balsamita*)

Family—Compositae (daisy)

Synonyms—Bible leaf, sweet mary, alecost

Description—Oval-shaped leaves growing to 7 inches long. I think it has the aroma of bubblegum when caressed. Flowers (if the season is long enough) are small, yellow buttons that dry well. The name *alecost* comes from its use in olden days to clarify ale. Called *Bible leaf* because it was used as a bookmark for Bibles. Called *sweet mary* for its sweet scent and to honor the Virgin Mary.

Cultivation—Likes most soils with good drainage, and full sun. Keeping it trimmed will keep it from becoming weedy looking.

Propagation—Seeds (germination not good), root division in spring is best method. Dry on screens or press in books for bookmarks and to give the book a pleasant scent.

Part Used—Leaf and flowers

Uses—Culinary: a good tea herb. Use as a seasoning with beef, chicken, or desserts; I often put a whole leaf in the bottom of a cake pan and pour the batter over it. The costmary will flavor the cake.

Fragrance: scent for potpourri and sachets.

Cosmetic: use in bath water, in the form of vinegar or waters.

Orris Root *(Iris florentine)*

Family—Iridaceae (iris)

Synonyms—None

Description—Long, blade-like stems from a rhizome; produces pale blue to white flowers.

Cultivation—Full sun to partial shade with good drainage. Do not bury the rhizome deeply; you should be able to see some of it through the soil.

Propagation—Division of rhizomes in early spring or late summer

Part Used—Rhizomes

Harvest—The rhizomes in third year; cut and dry at once or they become hard as a rock and impossible to cut; powder with mortar and pestle.

Uses—Used as a fixative in potpourri and sachets. *Never* is it taken internally. Nice garden plant for pleasure along with other iris species.

Mints *(Mentha spp.)*

Family—Labiatae (mint)

Description—There are over two hundred species of mints and quite a few crossbreeds. Mints are probably one of the most difficult herbs to categorize. Give three experts the same herb and you may get three different names for the herb. I must confess to being a lover of these very invasive herbs.   Among those that I grow are the following species and their synonyms:

- Applemint—M. Roundifolia (Egyptian mint)
- Peppermint—M. x Piperita (brandy mint)
- White Peppermint—M. x P. Officinalis (not invasive)
- Spearmint—M. Spicata (green mint or garden mint)
- Orange Mint—M. x P. Citrata (bergamot mint and Eau-de-cologne mint)
- Pineapple Mint—M. Roundifolia (variegated)

Cultivation—Full sun to shade. The problem is usually not how to grow, but how to *control* the mints' invasion habits once you plant them. Some mints may develop a rust on them (in nine years of growing mints this has happened to me only once). If you get rust, cut the entire herb back to the ground and destroy the foliage. If it gets rust again, then you must destroy the entire plant and start a new strain in a new area.

Propagation—There are seeds available for some species, but I do not recommend them They may not be true to the strain. Root division is the only way to get the true species you want. I have not had success with cuttings.

Part Used—Leaf

Harvest—Just as they are coming into flower. Hang or screen dry.

Uses—Culinary: in a tea, made into jellies, or as seasoning for fish, lamb, poultry, or desserts. Apple mint is the mint used for the famous mint julep drink. Spearmint is preferred for lamb.

   Fragrance: potpourri and sachets; all the mints can be used and you will probably have a favorite.

   Medicinal: Mints are applied to bee stings to ease the pain and swelling; a medicine for stomachaches, but overuse may cause nausea. Peppermint is used for mouthwash, gargle, and whitening teeth.

Clove Pink *(Dianthus caryophyllus)*

Family—Caryophyllaceae (pink)

Synonyms—Gillyflower, clove carnation

Description—Blue-green, narrow leaves; pink, clove-scented flowers. Shakespeare mentioned gillyflower in his works. Pink flowers have been used to float in wine since early cultures; they were popular at weddings and coronations.

Cultivation—Medium soil in full sun with good drainage; likes an alkaline soil and needs to be weed free.

Propagation—By seed, start 6 weeks before last frost in your area; usually will produce flowers first year.

Part Used—Flowers

Harvest—Full bloom; use fresh or store in vinegar or ice cubes.

Uses—Culinary: can be used fresh to decorate salads, cakes, or desserts. Float in beverages.

Fragrance: colorful and scented in potpourri; nice in fresh arrangements.

TWELVE

Green Faces and Marshmallow Hands

(How to Use Herbs for Beauty Care)

DURING THE 17TH CENTURY, some of the cosmetics that were used were very dangerous; skin was whitened with powdered lead, and rouge was made from a lead base. Deadly nightshade was used to dilate the pupils of the eyes, since this was considered attractive. In the 20th century we are also applying some dangerous chemical compounds to our faces and bodies for the sake of beauty. Many cosmetics sold over the counter contain chemicals and preservatives; just read some of those labels. The amount of an ingredient is not usually listed on the label; for example, when a product states that is contains strawberries as an ingredient, does it contain real strawberries or an artificial scent or drop of oil? The cosmetic industry is badly regulated by the FDA, as far as labeling is concerned.

Science has proven that what we apply to our skin is absorbed into the blood stream. By making your own natural cosmetics, *you* are in charge of what goes on and *in* your system, and you can save a lot of money while you are watching out for your health.

In the 1960s and 70s, there was a trend towards using more natural products in our daily living habits. Perhaps this was because of a desire for a simpler lifestyle or because of side effects from certain chemical products. But be aware that certain skin types will also be sensitive to certain natural products. Any new product should be tested by applying a small amount to the inside of the elbow; if a rash or burning sensation occurs, do not use the product. Very light-skinned people are apt to be sensitive to those products containing real strawberries; rue and St. Johnswort may cause a reaction in some people.

In the 1980s, people became more knowledgeable about the side effects of the chemical products used on our bodies and in and around our homes. Everyday there are newspaper and television articles on these dangers, with bans being put on certain chemicals. We know that cigarettes and the sun are enemies to our skin and that pollution from the air is increasing. These are just a few reasons why we must be as natural as possible in our daily living habits. Making your own home-grown natural herbs, flowers, and vegetables into cosmetics will give you an edge on health and beauty.

Your Herbal Bath

Chapter 3 tells you about some of the herbs to plant in your cosmetic garden. This chapter suggests ways to use these herbs in your beauty routine. Keep in mind that these botanicals are all natural products with

Herbs, oil, loofah sponge, and spices all add to the pleasure of the bath.

no chemical preservatives being added so they must be kept in the refrigerator or made in small amounts which are used right away. Do not use aluminum products when mixing or storing, as they may cause a chemical change in the mixture, resulting in an adverse reaction. Most of the ingredients in this chapter can be grown in your own back yard for fresh use. They can be preserved for winter in oils, vinegars, and salt packs, or they can be frozen or dried.

Showers are great for a quick cleanup but a long soak in an herbal bath will nourish both body and mind. Make time for your own special bath-beauty spa once a week, or more often if you can. Have a pleasingly decorated bathroom for serene atmosphere; surround yourself with soft rugs, live plants, soft music, and things you enjoy having around. Cleopatra bathed in a swan-shaped tub full of asses' milk. Mary Queen of Scots added red wine to her bath, while Madame de Pompadour and Catherine the Great bathed in strong herbal concoctions. For your special spa, have a certain time and follow your personal ritual. I like to read while relaxing in the tub; others may prefer doing their nails or just relaxing to the sound of their favorite music with a glass of wine (elderberry?)

Herbal Waters

Pour boiling water over your herbs and let them steep overnight so you get all of the essential oil out of the herbs. Strain the herb water. You can make a quart of the water for immediate use or a gallon to keep in the refrigerator for up to three weeks. About one quart of herbal water is used per bath. Herbal water can be made with one herb or a combination of several. See the herb list in Chapter 3.

Love Bath Water

Mix together and let age for two weeks before using. Use ½ cup herbs to 1 quart of water; let steep overnight, then add to bath. Keep dried mixture in airtight container.

1 cup rose petals—for love and scent
1 cup elderflower—for softening the skin
1 cup marshmallow leaves—for moisturizing the skin
1 cup sage leaves—for healing and as an astringent

Herbal Vinegars

Cider vinegar softens the skin and helps soothe aching muscles. Always dilute it with water because using it full strength may irritate the skin. See Chapter 8 for directions on making herbal vinegars. One recipe for your vinegar bath is:

Fragrant Bath Vinegar

Using the general method of making herbal vinegar, use equal amounts of the following herbs. Use *2 cups of vinegar* per bath.

> *peppermint*—cooling and astringent
> *fennel seed (or leaf)*—tonic
> *lovage*—acts as a natural deodorant
> *comfrey*—for healing

Bath Oils and Salts

Bath oils are used to soften and moisturize the skin. To make oils, put selected herbs in a glass jar and pour oil over them, just enough to cover. Let set in a sunny window for ten days, shaking daily. Strain out the herbs and put the oil into a bottle. Use good oils such as olive oil, peanut oil, sunflower oil, or almond oil. Use one tablespoon of oil to a tub of water. Most oils do not disperse in the water so only a small amount is needed. Castor oil will disperse in water and does not leave a ring around the tub.

An herbal salt mix also makes a nice addition to your bath. The soda base neutralizes the acid secreted by the skin so that the herb fragrance clings to the skin. Soda also helps to soften hard water.

Bath Salt

Mix together:

> *2 cups of baking soda*
> *½ cup powdered herbs*
> *½ cup sea salt*
> *3 drops of essential oil to match herb fragrance.*

Mix and store in an airtight container for one week before using. Use ½ cup of mixture per bath (in cheesecloth bag).

Mugwort Muscle Relaxer

After a long day in the garden this bath infusion will help to relax those tired muscles. Infuse in *2 cups of water:*

> *1 tbsp comfrey*
> *2 tbsp mugwort*
> *1 tbsp chamomile*
> *1 tbsp sage*
> *1 tbsp marshmallow leaf*

Spicy Calendula Mix

Mix together:

> 1 cup cinnamon chips
> ¼ cup whole cloves
> ½ cup calendula flowers
> 1 cup mineral oil

Let stand for 10 days. Strain out herbs and put in bottle. For a nice gift add a cinnamon stick in the jar and tie a pretty ribbon around it. Use 1 tablespoon of oil per bath. Very good for those with oily skin as the mineral oil does not penetrate the skin.

Lavender Softener

Mix together:

> 2 tbsp lavender flowers
> 3 bay leaves
> 4 tbsps oatmeal
> 4 tbsps bran
> 1 tbsp rosemary
> 2 whole cloves

Simmer mixture in 4 cups of water in a covered pan for 30 minutes (do not boil). Strain and add all of it to the bath water. Will soften the skin.

Rosemary Bath Salts

Make an infusion of the following herbs in 2 cups of water:

> 2 tbsps rosemary
> 1 tbsp comfrey
> 1 tbsp rose petals
> 1 tbsp lemon balm

Strain and add to the bath water, along with 2 cups of sea salt. Use all of the mixture at once.

Herb waters are usually made by the infusion method and then added to the bath water. Another way is to make little bags out of cheesecloth and fill with the herbs; tie a ribbon (one that is colorfast) around the bag and float it in the tub, releasing the herbal properties as you soak. The following recipe is one I use; it calls for large amounts in order to have enough to make up as gifts.

Greenleaf Bath Bags

Mix dried herbs together and let age for two weeks, then put in cheesecloth bags:

3 cups patchouli	1 cup strawberry leaves
3 cups orange-scented geranium leaves	½ cup pennyroyal
	1 cup rosemary
2 cups white peppermint	2 cups oatmeal
2 cups sage	4 whole cloves

Herbal Cosmetics

There are two kinds of base oils usually used in cosmetics, *penetrating oil* and *non-penetrating oil*. Penetrating oils are oils right off the cupboard shelf, including olive, almond, peanut, and sunflower oil. Jojoba oil and vitamin E oil can be purchased at the health food store. These oils also penetrate the skin, softening and protecting. These particular oils are not good for people who have oily skin to begin with, but dry and aging skin will benefit from penetrating oils.

Non-penetrating oil, such as mineral oil, is used in many commercially made cosmetics simply because it is cheap and has a long shelf life. It is very good for those with oily skin as it does not penetrate and add more oil. It will not help those with dry, aging skin.

Essential oils and fragrant oils were discussed in Chapter 11 for their use in potpourri. Several of these oils are also used in cosmetics. First of all, remember that these oils are highly concentrated and they should not be applied directly to the skin as they will cause rashes and burning sensations in some persons. Dilute these oils with other oils (olive, almond, etc.), vodka, or alcohol. A small amount can also be added to hair rinses, bath waters, and massage oils. I like the oils of lavender, rose, ylang ylang, sandalwood, and rose geranium.

Skin Care for Gardeners

We gardeners subject ourselves to the harsh rays of the sun and daily work in dust and dirt so we need a good skin care program to keep our skin healthy and clear.

Our skin is a complex system, not just a covering to keep everything else inside. It acts as a temperature regulator and protector for our whole body. Sebum is a fatty substance that is excreted through the pores to aid in keeping our skin soft and moist. During cold weather, when the sebum reaches the surface of the skin it often congeals, giving us dried, chapped skin. The skin is normally acid and that acid balance, like the pH in the garden soil, is important to good health. The skin's acid mantle, as it is called, acts as a protection against bacteria entering the body. When too much or too little sebum is produced, then we have skin that is either too oily or too dry and the acid balance is upset. Excess sebum is the cause of blackheads and acne.

Our skin is always breathing and excreting the toxic properties from our body. Keeping our skin in good condition aids in letting the skin do its job more efficiently.

The skin is made up of several layers that are constantly changing. The outer layer, the epidermis, flakes off and we have a change in the skin about every thirty days. Use a loofah sponge to help remove the flaky skin. The following program will help you have more healthy skin.

The Skin Care Program

1. Complete cleansing and rinse
2. Steam skin facial (unless you have a problem with red thread veins or very sensitive skin)
3. Facial for tightening and pore cleansing
4. Rinsing and astringent
5. Moisturizing

Cleansing—*Oily skin:* Wash with soap and water or witch hazel lotion.

Dry and aging skin: Wash with soap and water or the herbal cleanser described below.

Always use a non-alkaline soap to prevent the harsh activity of an alkaline soap on the acid mantle.

When you have thoroughly cleansed the skin, rinse with:

Oily skin: an herbal vinegar made with sage or yarrow. (Always dilute vinegar when using on skin).

Dry, aging skin: an herbal water made of calendula and lemon balm.

Herbal Cleanser

Mix and let set for two days; strain and bottle:

6 tbsp witch hazel
6 tbsp sunflower oil
3 tsp thyme
3 tsp oregano
3 tsp sage

Steam Facial—A steam on the skin will open the pores and help release the oils. Do not use this step if you have problems with red thread veins on your skin. Facial steam appliances are commercially available and inexpensive. Or, you can make your own at home as follows: Fill the sink or a bowl with boiling-hot herbal water (using chamomile or peppermint water has a cleansing action). Put your face near the steam and cover your head and the bowl with a towel to hold the steam in. Another way is to fill a bowl with hot water and soak washcloths in it, then apply to your face, alternating hot cloths as they become cool.

Facials—A facial will further cleanse, soften, and nourish your skin when certain products are used. Before applying the facial, apply a thin layer of penetrating oil under the eyes as this area is very sensitive and should not have the tightening effect of the facial material on it. Prepare your facial mixture and apply generously to the face and neck. Soak cotton balls in an herbal infusion of fennel or wormwood, or even black tea bags. Lie down for fifteen minutes with your legs elevated. Clean off the facial with water and use a rinse suitable for your skin type.

Rinse—To improve the skin's acid balance, rinse with an herbal vinegar diluted half and half with water. Some herbs to use for a skin rinse or as an astringent include:

Oily Skin	Dry or Aging Skin
basil	agrimony
calendula	coltsfoot
mints	elderflower
rosemary	lady's mantle
sage	marshmallow
yarrow	parsley

If you have sensitive skin you may want to use just herbal waters and not the herbal vinegar.

Moisturizing—The first commercial skin lotion was produced in the 17th century by Gervase Markham. It contained fennel, feverfew, violets, and nettles, and it needed to be diluted with milk for use. Today there is every kind of beauty cream available you can think of.

The outside of the body needs nourishment in order to keep the skin healthy and soft. Apply a good moisturizer daily, after your cleansing program. Use a light lotion for day wear and a heavier one (cream) for the nighttime. The following natural lotions and creams should be made in small amounts and kept in the refrigerator. Remember, we are working with natural products that are not full of chemical preservatives and so they do not have a long shelf life.

Herbal Cosmetic Recipes

Cleansing Cream for Oily Skin

Infuse herbs in ½ *cup of witch hazel* for 10 days, strain and bottle.

> *1 tbsp elderflower*
> *1 tbsp comfrey*
> *1 tbsp mint*
> *1 tbsp rosemary*

Skin Cleanser for Dry or Aging Skin

Mix all ingredients together; let set for 10 days. Strain and bottle.

> *¼ cup witch hazel*
> *¼ cup almond oil*
> *$^1/_8$ cup thyme*
> *$^1/_8$ cup oregano*
> *$^1/_8$ cup sage*

Cleanser for All Types of Skin

> *1 tbsp beeswax*
> *2 tbsps lanolin*
> *½ cup olive oil*
> *3 tbsps herbal water (infusion of elderflower, parsley, and salad burnet)*

Melt wax and lanolin over low heat. Remove and beat in olive oil with a wooden spoon, mixing well and adding herbal water slowly. Stir well until cool.

Facial Masks

Good for dry skin. Mix well:

> *1 egg yolk*
> *1 tbsp honey*
> *1 tbsp marshmallow infusion*
> *1 tsp olive oil*
> *1 tsp cornmeal*

Good for oily skin. Mix well:

> *2 tbsps dried milk*
> *1 tbsp honey*
> *1 tbsp yarrow infusion*
> *1 tbsp cornmeal*

Good for normal skin. Mix together:

> 2 tbsps lady's mantle infusion
> 3 tbsps bran
> 1 tbsp oatmeal
> 1 tbsp honey

Good for any skin. Mix together:

> 1 tsp honey
> 1 tsp vitamin E oil
> 1 tbsp powdered brewer's yeast
> 1 tsp milk
> 1 tsp calendula infusion
> ½ tsp salt

A Blue Facial. Mix together 2 tablespoons of blueberries into 2 table-spoons of water. Heat and crush. Add:

> ½ cup plain yogurt
> 1 tbsp honey

Green Clay Facial. Mix together:

> 1 tbsp green clay
> 1 tbsp honey

Add enough herbal water to make a paste but keep it soft enough to apply to the skin, but not runny. Use any herbs of your choice which are compatible with your skin type.

Facial mask mixtures do not keep well so make only small amounts as mentioned above. To nourish the skin, add strawberries, cucumber, apricots, or bananas (mashed and added to the facial for any skin).

Herbal Rinses

Herbal rinses are used after the cleansing program, after facials, or anytime just because they feel good. Keep them refrigerated. All are made by the infusion method. For dry, itchy, or aging skin, an infusion of:

> 3 tbsps comfrey
> 3 tbsps licorice root
> 2 tbsps chamomile
> 1 tbsp red clover flower
> 1 tbsp thyme
> 1 tbsp lady's mantle
> 2 cups water

For oily skin. Infusion of:

> *½ cup chamomile flowers*
> *¼ cup coltsfoot*
> *1 cup witch hazel*

For all types of skin. Infusion of:

> *2 cups water*
> *1 tbsp comfrey*
> *1 tbsp lemon peel*
> *1 tbsp peppermint*
> *1 tbsp parsley*
> *1 tbsp rose petals*

Steep for 1 hour, strain, and use.

Moisturizers

Use your moisturizers daily to keep skin soft and supple.

Moisturizer 1. Mix:

> *1 tbsp mayonnaise*
> *3 drops marshmallow oil*

Moisturizer 2. Melt *¼ cup of beeswax* over low heat. Mix in:

> *1 cup almond oil*
> *¼ cup herbal infusion (made with ¼ cup water, 1 tbsp each of*
> *agrimony, borage, elderflower, and rosemary).*

Moisturizer 3: Bedtime cream. Warm over low heat:

> *4 tbsp lanolin*
> *¼ cup almond oil*
> *¼ cup vitamin E oil*

Remove from heat, then add *1 tbsp of honey* and *2 tbsp of elderflowers* (powdered). Let set until cool. Refrigerate.

Spice aftershave. Make an infusion of:

> *1 tbsp crushed coriander seeds*
> *¼ cup cinnamon chips*
> *4 whole cloves*
> *2 cups boiling water*

Let steep overnight. Strain and add *1 tablespoon of alcohol.*

Herbal aftershave. Make an infusion of:

> *½ cup thyme*
> *¼ cup mint*
> *2 cups boiling water*

Friction rub. Use at least once a week to get rid of flaky skin; also good to help remove blackheads. Mix:

> *¼ cup milk*
> *1 tbsp cornmeal*
> *1 tbsp yarrow or parsley infusion*

Pale, greasy skin: Make a strong infusion of parsley by steeping overnight. Apply to the skin several times a day. Prepare fresh infusion daily. Sage tea is also beneficial.

Blackheads and acne: This problem is usually caused by overactive sebum. The friction rub above will be useful. Follow the skin cleansing program at least once a week and use parsley tea several times a day.

Freckles and brown spots: Lemon juice bleaches the skin and must be used daily for results. Some herbalists recommend applying a tea made from burdock root to the affected area to soften the color of freckles.

Hand and Foot Care

My intention every spring is to wear garden gloves to protect my hands from the grit and grime of weeding, but after a short time in the garden the gloves come off. Tricks I have learned to help my hands afterward are:

- Dig the fingernails into a bar of soap before going out to weed.
- Use an herbal rinse after every hand wash. This is made with an infusion of marshmallow, fennel, lady's mantle, comfrey, chamomile, or a combination of any of these herbs.

Gardeners are often seen in shorts and barefooted. This causes us to have rough knees and feet. Knees that are dirty-looking even after a bath can be bleached by rubbing a fresh lemon on them followed by an almond oil massage. If your feet are tired or swollen, soak them in this herb bath:

Mugwort Foot Relaxer

Make an infusion in *1 gallon of hot water* using:

> *½ cup mugwort*
> *½ cup rosemary*
> *½ cup peppermint*

Hair Care for the Gardener

The sun bleaches out the hair and the ends break; dust and dirt are a constant hair problem. But with herbs growing in the garden you have a supply of help near at hand. Herbs were once the mainstay products used for the hair. Henna, used by the Egyptians, can be found on the health food store shelf today. For a simple hair color aid, use sage or rosemary for dark hair and calendula for lighter hair. However, they must be used continuously for good results.

Hair Care Recipes

Shampoo—Use pure castile soap or baby shampoo (unscented) to make your own herbal shampoo as follows:

1. Fill a jar with herbs.
2. Cover with castile or baby shampoo.
3. Let set for 10 days, shaking daily.
4. Strain and bottle.

Use any of the following herbs alone or in combination:

Dark hair—sage, rosemary
Light hair—calendula
Itchy scalp—chamomile
Dandruff—burdock root, southernwood, parsley
Oily hair—yarrow, parsley
Dry hair—marshmallow, soapwort

Herbal Hair Rinse—Using a diluted vinegar of your favorite herbal scent will leave your hair squeaky clean and shining. Choose from the list for shampoo, or use favorites such as roses, lavender, or mints.

Herbal Hair Conditioner—For split ends, very dry hair, and weather-worn tresses, give yourself a weekly hair conditioning treatment. Use the conditioner just before shampooing. Note that olive oil may slightly darken the hair.

Oil conditioner—Apply warm oil to the hair and scalp; use olive, almond, peanut, vitamin E, or jojoba oil. Apply hot towels to the head for 15 minutes. Rinse well, shampoo, and then rinse with an herbal vinegar.

Egg conditioner—Beat 2 egg whites in ¼ cup parsley herbal water. Apply to hair and scalp and leave on to dry for 30 minutes. Shampoo, then rinse with herbal vinegar.

Plant Profiles

Lady's Mantle *(Alchemilla vulgaris)*

Family—Rosaceae (rose)

Synonyms—Lion's foot, bear's foot

Description—Lady's mantle is one of the herbs that has come into general use by the landscaping business. Its beauty alone makes it a good specimen plant. The large, fan-shaped, pleated leaves catch the morning dew, and legend would have us believe that eyes washed with this dew will be strong and healthy. Flowers (in June) are yellow-green; growing in a mound shape, this herbaceous perennial is about 20 inches tall. An old herb (since the 1500s), the leaves are said to represent the Virgin's cloak, hence its name lady's mantle. Said to be dedicated by the Virgin as a help for all women's problems.

Cultivation—Likes good drainage in full sun; add wood ashes, bone meal, or lime yearly. The thick center of the herb chokes out the weeds. Cut off flowers after long blooming period is over to keep the herb neat and trim looking.

Propagation—Seeds are slow to germinate and it takes two years for maturity. Spring divison of roots is the best way to propagate. It sometimes self-seeds if flowers are left on the herb.

Part Used—Leaf and flowers

Harvest—Leaves all season; flowers in full bloom. Dry flowers by the hanging method, screen dry leaves.

Uses—Medicinal: Its medicinal use is dedicated to women for help with their medical problems. Leaf is taken in the form of a tea; it stops excessive bleeding during the menstruation period. It helps to reduce hot flashes during the menopause period. *Caution:* Lady's mantle tea should not be used in excess; limit yourself to not more than two cups of the tea a day. As with all herbs taken internally, you may want to consult a holistic doctor first.

Miscellaneous: Excellent for fresh or dried floral arrangements and wreath making.

Mugwort *(Artemisia vulgare)*

Family—Compositae (daisy)

Description—Herbaceous perennial to 6 feet tall. Toothed leaf, dark green on top, gray underneath. Flowers insignificant, brownish-gray in late

Mugwort

summer. Crowns of mugwort and St. Johnswort were used in Midsummer's Day rituals. They were thrown in the fires at the end of the day to bring good luck for the following year. Also, they were hung above the doors because it was thought that they would bring good luck and protection from any evil entering the home. Another legend tells us to put mugwort in our shoe and we will be able to walk forty miles before noon without tiring. Also reputed to attract money when carried in the pocket; when I tell this legend on my garden tours, everyone picks a leaf to carry in their pocket. Mugwort has been used throughout history to bring good luck and ward off evil spirits.

Cultivation—Easy to grow anywhere, can be slightly invasive; likes full sun to partial shade

Propagation—Easy to seed and will self-seed everywhere. Cut flowering head to prevent invasion by seeding. Division of roots can be done in the spring.

Part Used—Leaf

Harvest—Leaf all season; hang or screen dry

Uses—Once popular as a culinary herb with poultry, fish, and fatty meats. Tea for pleasure, but be reminded that *it has been banned by the FDA for sale for internal use.*

Medicinal: As a diuretic; and modern herbalists believe its medicinal use includes being a tonic, stimulant, and likely to have some effect on relieving congestion in the brain. Mugwort is used extensively in Chinese medicine.

Crafting: Mugwort makes a good base for wreath making; its brown color contrasts with pink flowers. An ingredient for making moth bags and sachets.

Miscellaneous: For household use, it deters moths and other insects as do all members of the artemisia family.

Cosmetic: It is used in baths, facials, and as a soak for tired feet.

Coltsfoot *(Tussilago farfara)*

Family—Compositae (daisy)

Synonyms—Son-before-the-father, coughwort

Description—This unusual herb has yellow flowers that appear in early spring, before the leaves unfold. The flowers are followed by heart-shaped leaves, hence the name son-before-the-father. This herbaceous perennial is invasive and is found growing in the wild in the New England area, usually beside roadways. Makes a good ground cover in hard-to-care-for areas of banks or yards.

Coltsfoot is helpful in treating coughs and colds.

Cultivation—Prefers lean soil, full sun to partial shade. The richer the soil the quicker it spreads.

Propagation—Division of roots in spring when the leaves appear

Part Used—Leaf

Harvest—All season, dry on screens

Uses—Medicinal: for coughs and bronchial troubles. Recipes have been passed down through the generations, most using it in tea. Externally used as a poultice applied to wounds and sores, it is believed to be beneficial by some herbalists.
    Culinary: leaves are slightly bitter but can be added to salads.

Gipsywort *(Lycopus europeans)*

Family—Labiatae (mint)

Synonyms—Egyptian's herb, gypsyweed

Description—Herbaceous perennial to 2½ feet, deeply toothed, dark green leaves; pale pink in July. Like a true mint family member, it spreads quickly by underground root runners. History tells us that the gypsies painted their bodies with this plant to darken their skin.

Cultivation—Full sun to partial shade, good drainage. Keep in a contained area to prevent its taking over other herbs' territory.

Propagation—Easy by seed or with root division early spring

Part Used—Leaf

Harvest—All season, hang dry

Uses—A dye plant that yields black dye for wool and silk.
    Medicinal: It is reputed to have astringent medicinal properties, but much research needs to be done and I would *not* recommend its medicinal use at this time.

Scullcap

Family—Labiatae (mint)

Synonyms—Blue scullcap, hoodwort

Description—This herbaceous perennial is native to the New England area, often found in wet, marshy areas. The 12 inch herb has lance-like leaves of dark green, spreading quickly around the mother plant. The little blue flowers look like small snapdragons, flowering through July and August.

Cultivation—Adapts nicely to the garden, full sun or partial shade, and not fussy as to soil type.

Propagation—Start seeds 6 weeks before last frost date or divide in early spring from roots.

Part Used—Leaf

Harvest—All season

Uses—Medicinal: I have a friend who swears by this herb for a good night's sleep and for use as a general tonic; she is in her nineties. A calming herb reputed to lessen excessive emotions of anger and jealousy. Used by the Indian medicine man for nervousness. Although a calming herb, *overdoses will cause wakefulness and it should be used in moderation.*

THIRTEEN

Medicine Men, Modern Science, and Motherwort

(Using Nature's Plants for Medicine)

THE PURPOSE OF this chapter is to introduce you to the fascinating world of herbal medicine. The lore of how plants are used for medicine has been passed down to modern man from the beginning of recorded time. Some of this use is simply folklore but much of it has now been scientifically proven to have beneficial results for humans and animals. Many plants are still recognized in *United States and English Pharmacopia* (a book containing the official list of drugs used at the specific time of its publication). Yet unfortunately, many useful plants have been discarded and replaced over the last decade by stronger chemical drugs.

Philosophies and Practices of Herbal Medicine

The 1980s brought to the general public certain therapeutic ideas from other cultures. Since I cannot do justice in one short chapter to a subject as deep as medicinal herbs, may I suggest you visit your local library or bookstore to find books dedicated to the particular philosophy of medicine that interests you. The following is a brief summary of some of the philosophies that consider the use of herbs in their therapeutic practices.

Aromatherapy

Aromatherapy is a philosophy of using scents from the essential oil of herbs and flowers in the healing process of the mind and body. I guess the first time I tucked a cotton ball scented with rose oil under my pillow, I was practicing aromatherapy. The sending of scented flowers to a sick person is an indirect method of using aromatherapy to cheer up that person. A holistic approach is taken in aromatherapy, using the essential oils made by the distillation of herbs and flowers. These oils are taken in the form of teas, syrups, lotions, massage oils, ointments, plasters, tinctures, and capsules. Capsules are often prescribed for diseases while other methods are often used to prevent the disease from getting into the system in the first place. Essential oils are highly concentrated and must be used with caution at all times. Used improperly, some of them become toxic. For example, many experts believe that rosemary, sage, and hyssop, when taken in excess, may produce a tendency towards epilepsy in certain persons. Some oils, if not diluted, will cause burning of the skin. I set some undiluted pine essential oil in a plastic dish and forgot it until some time later. It had eaten a hole right through the plastic dish.

When we think of using aromatherapy in our lives, we think of nice fragrant herbs and flowers, but two very important herbs which are often used are garlic and onions. Both have been used for health since the ancient Greek and Egyptian civilizations. Garlic and onions are not prescribed as often in the oil form because they are readily available in natural form. However, the oils are available in health food stores. The workers who built the pyramids were given cloves of garlic to use as a tonic and for antiseptic purposes. Both my husband and I take garlic daily and find it does help in keeping colds to a minimum. To offset the effect of bad breath, eat parsley or drink teas of parsley, rosemary, or anise seed. Use garlic in salads and other cooked dishes, or eat it raw with a glass of milk as I do. Garlic and onions have been steeped in lard or oil and used externally to treat tumors of the skin and wounds (with success, according to some herbalists). Also, there is the folklore of wearing garlic around the neck to ward off colds. *Caution:* Nursing mothers should not eat garlic as it may spoil the milk and give the baby colic.

Onions can be used raw or cooked for use in so many different recipes that it would be impossible to mention them all here. They have antiseptic and diuretic properties useful in treating influenza, rheumatism, obesity, and diabetes. One book on aromatherapy recommends boiled onions served with olive oil as an aid in preventing gallstones.

Aromatherapy is a part of everyday cooking when the antiseptic herbs thyme, rosemary, garlic, onions, and cloves are used.

The first scientific research in aromatherapy was done in 1887, with work on using the antiseptic properties of herbs to cure the anthrax bacillus in cattle. Today we know that certain herbs *do* contain properties that can help in killing influenza germs. These include thyme, cinnamon, lemon, and pine needles. Using herbs and flowers in our daily living for cooking, teas, potpourri, and cosmetics may help to keep us in a healthy state of mind and body.

Ayurveda

This is an Eastern Indian philosophy which develops a holistic attitude towards using yoga, herbs and astrology. Striving for a harmonious lifestyle is perfected by the cosmic intelligence, called *mahat* in Sanskrit. This is a way of thinking in unity with nature: a way of seeing our inner self and spirit in harmony with nature. People are being drawn to ayurvedic medicine because it offers an approach to healthy living that is healing, calming, and effective, with the least danger of side effects. Even when the wrong herb is used for a certain disease, it will usually pass through the system naturally without harming us; but a harsh chemical may produce side effects to add to the impact of a disease. Followers of ayurveda believe that there is a definite reason for disease being present in an individual and that by adopting a healthy attitude, keeping good eating habits, and proper exercise, many diseases can be prevented and cured. This philosophy, of course, has been greatly simplified here in order to present a summary. As with all philosophies of medicine, a great deal of study and knowledge is necessary in order to fully understand and practice it. Chemical medicines are given out based on the *disease*, whereas ayurveda advocates an individual treatment for each person based upon *which characteristics are out of balance* in that person. Some of the herbs that might be prescribed in ayurvedic medicine include:

Parsley: A nutritional herb used to help treat chills and colds in some persons. Parsley acts as a diuretic, aiding in relief of menstrual problems, such as cramps and water retention. It may also help dispel kidney stones. However, if a kidney inflammation is present, it will irritate that problem.

Scullcap: An infusion of scullcap has calming properties that are reputed to reduce the emotions of anger, jealousy, and frustration. Some say it enhances awareness and perception. It is usually taken as a "nightcap" tea before retiring. It may also help relieve headaches.

Ginger: I was brought up on ginger tea for stomach cramps, colds, and headaches. I use the powdered form of ginger in a tea with milk and honey. It will produce perspiration so it should not be used when high fevers are present. *Caution:* Excessive or prolonged use may cause symptoms of poisoning. Those with bleeding ulcers or serious skin diseases should *not* use ginger as a medicine.

Chinese Medicine

China has one of the oldest recorded medicinal philosophies in the world and its therapeutic techniques are often used today in combination with Western medical practices. Acupuncture immediately comes to mind as an example of Chinese medicine; but many teas are used, usually in a combination of several herbs and flowers. One such formula for frostbite includes herbs of cinnamon, white peony, angelica, Chinese licorice, Chinese jujube, and ginger. Some herbs that may be taken in a form of tea for a general tonic are ginseng, agrimony, mugwort, and skullcap. Many potent herbs are taken only to cure a disease, then are discontinued after there has been a cure. Among these may be ephedra, sweet annie (the annual wormwood), and aconite. *Caution:* Aconite is a poisonous herb and is used *only in small amounts under medical supervision.*

Western doctors often treat the physical symptoms or the disease itself, whereas Chinese doctors treat the whole person in order to find the underlying cause of the disease. Like a healthy plant, a healthy body is not usually attacked by disease. Plants are often put in a weak condition by using chemicals on them. If a person is overstressed or run down physically or mentally, for example through the abuse of cigarettes, alcohol, drugs, or chemicals, then that person is a prime target for germs, bacteria, and disease. Herbal or holistic doctors believe that the treatment of the body and mind as a whole is necessary and that a small amount of medicine over a longer period of time is better than a large dose all at once. Substituting sage herbal teas for coffee, black tea, soda, and alcohol will eventually benefit your general health.

The American Indian Medicine Man

The medicine man was held in high esteem by his people and he was well versed in the techniques of medicine, which had been passed down through the generations by word of mouth. Certain rituals often accompanied treatments; some were in the form of prayers while others may have been designed to show the importance of the medicine man. In comparing the herbs used in various religious and medicinal philosophies, we often find the same herbs used for similar purposes. This alone has helped to prove that some of these herbs indeed are effective and not just figments of folklore. Among some of the American Indian native herbs are:

Catnip: This was used in earlier days, as it is today, for a nightcap. The Indians also used it to treat colds, fevers, and headaches. Catnip was one of the herbs they smoked, calling the leaves "shinnecock" in their rituals.

Purple coneflower: This was thought to be helpful in treating the bite of snakes. The juice of the plant was also applied to burns. The powdered root was put on an aching tooth to alleviate pain. Purple coneflower can be purchased in capsule or oil form in the health food store under its botanical name Echinacea.

Pennyroyal: There is some information that pennyroyal may be abortive in nature, but the Indian women used it for menstrual cramps and after a miscarriage. It was also used for gout, as a stimulant, and to provoke perspiration, but it is *not* recommended by this author to use pennyroyal internally. Rubbed on the skin, it will prevent mosquito bites for a short period of time.

Gumplant: This has become a favorite herb of mine. When I planted the seeds of this plant two years ago, I had no idea what it would look like or how hardy it would be in zone 4 in Maine. It was a pleasant surprise for me when it turned out to be hardy and to produce long-lasting, medium-size, yellow daisy flowers. The leaves were used by the Indians as a poultice for swellings and wounds.

Modern Science

The Europeans are well ahead of us on current research into the study of the properties of botanicals for medicinal uses. Even though some of us use herbs in our daily living and feel confident of their positive reactions, scientists are only recently proving some of these herbs safe and beneficial for medicinal use today. Yet many cultures and religious philosophies use botanicals in their rituals and medicines and have done so for many centuries. Among some of the herbs that are presently being studied or have recently been researched are:

Artemisia annua (The annual wormwood or sweet annie): Purdue University is doing research on this herb for its anti-malaria properties. It is already being used, as it has been for eons, in Chinese medicine.

Cartharanthus roseus (Madagascar periwinkle): Eli Lilly and Company has had success with the extract gamma-linolenic acid (GLA) in the treatment of tumors. So far, the main source of GLA has been produced commercially from the evening primrose (Oenothera biennis). The fatty acid has recently been found in borage seeds, so some research may soon begin on this herb. Extensive information can be obtained by writing to

Purdue University, Division of Continuing Education, West Lafayette, Indiana 47907.

Tanacetum parthenium (feverfew): This is a wild, single-petalled herb being researched at London University for its effects on migraine headaches. Feverfew has been recommended for centuries for headaches and I often eat a piece of the leaf when I have one. However, there are side effects experienced by a small percentage of users. These include mouth ulcers, indigestion, and stomachaches. These effects were experienced when three to four leaves a day are taken over a long period of time.

The Study of Herbal Medicine

The information contained in this book is purely for background knowledge and general information. It consists of data I have collected over the past ten years and my personal experiences. *It is in no way a substitute for professional medical help.* Using herbs for medicine requires many years of study under a guided practicioner. *Caution* should always be the priority when using any medicines, herbal or chemical. For the serious student of herbal medicine, the following list includes a few of the things that should be understood before using herbal medicines:

- Accurate identification and knowledge of plants
- Knowledge of what part of that plant to use
- Parts of the plant which may be toxic
- Knowledge of anatomy and diseases
- Correct diagnosis of a particular disease
- Possible cures of that disease and which one is best for that particular individual
- Form and dosage of the herbal medicine used
- What side effects, if any, may occur
- Will excessive use or prolonged use produce side effects?
- How, when, and where was the plant harvested?
- Which herbs are generally safe to use, which herbs are poisonous, and which can be used only under medical supervision.

Here are some herbs that should be used *only under professional medical supervision* because of their toxicity; these are *not* used by the layman:

- arnica—poisonous when incorrect dosage is used
- blue cohosh—dangerous to those with high blood pressure
- foxglove—may cause a heart attack if incorrect dosage is used
- pennyroyal—may be abortive and cause side effects
- St. Johnswort—causes photosensitivity in some persons and in cattle.

Preparation of Herbal Medicine

The following preparations are easily made at home. The herbs recommended are basic and generally safe for the average, healthy person. But take into consideration that each person has individual needs and allergies. Use a moderate dosage at first.

Tea—For internal use, a tea is often taken for medical problems. To make, pour boiling water over the herbs and let steep from 5 to 15 minutes to extract all the bitter principals. From one to three cups a day is generally recommended by most herbalists.

Oil—Herbs are placed in a jar with oil (such as olive, almond, or peanut) poured over them. Let set on the shelf for 10 days, shaking daily, then strain and store in an airtight container. The oil is used externally for sprains, swellings, and massage.

Vinegar—This is used for rubbing onto sprains, bruises, and in bath water. For preparation see Chapter 8.

Tincture (internal use)—Place fresh herbs in a glass jar and cover with 60 proof vodka. Set in a warm (but not direct sun) area for 12 days, shaking daily. This tincture is used in small dosages for internal problems. For example, coltsfoot might be used for bronchitis by taking 2 tablespoons three times a day. Dosage varies with the herb used. Check a good medicinal herb reference book.

Tincture (external use)—Made the same as above but pure rubbing alcohol or witch hazel is used instead of vodka. Used to rub on insect bites, swellings, bruises, or as a massage.

Syrup—Boil 1½ pounds of brown sugar with 1 pint of water, stirring constantly so it does not burn. Remove from heat when the desired consistency is reached, usually in 5 to 7 minutes. Add herbs and let steep overnight. In the morning, heat up and strain out the herbs. Used for colds and coughs, taken by the teaspoonful when needed.

Powder—Put dried herbs in a mortar and pestle, grind until they are in powdered form (large amounts can be done in your blender). Mix with unscented baby powder or arrowroot. Use on sores or as a foot deodorant.

Salve—Herbs that have been powdered are added to vaseline or a good grade of lard. Warm on low heat to melt, stirring in herbs; then let harden.

Cough Syrup

Mix together:

½ cup honey
¼ cup lemon juice
3 tbsps herb infusion of sage (or any of the following herbs: licorice
root, horehound, marshmallow root, rosemary, betony, coltsfoot,
elderflower, thyme, peppermint).

Note: The teaspoon of the syrup can also be taken in a tea to reduce cold symptoms.

Essential oils are often used instead of the dry herbs. Use externally only for wounds, bruises, and to soften skin.

Poultice—Make an infusion of the herb; soak a sterile cloth in the solution; apply to wound or swellings. The whole herb can also be put in hot water, wrung out, and applied directly to the skin.

Herbs to Use in Medicine

The herbs mentioned below are usually recommended for the named diseases or discomforts. Again, use with discretion as we all have our own individual reactions and some herbs will affect you differently than they would me. *Abuse, overuse, or prolonged use may cause serious side effects in some persons.* Herbs commonly used in our daily living, such as ginger, sage, or nutmeg can become *toxic* when misused in large quantities.

Coughs and Colds—There seems to be no way to prevent or cure a cold; it will go through its time cycle. However, the following herbs may help alleviate some discomfort. I swear by my cough syrup remedy for a sore throat.

Herbs Used As Sedatives—These herbs are reputed by some herbalists to aid in relaxing the mind and body. They are generally taken just before bedtime to help one get a good night's sleep. They should be used in moderation and not continuously over a long period of time: catnip, scullcap, motherwort, valerian (prolonged use will cause severe headaches). A recipe follows for a tea I often use on those sleepless nights.

Relaxer Tea

1 tsp valerian root
1 tsp peppermint
½ tsp chamomile
½ tsp lavender
½ tsp catnip

Mix and let age for one week before using.

Herbs for Common Health Problems

Indigestion—Who hasn't overeaten and ended up with indigestion? If indigestion is a way of life with you, change your eating habits and see a physician. Herb teas, served after a heavy meal, may aid the digestive process. And don't forget to eat that piece of parsley on the plate. Herbs that may help for digestive problems include:

anise	ginger root
caraway	mugwort
catnip	parsley
dill	peppermint
fennel	sweet cicely

Headaches—An occasional headache from stress or too much sun may be reduced by a relaxing cup of herbal tea. Continuous headaches may be a symptom that something is seriously wrong and should be checked by your physician. The following herbs are thought by several herbalists to be helpful for minor headaches:

catnip	lemon balm
chamomile	mints
feverfew	mugwort
lady's mantle	rosemary
lavender	sage

As with all medicines, these teas should be taken in moderation. Use alone or in combination with your favorites. For example, mugwort, rosemary, and lavender combined make a good tea.

Backaches from too much garden work—After several hours in the garden, I enjoy a long soak in an herbal bath, followed by a warm herbal oil massage. Herbs to use in your bath are discussed in Chapter 12. The oils I find especially helpful for me are mugwort, tansy, or mints. These, of course, can also be added in your herbal bath water.

Constipation—Keeping the bowels healthy is very important to our overall health. The following herbs are reputed to be helpful when taken as a tea or steeped in olive oil and taken in the morning (a tablespoon). Drinking lots of water and fruit juices will also be beneficial.

basil	Good King Henry
chicory	restharrow
horehound	sorrel

Diarrhea—The other extreme of bowel problems; it also may be helped by using herbal teas. Herbs that are useful are:

betony	hyssop
blackberry fruit and leaf	lady's mantle
catnip	rhubarb, stem only
comfrey	sage

Fever—A fever is a warning system to tell us that something is wrong within the body. It is not a disease in itself. Any extremely high or prolonged fever should be checked by your physician. Herbs taken in the form of tea that may prove helpful in reducing the effects of a fever are:

basil	goat's rue
borage	sage
catnip	violet leaf and flower

Female problems—Since prehistoric times women have used herbs to alleviate pain from menstruation, to help in labor, and for menopause. Rejecting chemical medicines for my entrance into the menopause age, I experimented with various suggested herbs and found them to be very helpful, with no side effects. Tea was the medium I chose because of its simplicity, but some of these herbs can be purchased at health food stores in the form of capsules. Those herbs I used successfully were lady's mantle, licorice root, rosemary, and elderflowers. These were often combined for extra flavor. I suggest using lady's mantle *with caution* as too much may produce side effects in some people.

Herbs suggested for fighting menstrual cramps are:

alfalfa	ginger root
catnip	spearmint
chamomile	valerian

Herbs that are diurètic in nature and may reduce water retention are mugwort and yarrow. Use with caution.

Calcium is important to women during all stages of life. According to herbalists who specialize in women's problems, some herbs contain calcium; these include comfrey, motherwort, and raspberry leaf.

Pregnancy and birthing—Women who are pregnant should be very careful of the herbs and foods they ingest. Certain herbs may be toxic and do damage to the fetus; included here are tansy, pennyroyal, golden seal, and blue cohosh. However, blue cohosh is often given to those in slow labor, but should only be taken under the medical supervision of a midwife or holistic doctor. The wrong dosage can be damaging to the baby and the mother.

Red raspberry leaf in tea form is reputed to prevent miscarriage.

Nursing mothers should not drink sage tea, but when they are ready to dry up their milk it will help in that process.

One chapter cannot do justice to this subject, so this is just a mere sampling of some herbs for women's problems. There are several good books on the subject, but contacting a holistic doctor will save you a lot of mistakes made because of incomplete or incorrect information.

The Herbal Medicine Chest

Keeping a good medicine chest will prevent frustrations when you become ill: that is no time to be running around looking for products for your discomforts. Be prepared with your own herbal medicines for minor illnesses and wounds. Herbs helpful for home remedies include:

aloe vera	motherwort
catnip	onions
coltsfoot	parsley
garlic	rosemary
ginger, ground	sage
horehound	scullcap
lady's mantle	thyme
marshmallow root	valerian

Also keep on hand:

cider vinegar	vitamin E oil
honey	vodka
lemon juice	witch hazel
olive oil	

Add a good medicinal herb book for reference and other herbs for your own particular problems.

Aloe vera is a must in every home; it helps heal burns and wounds and makes a good houseplant.

Plant Profiles

Betony *(Stachys officinalis)*

Family—Labiatae (mint)

Synonyms—Woundwort, bishopswort

Description—Herbaceous perennial with long, oval-shaped, light green leaves to 2 feet tall. It is not overgenerous with its pink spike flowers, but they stay in bloom over a long period of time; was once used in witchcraft to ward off the evil spirits.

Cultivation—Enjoys partial shade; grows neatly into a clump; nice for a wooded setting. Give good drainage and a yearly application of wood ash.

Propagation—Easy by seeds, start 6 weeks before last frost in your area; or, root division in early spring. Divide the betony clump every 4 years to prevent the roots from strangling themselves.

Part Used—Leaves

Harvest—All season, hang or screen dry

Uses—Culinary: as a tea for pleasure
   Medicinal: Tea is reputed to stop external bleeding of wounds and aids in healing them, hence its name woundwort. Tea (when combined with coltsfoot) may ease a headache and calm the nerves.
   Caution: overuse of betony can cause stomach irritation and it should not be used by those with ulcers.

Horehound

Horehound *(Marrubium vulgare)*

Family—Labiatae (mint)

Synonyms—hoarhound

Description—A herbaceous perennial to 15 inches tall; woolly, gray-green leaves, with a wrinkled, slightly sticky feeling; small white flowers on stems are followed by burrs.

Cultivation—Likes full sun with good drainage. Add some bone meal, wood ash, or lime yearly to keep the soil alkaline. For a low, neat herb, keep flower stalks cut off.

Propagation—Seeds are easy, start 6 weeks before last frost; or, division of roots in spring. During a winter with no snow cover it will probably die out, but it should produce small seedlings from self-seeding.

Horehound Candy Cough Drops

Boil 1 quart of chopped horehound leaves (picked before the plant comes into flower) in 1 pint of water. Boil for 10 minutes to make a strong decoction. Strain out leaves. Add 3 cups of sugar and bring to a boil. Add ¼ cup butter and continue cooking until the syrup forms a hard ball in cold water.

Pour in a shallow, buttered pan. When cool, break into pieces and store in an airtight container.

Part Used—Leaves

Harvest—Best harvested just before it comes into flower; dry on screens or hand dry, or just stand upright in a jar.

Uses—Medicinal: has a bitter taste and is used in making cough drops or syrup. There was a time when you could buy horehound drops in any store.

Miscellaneous: Horehound is reputed to discourage flies, so plant it near doors and under windows, and around animal houses. Hanging bunches in the home or using in arrangements will help discourage flies.

Valerian is used externally for wounds and rashes.

Valerian *(Valeriana officinalis)*

Family—Valerianaceae (valerian)

Synonyms—Allheal, phu, setwell

Description—Herbaceous perennial to 6 feet tall. Large, segmented leaves with white flowers that have a tint of pink blush; very sweet-scented flowers, sending their aroma up to twenty feet away. Used in love potions; it is said that if a girl were to wear valerian she would never lack for lovers. Reputed to be the herb used by the Pied Piper of Hamlin to take the rats away. It is used both for and against witchcraft.

Cultivation—Full sun to partial shade, not fussy as to soil. Being so tall makes it an excellent background plant.

Propagation—Easy by seeds or spring root division; once established it will self-seed invasively.

Part Used—Roots

Harvest—Fall, see Chapter 8 for harvesting process for roots.

Uses—Medicinal: it is used externally to wash wounds and rashes. Internally, it is a potent drug that should be used only under medical supervision. Said to be sedative and may cause headaches and nausea with overuse or continuous use.

Feverfew *(Chrysanthemum parthenium)*

Family—Compositae (daisy)

Synonyms—Featherfew, featherfoil

Description—A herbaceous perennial growing to 15 inches tall. Medium-size, toothed leaves with white flowers on the common herb species. There are other hybrid species of feverfew: double white flowers on one, a gold leaf with white flowers on another, and a new variety, with yellow flowers, called gold ball feverfew.

Cultivation—Full sun to partial shade for all varieties. Needs good drainage; likes bone meal, lime, or wood ashes added to raise the alkaline pH of the soil; will spread by self-seeding once established.

Propagation—Easy by seeds, start 8 weeks before last frost in your area; usually will produce flowers the first year when starting by seeds.

Part Used—Leaf and flowers

Harvest—Leaf all season, flowers in full bloom; screen and hang dry.

Uses—Crafting: flowers dry nicely for dried arrangement and wreath making.
   Medicinal: Long known as a remedy for headaches; modern research is proving this to be true. No more than one cup of tea a day is recommended at this time due to possible side effects in some persons.

Motherwort *(Leonurus cardiaca)*

Family—Labiatae (mint)

Synonyms—None

Description—Deeply cut, palmate leaves, white to pinkish flowers up the stalk with burr-like bristles following the flowers. Herbalist Culpepper says, "it is an herb to drive away the vapours of the heart including faintings and swoonings."

Cultivation—Very hardy and requires no special soil; as with most members of the mint family it is invasive from seed distribution.

Propagation—Seeds

Part Used—Leaves

Harvest—Just before it comes into flower; hang dry

Uses—Medicinal: It has been recorded as being in use since 1658 in Russia. It has always been used as a medicinal for weak hearts and cramps during menstrual and menopause periods. The colonial women used this herb for their menstrual problems and nervous hearts. As with all medicinal herbs, it must be used with discretion.

Appendixes

Recipe Guide

Plant Profiles

Index

Also from The Countryman Press

The Countryman Press and its associated companies, long known for fine books on nature and manuals for healthful living, offer a range of practical and readable books for those interested in herbs, gardening, and nature.

Herbs, Gardening, and Wild Plants

Perennials for the Backyard Gardener, $18.00
Earthmagic: Finding and Using Medicinal Herbs, $15.00
The Earth Shall Blossom: Shaker Herbs and Gardening, $18.95

Nature and Country Living

Backwoods Ethics: Environmental Issues for Hikers and Campers, $13.00
Wilderness Ethics: Preserving the Spirit of Wildness, $13.00
Sketching Outdoors in All Seasons, $20.00
Earth Ponds, $17.00
Surveying Your Land, $10.00
Backyard Bird Habitat, $9.95
Our Native Fishes, $14.95
Backyard Livestock, $14.95
Backyard Sugarin', $8.00
The Wines and Wineries of the Hudson River Valley, $14.95

Cookbooks for Healthful Living

The King Arthur Flour 200th Anniversary Cookbook, $21.00
The Best from Libby Hillman's Kitchen, $25.00
Seasoned with Grace: My Generation of Shaker Cooking, $13.00

We offer many more books on hiking, walking, fishing, canoeing, and bking as well as a full line of mysteries through our imprint, Foul Play Press. Our titles are available in bookshops or they may be ordered directly from the publisher. When ordering from Countryman Press, please add $2.50 for one to two books; $3.00 for three to six books and $3.50 for seven books or more for shipping and handling.

The Countryman Press • PO Box 175 • Woodstock, VT • 05091
800/245-4151